CIVIL RIGHTS
UNDER
REAGAN

CIVIL RIGHTS UNDER REAGAN

Robert R. Detlefsen

ICS PRESS

Institute for Contemporary Studies
San Francisco, California

Inquiries, book orders, and catalog requests should be addressed to ICS Press, Institute for Contemporary Studies, 243 Kearny Street, San Francisco, CA 94108. (415) 981-5353. Fax (415) 986-4878. For book orders and catalog requests call toll free within the contiguous United States: (800) 326-0236. Distributed to the trade by National Book Network, Lanham, Maryland.

The Institute for Contemporary Studies is a nonpartisan, nonprofit public policy research organization. The analyses, conclusions, and opinions expressed in ICS Press publications are those of the authors and not necessarily those of the Institute, or of its officers, directors, or others associated with, or funding, its work.

Designed by David Peattie. Indexed by Shirley Kessel.

Library of Congress Cataloging-in-Publication Data

Detlefsen, Robert R.
    Civil rights under Reagan / Robert R. Detlefsen.
        p. cm.
    Includes bibliographical references and index.
    ISBN 1-55815-111-7 (cloth) : $24.95
    1. Afro-Americans—Civil rights. 2. Afro-Americans—Social conditions—1975–   3. Civil rights—Government policy— United States. 4. United States—Politics and government—1981– 1989. 5. Reagan, Ronald.   I. Title.
E185.615.D48   1991   323′ .0973—dc20   91-2327   CIP

To my mother and my father

Contents

Foreword

Racial politics is volatile because it asks the most profound of questions: What is a just society? How should it be achieved?

The answers are uncertain, in no small part because "civil rights" has come to mean many things to many people. Its original concept is the classic liberal ideal of nondiscrimination, articulated so powerfully by the Reverend Martin Luther King, Jr., in his "I Have a Dream" speech and enshrined in the 1964 Civil Rights Act. Then there is the more recent and much more controversial idea of "affirmative action," or policies that favor members of defined groups (women, certain racial and ethnic minorities) at the expense of members of other groups.

Some believe these two visions are harmonious. Most Americans believe them to be radically opposed. When Ronald Reagan was elected president in 1980, he promised to end preferential policies and return the nation to a color-blind system. Eight years later, preferential policies remained. Why did President Reagan have so little success in actually changing civil rights law?

The question is important because it cuts to the heart of how we might go about creating a just society. Despite the inflamed public rhetoric over racial issues, the civil rights battle since 1964 has been waged largely in the courts, the branch of government least responsive to the wishes of citizens. The "legislation" of civil rights law by an elite group of judges, lawyers, and administrators has estranged an entire generation of Americans from questions of racial justice. In the end this book questions whether it is still possible for Americans to create, through democratic and self-governing institutions, a just society, one in which we will be judged by the content of our character and not by the color of our skin.

Robert B. Hawkins, Jr., President
Institute for Contemporary Studies

Acknowledgments

This work was originally written as a doctoral dissertation, and therefore I owe much to my faculty mentors in the Department of Political Science at the University of California, Berkeley. When, after finishing my qualifying examinations, I mentioned to Nelson Polsby the idea I had for a dissertation topic, he warned me about the risk to my career of challenging the academic conventional wisdom on a subject as sensitive as civil rights. When I assured him that I was willing to assume that risk, he volunteered to serve on my dissertation committee and urged me to get to work. In the years that followed he pointed me to valuable sources of information and commented constructively on preliminary drafts. Martin Shapiro of the Boalt Hall School of Law made good his promise to assist me in any way he could. William K. Muir, Jr., was a continual source of inspiration and support. Through numerous conversations he helped me to crystallize my thinking and reinforced me in my belief that I was on the right track.

My greatest debt by far, however, is owed to my principal teacher at Berkeley, Robert A. Kagan. Rarely did a week go by when he did not favor me with his time and formidable talent, whether in the form of handwritten notes and newspaper clippings that he regularly deposited in my departmental mailbox, long conversations in his office and on the telephone, or the immensely helpful and incisive critical comments he offered in response to initial drafts and outlines.

Revision of the dissertation for publication was made possible by the Program on Constitutional Government at Harvard University and especially by its codirectors, Harvey C. Mansfield, Jr., and R. Shep Melnick. They provided me with a stimulating and hospitable environment in which to work and not least, the luxury of an unconditional postdoctoral fellowship.

CHAPTER ONE

Introduction

The liberal world has come apart at the seams. The struggle for racial justice, which seemed to be going tolerably well, is at an impasse. There's no reliable way of telling who stands where anymore. Old standards no longer apply; old labels no longer fit. Friends, who once confidently shared a way of seeing the world and reacting to its problems, find themselves at odds—sometimes at bitter odds—over the question of affirmative action.

—John C. Livingston,
Fair Game? Inequality and Affirmative Action

This passage first appeared in the introduction to a work published in 1979, and since then the divisive controversy to which it alludes has only intensified. In the following year, 1980, the American presidency was captured by a man whose administration would be staffed in part by policy makers resolutely opposed to affirmative action, as well as to the more general trend toward an increasingly race-conscious, group-oriented jurisprudence, of which affirmative action is a product. This event was virtually without precedent. Previously, even as the theoretical debate over affirmative action was waged in the universities, in the journals of opinion, on the op-ed pages of leading newspapers, and in a few celebrated Supreme Court cases, executive administrations from Nixon's through Carter's uniformly supported the concept and, especially in the case of the Carter administration, expanded and extended its practical impact on the life of the nation.

There was ample reason to suspect that this trend would be reversed under the Reagan administration. One of the preeminent themes of Reagan's election campaign was encapsulated in the candidate's promise to "get the federal government off the backs of the American people." Reagan spoke to what he believed was a growing sentiment among the electorate that government—especially the federal government in Washington—had become so large, unwieldy, and intrusive that its effect was often to undermine both economic efficiency and personal liberty. Although the precise reasons for Reagan's electoral victory remain obscure in the minds of many political analysts, it is at least plausible to suggest that Reagan's repeated denunciations of "big government" struck a responsive chord among the voters.

To make good his promise to reduce the influence of the federal government in the domestic affairs of the nation, the new president was obliged to alter the scope and direction of many long-standing policies, programs, and procedures. Among obvious targets for reform were tax rates, which, as increased (in effect) by inflation, arguably were hindering economic growth. Another target was the complex regime of federal regulations aimed at minimizing environmental degradation, protecting consumers, and promoting health and safety in the workplace. Still another logical area for reform was federal civil rights policy, particularly its two most controversial features, affirmative action and busing to achieve "racial balance" in the public schools.

Indeed, to characterize affirmative action and school busing as "controversial" fails to capture the magnitude of public opposition to these policies. When the Gallup organization surveyed public opinion on affirmative action in 1977, for example, it found that only 11 percent of its sample agreed with the proposition that "to make up for past discrimination, women and members of minority groups should be given preferential treatment in getting jobs and places in college."[1] At the same time, 81 percent agreed with the alternative position that "ability, as determined by test scores, should be the main consideration" for employment or college admission.[2] These findings have been supported by subsequent surveys,[3] including one conducted in 1985, which disclosed that 77 percent of black Americans rejected the notion that race should be a major criterion.[4] As for busing, a 1973 Gallup poll revealed that although a large majority of Americans favored integration of public schools, only 5 percent (9 percent of blacks and 4 percent of whites) favored busing as a means of achieving integration.[5]

Given the overwhelming unpopularity of affirmative action and compulsory busing, their continued presence in public law and public policy would seem (at least from the standpoint of political conservatives who supported the Reagan candidacy) to epitomize the worst features of officious, unresponsive "big government," here seen as attacking such venerated institutions as the merit principle and the neighborhood school. Surely if the Reagan administration were to honor its apparent mandate, it would strive to eliminate such policies. Yet after eight years it was evident that this was easier said than done. A variety of factors constrained the administration's efforts, and it is clear that no sweeping changes occurred during Reagan's two terms in office. Affirmative action is still widely practiced by professional schools and employers, both public and private, throughout the nation. Large numbers of schoolchildren are still bused out of their neighborhoods to achieve "racial balance" at some distant school.

Bureaucratic inertia may be partially to blame, but it surely is not decisive in explaining the general failure to make any substantial reformulation of civil rights policy during the Reagan presidency. Key administration officials repeatedly voiced opposition to race- and gender-conscious, group-oriented civil rights policies. Of these, perhaps none was more outspoken than William Bradford Reynolds. As assistant attorney general for civil rights in the Department of Justice, Reynolds was probably better situated than any member of the administration other than the president himself to effect change in the scope and direction of civil rights policy. In a candid interview given in the summer of 1984, he outlined his agenda while acknowledging his failure to implement it:

> I think we should bring the behavior of the government on all levels into line with the idea of according equal opportunity for all individuals without regard to race, color, or ethnic background. In my view this means that we should remove whatever kinds of race- or gender-conscious remedies and techniques that exist in the regulatory framework, to ensure that the remedies that are put in place are sensitive to the non-discrimination mandate that is in the laws. We've got a ways to go before we get there.[6]

In terms of constitutional principle, Reynolds's position was a corollary of Justice John Harlan's famous dissent in the 1896 case of *Plessy v. Ferguson*:

> Our Constitution is color-blind, and neither knows nor tolerates classes among citizens. . . . The law regards man as man, and takes no account of his surroundings or his color.[7]

The administration would thus appear to have had in Reynolds a policy maker with a principled agenda for reformulating civil rights policy. Reynolds had been placed in charge of a division of the Justice Department that has been described as "the Civil Rights backbone of the federal government, [whose] activities and policies set the pace not only for other federal departments, but also for state, local, and private agencies."[8] Yet, as noted above, and as conceded by Reynolds himself, the administration was unable substantially to redirect civil rights policy toward its original goal of ensuring equal opportunity to each individual without regard to race, ethnicity, or sex.

The question that this book addresses is *Why?* Why was a reform-minded administration, backed by overwhelming majorities, unable to modify substantially or eliminate unpopular civil rights policies? More precisely, we want to ask, What factors impeded the administration's efforts? Two basic strategies seem available for attacking this question. One utilizes a kind of "micro" approach, emphasizing the salience of institutional and procedural impediments to policy reform. Here we would stress the significance of the internal structure and organization of the various administrative agencies responsible for implementing civil rights policy, their respective legislative mandates, their relative autonomy, their responsiveness to various interest groups, and other similar factors. Undoubtedly such an approach would have considerable utility when applied to the realm of civil rights policy making. Within the executive branch, four discrete agencies share responsibility for implementing and enforcing civil rights policy pursuant to a series of legislative enactments beginning with the Civil Rights Act of 1964. These agencies are the Civil Rights Division of the Department of Justice, the Office of Federal Contract Compliance Programs (OFCCP), which is a subunit of the Department of Labor, the Office for Civil Rights (OCR) in the Department of Education, and the Equal Employment Opportunity Commission (EEOC).

Considerable evidence suggests that the Reagan administration's failure to alter civil rights policy substantially was due in part to an inconsistency of purpose among these agencies and their staffs. In September 1985 John Bunzel called attention to "a number of confusions and divisions that have existed within the administration for the past five years."[9] Bunzel contended that

> [a] wide gap has existed between rhetoric and action—specifically with respect to what policies to pursue in light of Mr. Reagan's frequently expressed view that race, sex and color are inappropriate tests of an individual's worth and his belief in the colorblind concept of non-discrimination. It is as if there were a certain schizophrenia running through the administration's whole posture.[10]

At least some of that apparent schizophrenia can be attributed to the differing and occasionally conflicting policy agendas of the Justice Department's Civil Rights Division and the Equal Employment Opportunity Commission. The agencies disagreed, for example, over the issue of numerical goals and timetables for the hiring and promotion of minority and female workers. Thus, when the Justice Department submitted its own internal affirmative action plan to the EEOC as required by law, the EEOC rejected the plan because it did not include numerical goals and timetables.[11] On another occasion the two agencies clashed over a court case. The Justice Department, supported by the White House, sought to prevent the imposition of a promotion quota for black officers in the New Orleans police department through a consent decree that had been approved by a panel of the U.S. Court of Appeals for the Fifth Circuit. The Justice Department, as intervenor, asked the court to delete the quota from the consent decree, even as the EEOC was filing its own brief urging the court to maintain the quota. Ultimately the White House prevailed upon the EEOC to withdraw its brief,[12] but the incident nevertheless served to highlight the disunity that evidently existed within the administration with respect to basic civil rights policy issues.

This lack of agreement is in marked contrast to the experience of previous administrations. According to Drew Days, assistant attorney general for civil rights during the Carter administration, there had always been under Carter "a unanimity of views on the means to achieve affirmative action. There's a drastic difference now.... It appears to be an all-out war."[13] Eleanor Holmes Norton, who chaired the EEOC during the Carter administration, agreed:

> The EEOC was usually able to get the changes it wanted. There was no fundamental difference between the EEOC and the Justice Department. Even in previous administrations—with the Nixon or Ford administration—there's no precedent for that.[14]

As the Reagan administration entered its second term in 1985, there was little evidence that its internal confusion over the proper direction of civil rights policy had abated. Earlier the president had nominated Edwin Meese to become attorney general, but now he nominated William Brock to become secretary of labor, who would prove to be Meese's nemesis on civil rights issues. By all accounts Meese was a leading advocate of civil rights policy reform within the administration during the first term. By September 1985 he was presiding over the development of new rules for enforcing the Voting Rights Act that would shift the burden of proof in voting rights disputes from government officials to those alleging illegal voting discrimination, and that would permit changes in local election procedures and in legislative redistricting under some circumstances even if such changes resulted in a "dilution" of minority voting strength.[15] Moreover, Meese had taken to speaking out publicly against the use of racial preferences in employment and school admissions, telling one audience that

> [t]he idea that you can use discrimination in the form of racially preferential quotas, goals and set-asides to remedy the lingering social effects of past discrimination makes no sense in principle; in practice, it is nothing short of a legal, moral, and constitutional tragedy.[16]

In spite of this forceful statement, the administration continued to send conflicting signals about its civil rights objectives. The new labor secretary, William Brock, as if to distinguish himself from Meese and Reynolds, told delegates to the NAACP's annual convention in the summer of 1985 that the administration supported the use of numerical goals "set in different ways to respond to different situations."[17] As Bunzel later commented, Secretary Brock, far from clarifying administration policy, "merely confirmed that cabinet members march to the beat of different drummers."[18]

Inconsistency of purpose within the administration was not confined to the executive's three major players. In addition to the Justice Department, the EEOC, and the Labor Department, civil rights enforcement is also carried out by the Department of Education's Office for Civil Rights. This agency, which has responsibility primarily for enforcing Title IX of the Education Amendments to the Civil Rights Act, was portrayed by Jeremy Rabkin in 1978 as staffed to a considerable extent by doctrinaire zealots who were given to pursuing their antidiscrimination mandate in aggressively innovative ways.[19] One might have expected this posture to change during Reagan's tenure, but by May 1985 there was evidence that precious little change had occurred. In that month, the OCR filed a complaint against the University of California, Berkeley, over the presence of "sexist" language in its course catalog. Among the words the agency objected to were "mankind," "manpower," "manmade," and "grantsmanship."[20] University officials declared themselves to be "astonished that the Office for Civil Rights was able to waste its time and our money on matters of this sort."[21] The incident did seem to be all the more puzzling because it occurred under an administration pledged to curtailing bureaucratic heavy-handedness.

Undoubtedly the lack of a consistent, comprehensive agenda accounts to a considerable extent for the continuation of a race- and gender-conscious regime of civil rights. If the administration could not, even after five years, speak with one voice on civil rights, it is no wonder that no effort was mounted to persuade Congress to amend the Civil Rights Act to prohibit racial preference and reverse discrimination, or to modify or revise Executive Order 11246, which requires firms under contract to the federal government to practice race-conscious affirmative action in hiring and promotion. A valuable study might thus be undertaken on the sources of internal confusion and inconsistency within the administration—the role of interest groups, civil service holdovers from previous administrations, interpersonal and interagency rivalries, and the like—and would draw its theoretical insights from the burgeoning scholarly literature on organization theory and policy implementation.

There is, however, an alternative (and, to this writer, more interesting) approach to the question we have formulated. Rather than focusing on the factors that seem to have contributed to the Reagan administration's *failure to act* in ways that one might have anticipated, we plan to concentrate instead on those actions it *did* take in an effort to reformulate civil rights policy. Our focus will be primarily on the activities of the Civil Rights Division of the Justice Department, for this agency engaged in the most sustained and systematic attempt to reformulate civil rights policy during the Reagan presidency. Yet it achieved few victories for its efforts. The reason lies less in internal disunity (although there was no small amount of this) than in the response to the Justice Department initiatives from politically prominent, strategically influential elites outside the administration. Although the civil rights reforms pursued by the Justice Department were consonant with the results of public opinion surveys and arguably adhered to the letter and spirit of relevant statutory and constitutional provisions, they were strongly opposed by a sizable element of the American intelligentsia, particularly judges, journalists, academics, and virtually the entire organized "civil rights community."

The response of federal judges to the department's proposed civil rights reforms proved to be especially important, since these reforms were pursued largely through the courts. Because of the salience of courts in the civil rights arena, however, other members of the intelligentsia were highly influential as well. The power of ideas and intellectual criticism generally exerts itself more forcefully on the activities of the courts than on those of any other branch of government. This force is particularly felt when courts engage in constitutional adjudication, as is often the case when civil rights claims are at issue. In such circumstances, judges frequently come together with law professors, members of the media, and professional interest group advocates to form what Robert Bork has termed the "constitutional culture." According to Bork, "courts are part of a more general legal-constitutional culture and ultimately are heavily influenced by ideas that develop elsewhere in that culture."[22] The notion of a constitutional culture is paralleled in Richard E. Morgan's discussion of what he terms "the rights industry" in American politics. The introduction to his recent study of court-mandated social policy is especially pertinent:

> My political science training . . . made it clear that studying the [Supreme] Court in isolation was an inadequate way of understanding how civil liberties and civil rights were defined and judicially applied in American society. I came to see the Court as part, albeit the most important part, of a subsystem of constitutional politics in which activist lawyers, academic partisans, interest groups, and media publicists play important roles.[23]

The central message these writers convey is that, especially concerning law and social policy pertaining to civil rights, the American political system is disproportionately influenced by a relatively small segment of the population whose views are often at considerable variance with those held by popular majorities. In a constitutional system of government, where certain rights and liberties are explicitly codified in a written constitution, the insistence by a small elite upon the formulation of policies that respect and uphold those rights and liberties, even against the will of popular majorities, is vital.[24] However, a classic problem in democratic theory emerges when courts become mere conduits for enacting the subjective value preferences of the groups and individuals that make up Bork's "constitutional culture" or Morgan's "rights industry." To the extent that this occurs, representative self-government will gradually be supplanted by oligarchic rule.

It is rarely admitted that what might be called the "civil rights elite" has often used the courts to enact unpopular civil rights policies based, not on some clear statutory or constitutional command, but on their singular attitudes and beliefs. When one does encounter a candid acknowledgment of this phenomenon, it is worth quoting at length. Here is how Richard Neely, Chief Justice of the West Virginia Supreme Court, justifies judicial activism on behalf of unpopular civil rights policies:

> Certainly a majority of the educated elite, as reflected by the attitudes of the faculties, trustees, and student bodies at major universities, consider affirmative action, although predatory, morally justifiable. It is just as certain, however, that a majority of Americans disapprove. There is no theoretical justification for continued support of affirmative action other than the elitist one

that the courts know from their superior education that affirmative action is necessary in the short run to achieve the generally applauded moral end of equal opportunity in the long run. *That is probably not illegitimate, since judges are social science specialists and have available to them more information and have pursued the issue with more thought and diligence than the man on the street.* Courts should probably be accorded as much deference in their decisions over means as medical doctors, professional architects, or plumbers.[25]

What we learn from this passage is that the civil rights policies preferred by the civil rights elite are superior to alternative civil rights simply precisely because they are the policies the elite prefers.

Against this background, we may begin to appreciate the profound iconoclasm inherent in the Reagan program. Under Reagan, the Justice Department had departed from the record of previous administrations and repudiated the conventional wisdom that had been handed down by the civil rights elite. It had switched sides, becoming the "man on the street" in direct opposition to the preponderance of judges, media commentators, activist lawyers, and "social science experts." Throughout the first six years of the Reagan administration, the latter's reaction to the Justice Department's defection proved exceptionally vitriolic. A sampling of the frequently *ad hominem* calumny leveled at the administration generally, and at its principal civil rights policy makers in particular, may serve to indicate the intensity of opposition to the Justice Department's efforts. Here, for example, is how Ira Glasser, executive director of the American Civil Liberties Union, described Assistant Attorney General Reynolds after reflecting on his record as head of the Civil Rights Division:

> Mr. Reynolds is the moral equivalent of those Southern segregationists of a generation ago standing in the schoolhouse door to defend segregation. Today, he stands at the workplace gate, defending discrimination in employment. His efforts disgrace the American dream of equal opportunity.[26]

The columnist Anthony Lewis, after bitterly declaiming that "instead of fighting for the blacks and women who have been the historic victims of discrimination, the Justice Department is now 'emphasizing the rights of white males,'" concluded that Reynolds was "lawless and heartless" and labeled him a "white man's lawyer."[27]

In a similar vein, NAACP director Benjamin Hooks had this to say when, in early 1984, Reagan announced his nomination of Edwin Meese to succeed William French Smith as attorney general:

> Mr. Meese has been a key architect in the development of the administration's conservative ideology and programs. He has proven by everything he has said and done that he is anti–civil rights and an enemy of progressive social policy.
>
> By this action, Mr. Reagan is putting another anti–civil rights devil in charge of the agency responsible for protecting minorities.[28]

Referring to Reagan's apparently successful attempt to reconstitute the U.S. Commission on Civil Rights by appointing new commissioners thought to be more sympathetic to the administration's civil rights initiatives than those they replaced, the NAACP, in its annual report for 1985, expressed its resolve to "struggle to prevent the president from turning the Civil Rights Commission into a haven for political and social Neanderthals whose views of the Constitution are clouded by distortions of justice and a social Darwinist theory."[29] More generally, NAACP board chairman William F. Gibson simply denounced Reagan personally as "basically a reactionary and racist."[30]

Particularly striking has been the tendency of critics to focus, as in the Lewis quotation above, on the supposed impropriety of "emphasizing"—or even acknowledging—"the rights of white males." When Reynolds appeared before the House Judiciary Subcommittee on Civil and Constitutional Rights in May 1983, he startled chairman Don Edwards by divulging his intention to officially challenge "those practices that unfairly disadvantage women, Hispanics, and whites." His inclusion of whites among those who are arguably disadvantaged by certain practices prompted a rebuke from Edwards:

> You and I are white male attorneys. We came from families with some money and were educated in the right schools. Unless we behaved very stupidly, the family and institutional support systems guaranteed places for us. We benefited from a racial spoils system.[31]

The sentiments expressed by this view were echoed in 1984 by Mary Frances Berry and Blandina Cardinas Ramirez, two hold-over members of the reconstituted Civil Rights Commission, when they jointly wrote that

> civil rights laws were not passed to give civil rights protections to all Americans, as a majority of this Commission seems to believe. Instead, they were passed out of a recognition that some Americans already had protection because they belonged to a favored group; and others, including blacks, Hispanics, and women of all races, did not because they belonged to disfavored groups.[32]

Among many within the scholarly community, the administration's willingness to apply the civil rights laws' protections to white males is accepted as evidence of hostility toward civil rights. Consider, for example, the following passage taken from a recently published textbook for political science courses in constitutional law:

> [T]he Reagan administration's stance on civil rights . . . is at significant odds with the civil rights positions of the five previous administrations, all of which actively used their discretionary powers to pursue civil rights claims through the administrative process and to press civil rights claims in the courts. In sharp contrast, the Reagan administration has slowed to a near standstill or has actively opposed civil rights actions. For instance, in the 1983 Boston Firefighters Union case, the Reagan administration filed a brief in opposition to the NAACP, and in 1984, it filed a brief supporting the City of Birmingham's challenge to a 10 percent minority employment and purchasing requirement.[33]

What is interesting about this passage is that in each of the two cases cited by the authors to substantiate their assertion that the Reagan administration had "actively opposed civil rights actions," the administration had sided with plaintiffs who alleged that their civil rights had been violated by policies that deliberately discriminated against them on the basis of their race. An essentially identical allegation had been made by the plaintiffs in *Brown v. Board of Education*; indeed, a "civil rights action" is by definition one in which a plaintiff charges that a particular policy or practice violates the antidiscrimination mandate of the federal

Civil Rights Act or the Fourteenth Amendment's equal protection clause. This was the argument made by the plaintiffs in each of the cases cited in the passage quoted above, yet the Reagan administration's decision to involve itself on their behalf is regarded by the authors as direct evidence of *opposition* to civil rights actions. If this seems paradoxical, it is necessary only to point out that in both cases the plaintiffs represented the interests of white males who believed themselves to be victims of discrimination. What the quoted passage teaches, then, is that a civil rights action brought by white males is no civil rights action at all.

It is obvious that the Reagan administration's civil rights initiatives generated a debate that revealed more than just raw emotion and passion. Much of the rhetoric that issued from both sides can be understood to reveal stark differences in the way people think about civil rights. Antagonists disagreed not merely about the means to achieve generally agreed-upon ends; they also disagreed fundamentally about what the ends should be, and even about which ends are permissible. Even more fundamentally, they differed in their vision of the society to which civil rights policy is to be applied. This book seeks to explain—at least partially—the inability of the Reagan administration to reformulate national civil rights policy by developing a theory of elite attitudes and beliefs about civil rights. Our argument will be that the civil rights elite in America—a segment of the population that is roughly coextensive with Bork's constitutional culture and Morgan's rights industry—has developed an ideology of civil rights that necessarily demands the creation of a jurisprudence in which different kinds or levels of rights and privileges are allocated to individuals on the basis of their membership in particular social groups, defined according to racial, ethnic, and gender criteria.

We will argue further that the civil rights ideology remains ascendant in public law and policy—even in the face of executive opposition—because of the strategic prominence of its adherents, and because holders of the ideology have, in promoting their views, successfully managed to de-legitimate alternative strategies for securing civil rights based on race- and gender-neutral criteria. To this extent, we shall go beyond making the familiar distinction between the color-blind and color-conscious versions of civil rights by developing a theoretical explanation for the continued prevalence of one version over the other.

The content and sequence of the remaining chapters is as follows: The second chapter examines the intellectual genesis of the race- and gender-conscious version of civil rights, and traces its gradual infusion into public law and policy up to 1980. Chapter 3 presents a detailed analysis of several important court cases in which the Reagan administration challenged the legality of racial preference schemes in the hiring, promotion, and discharge of workers. Chapter 4 examines major legal controversies that arose in the realm of education, including the denial of tax exemptions to allegedly discriminatory private schools. Chapter 5 assesses the extent to which the policy process itself impeded civil rights reform, with particular attention to the controversies surrounding the civil rights commission, the executive order requiring federal contractors to engage in race- and gender-conscious employment practices, and the passage by Congress of an amended version of the Voting Rights Act. The sixth chapter analyzes the content and character of the contemporary civil rights ideology, and explains how the application of ideological principles influenced the outcome of the issues covered in the earlier chapters. Finally, an epilogue analyzes three important cases bearing on affirmative action and employment discrimination that were decided by the Supreme Court in the spring of 1989.

CHAPTER TWO

Civil Rights Doctrine from 1965 to 1980: A Critical History

> The adoption of quotas would be the most radical change one can imagine in the American ethos. The fact that it began to be implemented with no public discussion whatsoever and the fact that this change began to be implemented through the activity of bureaucrats is an astonishing feature of the national life at this time.
>
> —Norman Podhoretz, quoted in George Roche, *The Balancing Act: Quota Hiring in Higher Education*

To speak of civil rights in the 1970s was to speak of a patchwork of policies and practices, in both the governmental and private spheres, that were loosely denoted by the term "affirmative action." The term has generally been used to refer to a broad range of efforts to increase systematically the percentage of women and members of judicially and administratively designated minority groups in occupations and institutions in which they are statistically underrepresented relative to their numbers in the general population. As such, affirmative action is usually understood to operate within the context of employment and admission to professional schools. As shall be discussed in subsequent chapters, however, the principles underlying affirmative action in employment and professional school admissions had, by the early 1970s, also come to inform many prominent Americans' understanding of what is meant by "school desegregation" and "voting rights" as well, two other areas traditionally of concern to the civil rights movement in America. An understanding of the theory and practice of affirmative action is thus indispensable in considering the politics of civil rights during the Reagan presidency.

The purpose of this chapter is to provide that needed understanding by reviewing the history of applied affirmative action, and to evaluate some of the theoretical justifications that have been advanced in its behalf. The purpose of the latter undertaking is not to "score points" or to take sides in a partisan debate, but rather to meet two objections that might have been raised by the discussion in Chapter 1. One is that, notwithstanding the popular wisdom as revealed through public opinion polls, the propriety of affirmative action is so self-evident as to render it an inappropriate subject for principled debate. This is essentially the position articulated by Judge Neely in the passage quoted in the previous chapter; affirmative action is simply the right way of going about things, and those who disagree do so out of ignorance, bigotry, or both. To the contrary, we want to suggest that it is precisely the vulnerability of affirmative action doctrine and practice to persuasive, if not compelling, criticism that, when combined with popular and executive opposition, makes the persistence of affirmative action doctrine so puzzling.

Another objection we want to confront concerns the place of rights in a constitutional democracy. An argument could be made, indeed often *is* made, that civil rights are by their very nature inviolable, no matter how strongly opposed by popular majorities or elected politicians. In the American system it is the special duty of the judicial branch of government to ensure that civil rights are respected by the "political" branches, and affirmative action, although perhaps not a civil right per se, is at least necessary to facilitate civil rights that are fundamental and inalienable. Thus, the existence of popular or executive antipathy toward affirmative action is really quite irrelevant in attempting to explain the persistence of what is for practical purposes a bona fide civil right. Affirmative action persists for the same reason that freedom of speech persists for Communists and Nazis: because the judiciary is specifically empowered to protect the civil rights and civil liberties of unpopular minorities, without regard to popular or official sentiment.

Against this line of argument, we want to suggest that affirmative action itself may be regarded as a violation of civil rights, and that in any event it is extremely doubtful that it can properly be regarded as a civil right per se, or even as a necessary instrument for promoting civil rights. If valid questions can be raised about the moral and legal propriety of affirmative action, we can safely dismiss the proposition that affirmative action persists because it is unimpeachable on its merits or, alternatively, because it is compelled by the Constitution's special solicitude for minority rights. To that end, let us first trace the history of civil rights and affirmative action in America.

Civil Rights in American History

The term "civil rights" does not appear in the Bill of Rights, nor in the original Constitution, nor in the Declaration of Independence. The term, in fact, was rarely used in American political discourse until after the Civil War. Congress enacted the first measure called by the name "civil rights" in 1866. Records of the debates surrounding the bill's passage make clear that politicians of the day understood the term in light of the political principles of the American Founding, which in turn were informed by ideas delineated in the works of those eighteenth-century political philosophers we today identify with classical liberalism. One of the principal sponsors of the 1866 Civil Rights Act described civil rights as "the absolute rights of individuals, such as the right to personal security, the right of personal liberty and the right to acquire and enjoy property."[1] Jeremy Rabkin elaborates:

> The central idea behind "civil rights" was that the government must be restrained in its power to manage society, to coerce private preferences; a government that respected civil rights would, for the most part, have to allow the character of society to emerge from a multitude of individual choices and private initiatives.[2]

By the middle of the nineteenth century these values were already embedded in federal and most state law, at least as far as white males were concerned. In the immediate aftermath of the Civil War, Congress rightly feared that judges and other officials of the federal government might question whether respect for civil rights should properly extend to the thousands of newly emancipated slaves, and so the Civil Rights Act of 1866 was enacted to reaffirm the basic principles associated with civil rights and to emphasize that such rights were henceforth to be enjoyed by blacks as well as whites. Congress understandably was even more fearful that state governments—particularly those that had joined the Confederacy—would run roughshod over the civil rights of blacks, and so it attached the Fourteenth Amendment to the Constitution which included a clause that explicitly forbade any state to "deny to any person within its jurisdiction the equal protection of the laws." The intent clearly was to ensure that those state laws which protected the personal rights of white citizens would apply with equal force where the personal rights of black citizens were concerned.

Shamefully, the provisions contained in the Civil Rights Act of 1866 and in the Fourteenth Amendment's equal protection clause were routinely ignored and violated in the case of blacks, particularly in the South, until the 1950s, when the U.S. Supreme Court began using the equal protection clause to strike down governmentally compelled segregation (later to be known as "de jure" segregation) in state-supported colleges and professional schools. This line of decisions culminated in the famous case of *Brown v. Board of Education*,[3] in which the Court repudiated the "separate but equal" doctrine that had governed consideration of challenges to state-enforced segregation since the Court's infamous decision in the 1896 case of *Plessy v. Ferguson*.[4] A good deal more will be said about *Brown* and its legacy in Chapter 4; here it will suffice to say that the main thrust of Chief Justice Earl Warren's notably opaque majority opinion was to prohibit state officials from deliberately assigning black and white pupils to separate schools according to their race.

On the legislative side, the burgeoning black civil rights movement of the early 1960s achieved what was widely regarded as a supreme victory when Congress enacted the Civil Rights Act of 1964. This omnibus legislation differed from previous federal civil rights statutes chiefly in that it proscribed many forms of *private* racial discrimination (for example, in employment and with respect to public accommodations), and in its creation of a new set of federal administrative agencies whose specific mandate was to monitor compliance with the provisions of the act and to initiate legal proceedings against violators. Most importantly, the act provided for the withholding of federal subsidies from private and governmental entities that failed to comply with its terms.

Although passage of the Civil Rights Act of 1964 was generally regarded as a major triumph for the increasingly influential civil rights movement, there were some doubters. Interestingly, one such skeptic was the political scientist Willmoore Kendall, who, in an article published in 1967,[5] argued that the enactment of the Civil Rights Act of 1964 and the Voting Rights Act of 1965 (outlawing racial discrimination in voter registration) had effectively "killed" the civil rights movement. Kendall was, of course, aware of the paradoxical nature of his claim. He wrote:

> Political movements usually thrive on successes, whether electoral or legislative—as, at first blush, we should expect them to: such a movement, having shown its muscle by gaining first this objective (the opening of public accommodations to Negroes) and that objective (a voting rights act whose intended purpose is to get hitherto-disfranchised Negroes on the voting rolls)— what more natural than it should proceed, propelled now by forward inertia, to use that same muscle for gaining still further objectives and do so successfully?[6]

This rhetorical question contained an important insight that apparently was not generally understood at the time; to wit, that the civil rights movement's ultimate objectives transcended the elimination of formal inequality—that is, inequality with respect to the "protection of the laws." For one thing, formal inequality had for the most part been a Southern phenomenon. As Kendall put it,

> the Civil Rights Act and the Voting Rights Act outlawed the major *legal* disabilities of Southern Negroes. They went a long way toward putting the Southern Negro in the same legal position as the Negro north of the Mason-Dixon line—not all the way, of course, but at least far enough to drain most of the drama off the Civil Rights leaders' onslaught against Southern legislatures and city councils, Southern courts, and Southern law enforcement.[7]

Moreover, the goal of eliminating formal, or legal, inequality could not in itself have inspired such a formidable political movement. Ultimately the movement's success would be determined by the extent to which it managed to achieve for its constituents an equality of condition or status—what Kendall called "substantial equality"—and he well understood what this would entail:

> Winning *substantial* equality for the American Negro, once you have won for him his equality before the law, means first getting him out of the ghettos in Chicago, Los Angeles, Detroit, Philadelphia, and New York (to say nothing of helping him penetrate the white ghettos characteristic of Northern conurbations . . .), and, second, putting money in his pockets; and both of these are "objectives" that are going to require drastic action that must, on pain of killing the movement off, show "results" in the short term.[8]

What sort of "drastic action" would suffice? Kendall put it succinctly:

> The Civil Rights movement must henceforth, if it is to deliver the goods to its supposed constituents, go into the business simultaneously of reforming—nay, remaking—the American economic system, and of eliminating the existing American bias (by no means a monopoly of American whites) against desegregated housing. And this must force the movement to pit itself against resistances of a kind it never had to face when its target was the South, and its rhetoric the rhetoric of equality before the law. To ask the nation to help force the Southerners to stop using the American legal system for purposes of discrimination against Negroes is one thing; to ask it to surrender its own strongly-held prejudices, and to launch itself on unprecedented experiments with a deeply-cherished economic system, is quite another—if only because the movement doing the asking acquires, overnight, tens of millions of opponents, many of them occupying positions of power, who yesterday may well have seemed its friends.[9]

Kendall believed that the civil rights movement's success as of 1965 was attributable to the fact that, despite its seemingly revolutionary rhetoric—exemplified by the demand that legal equality be extended to blacks *immediately*, accompanied by public warnings from the movement's leadership that they would not take "No" for an answer—in reality it asked little more than that a series of legal anachronisms that had been practiced almost exclusively in one geographic region of the country be given up. The political system could accommodate this demand because the abuses that were cited were anomalous even according to the system's own rules. Kendall further believed, however, that the movement's larger, transcendent agenda, which emphasized the more ambitious objective of obtaining substantive (or "substantial") equality for its constituents, would not be treated nearly as generously by the system. For the "system," wrote Kendall, "is likely to take steps (not necessarily punitive, or at least not openly punitive) to cut the movement down to size, to bring it back into the system's fold and so to speak, resubordinate it to the system's rules."[10]

Kendall was undoubtedly correct in setting up the problem as he did. Until roughly 1965 (a convenient benchmark because that year, as noted above, marked the enactment of the Voting Rights Act, the last of the major federal statutes aimed at granting legal equality to blacks), the movement succeeded in large part because it asked little more than that the system honor its own accepted rules. (To be sure, in doing so it also asked white southerners to give up a deeply ingrained and cherished way of life. So long as resistance to the changes the movement sought was confined to one geographic region, however, the system could handle the resulting turmoil.) Once the movement began to pursue in earnest the goal of substantive equality, it would necessarily find itself demanding basic systemic changes,* changes in the system's rules as they pertained to the operation of the economy and to Americans' historic proclivity toward residential segregation—changes that would perforce be national in scope. In effect, the civil rights movement reached a crossroads in 1965. Either the movement would accommodate itself to the political system's rules (or, in contemporary parlance, permit itself to be "co-opted" by the system), or the system's rules would have to yield so that the system could accommodate itself to the movement.

Kendall regarded the former scenario as much more likely than the latter, and in 1967 the former scenario probably *did* seem more likely. In retrospect, it is clear that Kendall was less than prophetic. The story of affirmative action, and of race-conscious

---

*Of course, having succeeded in obtaining full legal equality for its constituents, the movement might have been content to rely on a combination of an improving economy, individual initiative, and chance to gradually achieve substantive equality, but then it would have ceased being a *political* movement.

social policy generally, is in one important respect the story of how the system's rules were substantially changed over a relatively brief period to accommodate the civil rights movement's demand for substantive equality for its constituents. The changes that occurred were not as sweeping or as cataclysmic as one might have imagined; the U.S. economy was not converted to socialism, direct monetary reparations were not paid to blacks, and massive numbers of people were not systematically driven from their homes and forced to relocate in order to break up traditional patterns of residential segregation. Nor were the systemic "rule changes" that did occur the result of a broad public consensus operating through established institutions of representative self-government—in this respect Kendall's prescience has been borne out. He failed, however, to anticipate fully the emerging critical role of courts and the federal bureaucracy in the development of national social policy. In the late 1960s and throughout the 1970s, the systemic "rule changes" that the profusion of affirmative action and race-conscious social policy represent were brought about principally through the agency of these nonelected, nonrepresentative institutions.

The Evolution of Affirmative Action

The term "affirmative action" has at various times meant different things to different people. This should surprise no one, since the term seems almost deliberately ambiguous. Taken literally, affirmative action could mean almost anything. In the context of civil rights, a variation of the term first appeared in the wording of Executive Order No. 10925, issued by President Kennedy in 1961. Executive orders are rarely cast as specific policy directives, and Kennedy's use of the term was typically imprecise, indicating merely that "it is the policy of the executive branch to encourage by positive measures equal opportunity for all persons . . . " and that federal contractors should take "affirmative steps" to ensure that objective.[11] President Johnson expanded the scope of the coverage of the contractual provision of the earlier executive order when he signed Executive Order No. 11246 in 1965. That order also transferred authority for supervising the implementation of the order's equal opportunity mandate to the Department of

Labor, which in turn created the Office of Federal Contract Compliance Programs (OFCCP) to carry out that function.

Although its supporters often locate the origin of affirmative action in Executive Order No. 11246, and accordingly regard affirmative action as one of the great civil rights victories of the Johnson administration, the Johnson order itself did nothing to alter the common understanding that affirmative action meant nothing more than that employers, in addition to hiring without regard to the race or ethnicity of job-seekers (both the Kennedy and Johnson executive orders are unequivocal on this point), should also publicize job vacancies and seek to encourage job applications from members of those groups (principally blacks) who might otherwise be discouraged from applying because of widespread discrimination against them in the past. In other words, "affirmative action" was understood to mean that employers should aggressively spread the news that the bad old days of racial discrimination were over, and that now all applications for employment would be treated in the same manner. The first indication that affirmative action might mean something other than this came in 1967 from Edward C. Sylvester, the director of OFCCP, who explained that

> [t]here is no fixed and firm definition of affirmative action. I would say that in a general way, affirmative action is anything that you have to do to get results. But this does not *necessarily* include preferential treatment. The key word here is "results" . . . affirmative action is really designed to get employers to apply the same kind of imagination and ingenuity that they apply to any other phase of their operation.[12]

In the following year President Johnson added "sex" to the list of prohibited forms of discrimination mentioned in Executive Order No. 11246, and OFCCP issued implementing regulations which for the first time required that all government contractors with contracts worth at least $50,000 develop written affirmative action plans. (By 1986, this group included some 15,000 companies employing 23 million workers at 73,000 installations.[13]) The regulations also expanded further upon the meaning of affirmative action:

> A necessary prerequisite to the development of a satisfactory affirmative action program is the identification and analysis of

problem areas inherent in minority employment and an evaluation of opportunities for utilization of minority group personnel. The contractor's program shall provide in detail for specific
steps to guarantee equal opportunity keyed to the problems and
needs of minority groups, including, when there are *deficiencies*,
the development of specific goals and timetables for the prompt
achievement of full and equal employment opportunity. Each
contractor shall include in his affirmative action compliance
program a table of job classifications. . . . The evaluation of utilization of minority group personnel shall include . . . an analysis of minority group representation in all categories.[14]

This description of affirmative action still leaves much to the imag-
ination, but it does—at least in retrospect—enable us to glimpse
the shape of things to come. For example, the regulations' use of
the word "deficiencies" foreshadows, albeit cryptically, one of the
guiding presuppositions of affirmative action doctrine—that in
the absence of discrimination, statistical parity among racial and
ethnic groups would be the norm. Although not explicit, a "defi-
ciency," as the word is used here, would seem to denote any state
of affairs in which this norm is not realized. It remained for yet
another set of guidelines, issued in 1971 as Revised Order No. 4,
to confirm this interpretation. Retaining much of the wording of
the previous guidelines, this one required employers additionally
to undertake

an analysis of all major classifications at the facility, with explanations if minorities and women are currently being underuti-
lized in any one or more job classifications. . . . "Underutilization"
is defined as having fewer minorities and women in a particular
job classification than would reasonably be expected by their
availability.[15]

The concept of "underutilization" introduced here was to give
an enduring teleological cast to the idea of equal opportunity, in
that it essentially proclaimed that equality of opportunity would
lead, inexorably and invariably, to equality of result, a necessary
condition of substantive equality. It is teleological in the sense that
much of biology is teleological: An acorn, given the requisite
amounts of water, sunlight, and soil nutrients, will inexorably and
invariably grow into an oak tree. Similarly, a minority group

whose members constitute, say, 10 percent of the carpenters in a particular labor market will, given the requisite amount of equal opportunity (so to speak), inexorably and invariably make up 10 percent of the carpenters in each and every firm that employs carpenters. In the event that the percentage of minority carpenters employed by such a firm amounts to less than 10 percent, the firm is said to be "underutilizing" minority carpenters.

One example of how the OFCCP regulations work is provided by the experience of a small Kansas construction company that employed fifteen hourly workers, including two truck drivers who were white males, as well as three workers of minority background. Following a Labor Department investigation, the company received a letter from the department accusing it of having "failed to exert adequate good faith efforts to achieve the minimum minority utilization goal of 12.7 percent for truck drivers and minimum female utilization goal of 6.9 percent for carpenters, heavy equipment operators, iron workers, truck drivers, and laborers." The letter noted that the "remedy" was to "recruit and hire qualified minorities and females until such time as the required utilization goals have been met."[16] OFCCP regulations provide for the debarment of contractors who fail to effect the prescribed remedies for documented instances of minority and female underutilization.

The OFCCP regulations issued in 1970 and 1971 were doubtless encouraged by the Nixon administration's experience with what has come to be known as the "Philadelphia Plan." Instituted by the Labor Department in 1969 and named for the city in which it was first applied, the plan required contractors bidding on federal or federally assisted construction projects to submit goals for minority employee utilization in a variety of job categories, including ironworkers, plumbers, pipefitters, and electricians.[17] Announcement of the program immediately raised eyebrows in Congress and elicited a letter from John L. McClellan (D–Ark.) to Comptroller General Elmer B. Staats, asking the latter to render an opinion on the legality of the program. In his letter, the senator charged that the Labor Department was requiring the use of an illegal racial preference scheme. Staats replied that the Philadelphia Plan was indeed illegal because it established quotas in violation of Title VII of the Civil Rights Act of 1964. But Staats was effectively overridden by Attorney General John N. Mitchell, who issued his own opinion one day before the implementation order for the Philadelphia Plan was issued. Mitchell declared the plan to be lawful, arguing that

> it is now well recognized . . . that the obligation of nondiscrimination . . . does not require, and in some circumstances may not permit, obliviousness or indifference to the racial consequences of alternative courses of action which involve the application of outwardly neutral criteria.[18]

In this pronouncement of the attorney general we have the first official rendition of Justice Harry Blackmun's oft-quoted dictum that "in order to get beyond racism, we must first take account of race."[19]

Despite further congressional resistance to the Philadelphia Plan, which took the form of a proposed rider to an appropriations bill that would have made the appropriation of funds for federal programs contingent upon the judgment of the comptroller general that the program was not in contravention of any federal statute, the Philadelphia Plan was sustained when both the House and Senate rejected the rider following a personal appeal from President Nixon, who urged Congress to "permit the continued implementation of the Philadelphia Plan. . . . "[20] With the Philadelphia Plan in place, officials in the OFCCP could confidently move forward in promulgating regulations based increasingly on a norm of statistical parity among racial groups and equality of result.

As an aside, we should note that the foregoing discussion suggests that the history of federal affirmative action (at least to the extent that it can be identified with the executive branch) is rooted less in President Johnson's executive order than in the implementing regulations issued by the Department of Labor during the Nixon administration, with the unequivocal support of the Nixon Justice Department and of Nixon himself. Contrary to conventional wisdom, contemporary federal affirmative action policy owes far more to the likes of John Mitchell, George Shultz (Nixon's secretary of labor), and Richard Nixon than to Lyndon Johnson, a fact that stands in sharp contrast to the typical caricatures of Johnson and Nixon one finds in contemporary political folklore.[*]

---

[*]See, for example, Joseph A. Califano, Jr., *Governing America: An Insider's Report from the White House and the Cabinet* (New York: Simon and Schuster, 1981), p. 212: "And I had watched, with frustration and anger, as Nixon's Southern strategy eroded the gains of the Johnson years and interrupted the blacks' march to equality."

The Legitimacy of the New Regime

At this stage we may pause to make two observations. First, the developments that occurred between 1965 and 1971 with respect to the executive's interpretation and implementation of Executive Order No. 11246 succeeded in substantially altering the political system's rules. Earlier we noted that in making legal equality and nondiscrimination the law of the land, the Civil Rights Act of 1964 and the Voting Rights Act of 1965 were intended not to effect fundamental changes in the systemic rules governing the distribution of wealth and status in America, but rather to ensure that the traditional rules would be applied with equal force to all citizens without regard to their race or sex. By 1971, however, a new regime of rules had emerged, substituting "underutilization" for "discrimination" as the evil that offends civil rights. Concomitantly, civil rights policy was becoming increasingly prescriptive, where once it had been entirely proscriptive. Essentially, the Civil Rights Act is a compendium of the various practices and policies that organizations and institutions are *prohibited* from undertaking. The emerging regime, on the other hand, assigned to such entities an *obligation* to produce equal outcomes among various groups. It is most significant for our purposes that the fundamental changes made in the rules of the game—changes that would affect the lives of millions of people—proceeded according neither to some constitutional command nor to a broad public consensus. Rather, the changes merely reflected the preferences of officials in the executive branch.

As the architects of a quintessentially conservative form of government, the American Founders believed that the capacity of the national government to coerce social change should be severely circumscribed, and it was with this in mind that they devised the system of federalism, which limits the authority of the national government, and, within the national government itself, the separation of powers among three distinct branches. The original Constitution established a legislative process whereby a bill could become law only if it successfully surmounted a host of obstacles deliberately placed in its path. The most notable of these include the bicameral legislature (one of whose chambers is not elected on the basis of population, thereby giving disproportionate influence to the inhabitants of the smaller states) and the presidential veto. By 1971, affirmative action had become a national social policy without ever being subjected to this process. The Civil Rights Act of 1964, by contrast, was a product of the conventional legislative process and, as noted, did nothing more than extend legal equality to all Americans. As if to emphasize this, Section 703(j) of the act expressly prohibits giving

> preferential treatment to any individual or group . . . on account of an imbalance which may exist with respect to the total or percentage of persons of any race, color, religion, sex, or national origin employed . . . in any comparison with the total number or percentage in any community, state, section or other area or in the available workforce or community.

What is most striking about this language is the remarkable prescience with which it anticipates the Philadelphia Plan and the OFCCP regulations implementing Executive Order No. 11246. It is as if the Nixon administration, in effect, unilaterally repealed an act of Congress and replaced it with its own contrary policy. When confronted with the fact of executive hegemony in the enactment of race-conscious social policy, supporters of affirmative action usually reply that Congress had the opportunity to kill the Philadelphia Plan (and thus, preemptively, the OFCCP regulations as well) when it voted on the appropriations bill rider in 1969 at the behest of Senator McClellan. Yet Congress voted to defeat the rider. Thus, concludes Barry L. Goldstein, assistant counsel to the NAACP Legal Defense and Education Fund, "the use of affirmative action and goals and timetables in the executive order program had survived after an extensive congressional debate."[21] If by this Goldstein means that affirmative action can be presumed to have the level of broad public support ordinarily associated with acts of Congress, he has seriously misunderstood the nature of the American system of government. As noted above, because of the system's inherent bias against government-coerced social change, the legislative process is, by design, slow and methodical, even to the point of being inert in the absence of a broad, stable (as opposed to ephemeral) public consensus. These characteristics are, of course, every bit as evident when Congress considers repealing a government policy as when it considers enacting one. That is why those who say that congressional acquiescence in an administratively or judicially created policy is tantamount, as an expression of consensus, to a congressional act are, in the words of the political scientist Richard E. Morgan,

> either naive or disingenuous. The same set of interest groups that are insufficient to persuade Congress to adopt a policy in the first place may be quite sufficient, if the policy can be put in place judicially or bureaucratically, to keep the legislature from disestablishing it. In assemblies it takes a good, healthy, stable majority to act and properly so; but a skilled minority can stop action.[22]

Our second observation has to do with the validity of the presuppositions underlying the notion of group underutilization and the goal of statistical parity among groups. When we say that affirmative action is predicated on the teleological belief that equality of opportunity would lead inexorably and invariably to equality of result, we use the words "inexorably" and "invariably" advisedly. Assuming equal opportunity, then equality of result, here indicated by statistical parity among designated social groups, is "inexorable" in the sense that it flows *necessarily* from equal opportunity. Moreover, statistical parity among groups will be the norm "invariably," that is, in virtually every conceivable category. Put otherwise, statistical group parity with respect to, say, the construction trades will be observed (or so it is assumed) not merely within the construction trades generically; not merely within each particular species of the construction trades (carpenter, welder, electrician, heavy-equipment operator, and so forth); not merely within each particular construction trade within each and every local labor force; but within each particular construction trade within each and every individual *firm* that employs said construction trade.

As noted in the example of the Kansas construction company cited earlier, even a firm with as few as fifteen employees is expected to conform to the norm of statistical group parity. This, argues the philosopher Alan H. Goldman, is simply not reasonable, mainly because "the programs are drawn up and the [minority and female utilization] goals applied on an institution by institution basis, and the statistical samples taken individually are too small in relation to the whole market to expect them to mirror the overall ratio by a specific date after fair competition begins."[23]

This point is made in a slightly different way by the economist Thomas Sowell, who performed a particularly edifying experiment designed to illustrate the effect of *statistical variance*. Sowell proposed to "consider some process where racial, sexual, or ideological factors do not enter, such as the flipping of a coin."[24] He then proceeded to flip a coin one hundred times, recording the ratio of heads to tails in each increment of ten coin flips. We would, of course, expect that the greater the total number of coin flips, the more closely would the ratio of heads to tails approximate a one-to-one relationship. Having flipped a coin one hundred times, Sowell noted that it came up heads 41 percent of the time and tails 59 percent of the time—fairly close to what one might expect given the total number of coin tosses. When the results of the coin tosses were tabulated in increments of ten, however, the incremental ratios varied significantly:

Heads	3	4	3	4	6	7	2	4	5	3
Tails	7	6	7	6	4	3	8	6	5	7

"At one extreme," Sowell observed, "there were seven heads and three tails, and at the other extreme eight tails and two heads. Statistics not only have averages, they have variance."[25] Then he explained the implications of his experiment:

> Translate this into employment decisions. Imagine that you are the employer who ends up with eight employees from one group and two from another, even though both groups are the same size and no different in qualifications, and even though you have been unbiased in selecting. Try explaining to EEOC and the courts [or, for present purposes, OFCCP] that you ended up with four times as many employees from one group by random chance! You may be convicted of discrimination, even if you have only been guilty of statistical variance.[26]

The Role of the Equal Employment Opportunity Commission

If by the early 1970s the Office of Federal Contract Compliance Programs (OFCCP) had developed a regime of rules for enforcing "civil rights" that managed to equate statistical variance with illegal race and sex discrimination, an even more radical regime of rules was simultaneously being developed by the Equal Employment Opportunity Commission (EEOC), yet another executive branch administrative agency. Unlike the OFCCP, the EEOC has jurisdiction over all employers with fifteen or more employees, regardless of whether they have contracts with the federal government. The EEOC was created by Congress in 1964 as the primary agency responsible for enforcement of Title VII of the Civil Rights Act, which bans discrimination in employment. In response to criticism of the proposed title during the Senate debates that preceded its passage, the act's floor leader, Hubert Humphrey (D–Minn.), declared: "Contrary to the allegations of opponents of this title, there is nothing in it that will give any power to the Commission [EEOC] or to any court to require hiring, firing or promotion of employees in order to meet a racial quota or to achieve a certain racial balance."[27] Senator Joseph Clark (D–Pa.) further reassured his colleagues that "an employer may set his qualifications as high as he likes, he may test to determine which applicants have these qualifications and he may hire, assign, and promote on the basis of test performance."[28]

Because the use of standardized hiring and promotion tests had become so prevalent in the American workplace, this reassurance was very important. Indeed, without it the Civil Rights Act might not have passed, for there was reason, even in 1964, to be concerned about its possible effect upon the use of such tests. In that year a hearing examiner in an Illinois Fair Employment Practice Commission case, *Myart v. Motorola, Inc.*, ruled that Motorola's test for radio repairmen—which the complainant, a black man named Leon Myart, had failed—was racially discriminatory because it "was normed on advantaged groups" and failed to "reflect and equate inequities and environmental factors among the culturally disadvantaged and culturally deprived groups."[29] Implicit in the ruling of the hearing examiner, Robert A. Bryant, was the notion that a test's adverse impact on minority job applicants is a basis for establishing that the test is racially discriminatory.

During the congressional debate over the Civil Rights Act, Senator John Tower (R–Tex.) argued vigorously against inclusion of any provision reflecting the rationale of *Myart v. Motorola, Inc.*[30] The act's Democratic leadership, specifically Senators Humphrey and Clark, agreed, with Clark declaring that there would be "no requirement in Title VII that employers abandon some bona fide qualification tests where, because of differences in background and education, members of some groups are able to perform better on these tests than members of other groups."[31] In short, the determination as to whether a professionally developed ability test was discriminatory could not turn on unintended effects. With this in mind, Section 703(h) was written into the Civil Rights Act. It is the sole provision according to which the EEOC was granted authority to issue guidelines on employment testing. It reads as follows:

> . . . nor shall it be an unlawful employment practice for an employer to give and to act upon the results of any professionally developed ability test provided such test, its administration or action upon the results is not designed, intended or used to discriminate because of race, color, religion, sex or national origin.

Almost from the moment of its inception the EEOC began issuing regulations that violated both the language and the spirit of this provision, but as in the case of the OFCCP regulations, the worst abuses did not occur until the advent of the Nixon administration. In 1970 the EEOC issued revised employment testing regulations inspired by the personal campaign of William H. Enneis, the agency's chief psychologist and the man in charge of its testing policy, to rid the American business community of "the cult of credentialism . . . in whatever form it occurs."[32] Phil Lyons describes the methods that propelled Enneis's crusade:

Commonly regarded as the high-water mark of Enneis and his colleagues' campaign for "socially responsible" testing standards, the 1970 guidelines' declared objective was identical rejection rates for minority and nonminority job applicants. The Commission sought to achieve this objective by discouraging employers from using any but its own preferred validation methodology and by adding three new hurdles: a test with different success rates for minorities and nonminorities had to be "fair"; it had to conform to "utility requirements"; and it had to be shown that no other suitable tests with lower minority rejection rates were available. With these new guidelines, all the arcana of psychometrics were drawn into the determination of a firm's compliance. So the 1970s became boom times for industrial psychologists: no large firm could afford to be without its own in-house team to defend company selection procedures against EEOC challenges. Still, even with the most sophisticated psychological expertise, no employer could be certain that his procedures would pass muster.[33]

When it became clear that the EEOC had begun to overtake the other federal civil rights agencies in the development of affirmative action doctrine, Congress enacted the Equal Employment Opportunity Act of 1972, which established an Equal Opportunity Coordinating Council (EOCC) consisting of representatives from the OFCCP, the Justice Department, the Civil Service Commission (CSC), and the EEOC. The council was ordered to draft uniform guidelines on employee selection procedures, thus enabling the federal government to speak with one voice on the issue of employment discrimination. In one of its first decisions, the council agreed that any uniform guidelines should extend to both public and private employers, but there was little agreement on the actual content of the proposed guidelines. The EEOC's representatives "wanted to retain the whole armamentarium of technical devices they developed to hold employers' feet to the civil rights fire."[34]

One such device was the 1970 guidelines' requirement that every test with "disproportionately high" adverse impact on minority job applicants be validated. To avoid the vagueness inherent in the phrase "disproportionately high," the negotiators for the OFCCP, the CSC, and the Justice Department wanted to establish a definitive ratio between minority and nonminority selection rates (4 to 5 was the ratio chosen) beyond which employers would not be subject to the guidelines' validation requirement. This recommendation (which came to be known as the "four-fifths rule") was rejected by the EEOC negotiator. Finally, when the other agencies' negotiators produced scientific evidence questioning the "viability" of the guidelines' requirement that tests be validated separately for minorities and meet standards of "fairness," the EEOC's negotiator recommended that the commission withdraw from the council. In a letter to his superiors, the negotiator wrote that "it would not be in the interests of the groups EEOC was interested in" to remain involved in the face of "research findings that were continuing to build the case against differential prediction."[35] In 1975 EEOC officials acted on this recommendation and advised that negotiations be broken off "on the grounds that agreement on a set of principles consistent with EEOC's principles was impossible."[36] This position prompted the Justice

Department's negotiator to conclude that racial quotas were its true goal:

> An unstated or covertly stated reason may underlie the apparent EEOC refusal to modify its present guidelines. Under the present EEOC guidelines, few employers are able to show the validity of *any* of their selection procedures, and the risk of their being held unlawful is high. Since not only tests, but all other procedures must be validated, the thrust of the present guidelines is to place almost all test users in a posture of noncompliance; to give discretion to enforcement personnel to determine who should be prosecuted; and to set aside objective selection procedures in favor of numerical hiring.[37]

The movement to create a regulatory environment in which quota hiring would ultimately replace hiring on the basis of test performance accelerated under the administration of President Carter. Responding to intense lobbying by the NAACP, the Leadership Conference on Civil Rights, the National Women's Political Caucus, and the Women's Legal Defense Fund, Congress enacted the Reorganization Act of 1978, which established the EEOC as having exclusive authority within the executive branch to interpret Title VII.[38] Carter appointed Eleanor Holmes Norton to chair this increasingly powerful agency. In expressing her dismay at the success with which employers were increasingly able to validate their tests, Norton unabashedly served notice that for her, Title VII's purpose was not so much to combat discriminatory employment practices as it was to guarantee jobs to the designated "bodies." "My hat is off to the psychologists," she said, referring to the growing incidence of successful test validation. But at the same time she complained that the vindication of employment tests had not been accompanied by "comparable evidence that validated tests have in fact gotten black and brown bodies, or for that matter, females, into places as a result of the validation of those tests." Then she added ominously,

> I see some positive advantages I must say in encouraging an employer to look at what the ultimate goal is. That is to say, did your workforce have some minorities and females before the test has been validated? And if you really don't want to go through that, but you are interested in getting excluded people in your work force, we would encourage you to do so.[39]

The implication of these remarks could hardly have been more obvious. The EEOC chairman was, in effect, telling employers across America, "Just hire the right proportion of black, brown, and female bodies and we won't bother you."

At this point in our discussion it seems appropriate to comment on the purported distinction between "goals" and "quotas." Unfortunately, the debate over affirmative action has all too often been sidetracked by an essentially semantic quibble over the meaning of these two words in the context of affirmative action. Opponents typically argue against affirmative action on the grounds that it amounts to a racial and gender quota system. On the other hand, supporters say that affirmative action has never made use of quotas; it merely sets flexible goals and timetables as a useful way (some say the only way) of measuring the extent of an employer's compliance with Title VII's nondiscrimination mandate. A typical expression of this view goes as follows:

> [A]ffirmative action isn't a bureaucratic inquisition aimed at enforcing a quota system. It hasn't meant the imposition of inflexible numbers. What it has meant [in the case of the OFCCP regulations] is that those businesses with which the Government [has contracts] must demonstrate a "good faith" effort to give women and minorities a fair share of the opportunities generated by Federal contracts.[40]

Furthermore, to the extent that "goals" may, in some settings, have been transmogrified into nonpermissible quotas, the fault lies not with the administrative rules and regulations that constitute the government's affirmative action effort, but rather with unscrupulous businessmen. Thus, Representative Don Edwards (D–Cal.) wrote in the *New York Times* that

> there are bound to be examples of employers who have used quotas to meet affirmative action obligations. Even today, there may be some Federal contractors who choose to use quotas. But the use of quotas in affirmative action programs has been, and remains, illegal. So if Federal contractors are indeed using quotas, it is up to the Administration to enforce the law and see that this stops.[41]

Our discussion so far has suggested that the clear intent of the OFCCP and EEOC regulations, with their focus on numerical results and their opposition to anything that tends to get in the way of statistical group parity (such as objective testing), together with the public statements of administrative officials such as former EEOC Chairman Norton, is to encourage—one is even tempted to say force—employers to treat "goals" *as if* they were quotas. There is thus something quite odd about suggestions that employers are to blame for adhering to the clearly discernible spirit of the regulation, as well as to the obvious predilections of those government officials who are responsible for their enforcement.

Ultimately the issue raised by affirmative action does not, as many scholars have recognized, revolve around the alleged distinction between goals and quotas.[*] Rather, the issue concerns the propriety of governmentally coerced racial and gender preference schemes, for it is axiomatic that the OFCCP and EEOC regulations encourage employers to prefer minorities and women over white males. At the most elemental level, this is indicated by the fact that an employer who fails to meet the minority or female goal is, at the very least, subject to an investigation, while the employer who does meet the goal is left unbothered. As we have seen, failure to meet a goal may be attributable to nothing more sinister than statistical variance. Since affirmative action does not recognize the concept of statistical variance, however, the employer is obliged to artificially adjust each instance of minority or female "underutilization" in favor of these groups, even if statistical variance is the cause of the supposed underutilization. (Of course, none of the executive agencies have guidelines for dealing with "underutilization"—or,

---

[*]Among opponents of affirmative action, see Thomas Sowell, *Civil Rights: Rhetoric or Reality* (New York: William Morrow and Co., 1984), and Nathan Glazer, *Affirmative Discrimination: Ethnic Inequality and Public Policy* (New York: Basic Books, 1975). Among proponents, see John C. Livingston, *Fair Game? Inequality and Affirmative Action* (San Francisco: W. H. Freeman and Co., 1979), p. 12: "The manipulative defense of affirmative action had sought to evade both the adverse effect on white interests and the ideological and moral issues involved. Even the label attached to the programs—affirmative action—reflects the approach of the image-makers. A transparent euphemism for preferential treatment, it seeks to conceal the fact of preference, as well as the hard and obvious truth that non-whites can be treated preferentially only at the expense of whites. And when the opponents of affirmative action invented the phrase 'reverse discrimination' to describe that truth, its supporters sought to conjure it away by inventing a distinction between quotas and goals."

for that matter, any form of discrimination—involving non-minorities and males.) When employers make such adjustments, they are engaging in "reverse" discrimination, *even* if one accepts the improbable teleological view of equal opportunity.

Affirmative Action and the Judiciary

So far we have seen that the federal affirmative action effort throughout the 1970s was for the most part undertaken unilaterally by executive agency personnel, frequently in direct contravention of both the letter and the spirit of the very Civil Rights Act and the very executive order these agencies were charged with implementing. A person with a text book understanding of American constitutionalism, with its separation of powers and its provision for a neutral, independent judiciary, might reasonably expect that a state of affairs such as the one we have described is precisely what the judiciary is supposed to correct. Though not explicitly authorized by the Constitution, the federal judiciary has exercised the power of judicial review since the tenure of Chief Justice John Marshall. Over time, the doctrine of judicial review has come to signify the power of courts to overturn executive acts that violate some aspect of the federal Constitution or some provision of federal law. In light of the essential incompatibility of administrative affirmative action regulations and certain key provisions of the Civil Rights Act, one might have expected the federal judiciary, when presented with appropriate cases, to fulfill its historic role and summarily strike down those rules and regulations that contravened the Civil Rights Act, not to mention the equal protection clause of the Fourteenth Amendment. This, however, is not what transpired. In fact, throughout the 1970s the courts became increasingly vigorous exponents of affirmative action doctrine in their own right. Not only did they consistently uphold challenged aspects of the regulations that were promulgated by the administrative agencies, but judges also began to enact their own affirmative action programs under the guise of equitable relief, often in the form of judicially enforced consent decrees.

To understand how such a thing could have happened, one might begin by cataloging the dozens of cases in which judges either permitted or required the proliferation of affirmative action in public policy. Here we propose to take a more succinct and ultimately, we hope, more revealing approach: We will focus on two influential articles published by eminent legal scholars during the 1970s. They attempted, on legal grounds, to reconcile the practice of affirmative action and its corollary, "reverse" discrimination, with the relevant provisions of statutory and constitutional law.

As we shall observe shortly, the writings of contemporary legal scholars are often more remarkable for what they reveal about the social policy preferences of their authors than for what they teach us about the law. Yet their policy preferences have a way of *becoming* law in the hands of sympathetic judges, who need only to be shown how the desired policies can be insinuated into existing legal instruments. A case in point is an essay by Ronald Dworkin entitled "How to Read the Civil Rights Act," which first appeared in *The New York Review of Books* in 1979. Dworkin was chiefly concerned with attempting to justify the Supreme Court's recent *Weber* decision,[42] in which the Court voted 5 to 2 to uphold the validity of an affirmative action program instituted "voluntarily" by a private employer, Kaiser Aluminum Corporation, in cooperation with the United Steel Workers of America. The Court had based its ruling on the premise that the Civil Rights Act permitted such racial preference schemes, which in this instance involved the establishment of a quota for blacks' admission to a lucrative apprenticeship program which led ultimately to promotion to a more highly skilled and better-paying position within the Kaiser organization. Ordinarily, admission to the apprenticeship program would have been determined by an employee's relative seniority, but under the disputed program seniority had been subordinated to race so that the quota for blacks could be met. The legal challenge to this practice was brought by a white male employee of Kaiser who, in his attempts to gain admission to the apprenticeship program, had been passed over in favor of less-senior black employees. For the Court's majority, the disposition of the case turned on the wording of Section 703(j) of Title VII of the Civil Rights Act (quoted above), which says that nothing in Title VII "shall be interpreted to require any employer ... to grant preferential treatment to any individual or to any group" in order to reduce racial imbalance in its workforce. Because Congress chose to use the word "require" rather than "permit," it therefore gave tacit permission to employers to give preferential treatment to underrepresented minorities to reduce racial imbalance in their workforce, so long as such action was not compelled by an agency or court, said the Court's majority.

Section 703(j), however, is not the only provision in Title VII that addresses the issue of racial preference. Section 703(a) declares that it is unlawful for any employer:

> (1) to fail or refuse to hire or to discharge any individual or otherwise to discriminate against any individual with respect to his compensation, terms, conditions, or privileges of employment, because of such individual's race, color, religion, sex, or national origin; or,
> (2) to limit, segregate, or classify his employees or applicants for employment in any way which would deprive ... any individual of employment opportunities or otherwise adversely affect his status as an employee, because of such individual's race, color, religion, sex, or national origin.

This is the language upon which the complainant, Brian Weber, rested his claim that Kaiser's practice violated the Civil Rights Act, and with which the Court's majority contended in rejecting Weber's complaint. In attempting to justify the Court's ruling against Justice Rehnquist's remarkably acerbic dissent, which emphasized the unambiguous clarity not only of Section 703(a) but of the intent of Congress as expressed through major sponsors of the Civil Rights Act such as Senators Humphrey, Clark, and Case, Dworkin adopts a twofold strategy. First he argues that, notwithstanding its "apparent" clarity, the meaning of Section 703(a) could not have been clear to a majority of the members of Congress, because if it had there would have been no need to attach Section 703(j) to the act to ensure its passage; the latter section would have been considered superfluous. Nor are the unequivocal statements of Humphrey, Clark, and Case disclaiming preferential treatment of any relevance in correctly interpreting the Act:

> There is no legislative convention that automatically turns the statements even of key leaders, even of "bipartisan captains," into preambles. If there were such a convention, it would not have been appropriate for opponents of the bill to voice fears

after the reassuring statements had been made. On the contrary, it would have been preposterous. Nor would it have been necessary to add Section 703(j). That would have been redundant, merely repeating what Senators Humphrey, Clark, and Case, and others had already added to the bill.

The fact that Congress added 703(j) shows that congressmen do not acknowledge a convention that turns the statements of important senators into amendments.[43]

It is at least as plausible to suppose that, having by 1964 experienced a good ten years of Warren Court–led liberal judicial activism, opponents who demanded the inclusion of Section 703(j) had quite reasonably surmised that some federal judges would be all too eager to ignore or traduce the plain meaning of Title VII, and concluded that a little redundancy might help restrain these proclivities. By this reading, the reservations voiced by congressional skeptics, even after having heard the reassurances given by the bill's key sponsors, would not seem "preposterous," but rather quite sensible. In any event, it is hardly certain that the voicing of such reservations, together with the addition of Section 703(j) to Title VII, "shows" what Dworkin says it shows; namely, that members of Congress did not *themselves* regard Section 703(a)'s absolute ban on racial preference as unambiguous and, more generally, that they did not accept the statements of key floor leaders as reliable indicators of legislative intent.

Having postulated a lack of congressional consensus on the meaning of Section 703(a) of Title VII, Dworkin proceeds to his next step, which is to recommend that whatever alleged ambiguities exist in the text of the Civil Rights Act be resolved in favor of the "disadvantaged group," to the detriment of white males such as Brian Weber, presumably because the latter are members of an "advantaged group."

Discrimination of the conventional sort, practiced against blacks in the United States for centuries, is wrong. But why? Is it wrong because any race-conscious distinction is always and inevitably wrong, even when used to redress inequality? If so, then it would be correct . . . to interpret Title VII as outlawing all such distinctions in employment. Or is traditional discrimination wrong because it reflects prejudice and contempt for a disadvantaged group, and so increases the disadvantage of that group? In that case, it would be sounder to attribute to Title VII the different program of outlawing such malign discrimination, and seeking to remove its inegalitarian consequences, and it would be perverse, rather than sensible, to understand the statute to bar private efforts in that direction.[44]

Dworkin's article is instructive because it evinces a style of jurisprudence that became increasingly influential among the federal judiciary throughout the 1970s. The passage quoted above contains all its essential features. First, a typology of different kinds of racial discrimination is introduced: There is "discrimination of the conventional sort," which is "wrong" and "malign" because "it reflects prejudice and contempt for a disadvantaged group." There is also a kind of discrimination that seeks "to remove [the] inegalitarian consequences" of "malign" discrimination. It would be "perverse," we are told, "to understand the statute to bar" this latter kind of discrimination. Secondly, it makes the determination as to whether a particular discriminatory practice is malign or benign contingent upon whether the victim of such practice is a member of a "disadvantaged group." Finally, it regards the Civil Rights Act as primarily an instrument for redistributing social goods, insofar as the act is said to countenance discrimination that "seeks to remove inegalitarian consequences."

If the Civil Rights Act's ban on the use of preferential treatment to achieve a racially balanced workforce could be "read" virtually out of existence, then so too could Section 703(h) of Title VII (which, as noted earlier, authorizes the use of "any professionally developed ability test" that is not "designed, intended, or used to discriminate because of race, religion, sex or national origin") be interpreted by judges to support the EEOC's quest to eliminate such tests. In its 1971 landmark decision in *Griggs v. Duke Power Co.*,[45] the Supreme Court held that at least where blacks had been overtly excluded from employment because of their race before the enactment of Title VII, the use of neutral employment criteria—in this case, performance on a general intelligence test and possession of a high school diploma—was *prima facie* unlawful if it produced, as between blacks and nonblacks, a "disparate impact" that was adverse to the blacks as a group. The Supreme Court ruled that the only way an employer could rebut the presumption of illegal racial discrimination implicit in the occurrence of a disparate impact was to prove to a court's satisfaction that the neutral criteria that produced it were "job-related." Writing for a unanimous Court, Chief Justice Burger decided (upon what basis is not clear) that

> Congress directed the thrust of the Act to the *consequences* of employment practices, not simply the motivation. More than that, Congress placed on the employer the burden of showing that any given requirement must have a manifest relationship to the employment in question.[46]

Expanding on this verdict, Burger declared that "good intent or absence of discriminatory intent does not redeem" employment procedures or testing mechanisms that operate as "built-in headwinds for minority groups and are unrelated to measuring job capability."[47]

Apart from the question of whether this decision can in any way be reconciled with the relevant statutory language or its legislative history, it is clear that the *Griggs* ruling is predicated on the dubious assumption that it is possible to distinguish empirically those criteria that are truly "job-related" from those that are not. Thomas Sowell has commented on the problematic nature of the Court's assumption:

> Nor can the "job-relatedness" of the standards be assessed in any mechanical way by the nature of the task. Standards that are *person*-related play the same economic role as standards that are *job*-related. If people who finish high school seem to the employer to work out better than dropouts, third parties who were not there can neither deny this assessment nor demand that it be proved to their uninformed satisfaction. It makes no difference economically whether this was because the specific task relates to what was learned in high school or because those who finish high school differ in outlook from those who drop out. Neither does it matter economically whether those who score higher on certain tests make better workers because the kind of people who read enough to do well on tests tend to differ from those who spend their time in activities that require no reading.[48]

In short, personal outlook, although not demonstrably "job-related," may nevertheless provide a reliable basis for predicting successful performance on the job.

Apparently oblivious to these considerations, the lower courts throughout the 1970s expanded significantly on the disparate-impact theory of discrimination as laid down by the Supreme Court. Soon the "job-relatedness" element of the *Griggs* decision evolved into what has become known as the "business-necessity" doctrine. The most rigid and widely followed definition of business necessity in the lower courts[49] was as follows:

> The test is whether there exists an overriding legitimate business purpose such that the practice is necessary for the safe and efficient operation of the business. Thus, the business purpose must be sufficiently compelling to override any racial impact; the challenged practice must effectively carry out the business purpose it is alleged to serve; and there must be available no acceptable alternative policies or practices which would better accomplish the business purpose advanced, or accomplish it equally well with a lesser differential racial impact.[50]

In *Griggs*, the Supreme Court's disparate-impact theory of discrimination was held to apply only to employers who had at one time practiced overt discrimination. That qualification was soon routinely ignored. Note too the stringency with which "business necessity" is defined: Employment criteria that produce a disparate racial impact may be sustained only if they are "compelling," which is to say, "necessary for the safe and efficient operation of the business." It is of no small import that this requirement is utterly unconnected to the reality of doing business in a highly competitive economy, where survival depends not only on a firm's ability to operate "safely" and "efficiently," but also upon whether it can provide a product or service consumers regard as superior to that offered by competing firms. Thus in 1971 a court held that an airline did not succeed in justifying its practice of hiring more women than men for the position of flight attendant, despite the existence of empirical studies showing that men did not comfort passengers as soothingly as did women, because, in the court's view, the "essence" of the airline's business was the safe transportation of passengers, not the creation of a pleasant environment.[51] The court may have been correct in locating the "essence" of the airline's business where it did, but anyone who has seen the advertisements put out by airlines knows that, aside from fares, the creation of a pleasant environment is largely what the competition between them is all about.

The lower courts also extended the *range* of employment criteria that were governed by the disparate-impact and business-necessity doctrines. *Griggs* spoke only of standardized tests and educational credentials, but by 1972 it was established that an employer could not refuse to hire applicants with multiple arrest records (unless he could prove the job-relatedness of this criterion) because national statistics revealed that blacks are arrested more frequently than whites.[52]

One important consequence of the increased salience of the disparate-impact theory of employment discrimination was the growing use of statistics as evidence. Because disparate impact renders the issue of discriminatory purpose or intent irrelevant, statistical evidence necessarily became the sole basis for advancing and rebutting allegations of unlawful discrimination. Assessing this trend, one scholar has concluded that "a survey of the case-law reveals that although the courts are committed to the use of statistical proof, too often their decisions display only a rudimentary and intuitive understanding [of statistics]."[53]

Generally, the courts have accepted three modes of statistical proof as sufficient to shift to the employer the burden of showing that his employment criteria are job-related.[54] First, the minority or female success rate on a challenged requirement, such as an exam, may be compared to the success rate of candidates not belonging to one of these groups. A second method compares the percentage of women or minorities within a relevant population who possess a certain requisite attribute, such as minimum height and weight or a high school diploma, with the percentage of males or nonminorities within that same relevant population who possess the requisite attribute. The third method is similar to that employed by the OFCCP in defining female or minority underutilization; the percentage of members of a plaintiff's class in the employer's workforce is compared to the percentage of that class in a relevant population.

Because both the second and third methods involve comparisons to "relevant populations," determining the appropriate geographical delimitation of that population may decisively affect the outcome of the case. Courts have shown themselves to be utterly capricious in this regard, however, inexplicably choosing to accept national statistics in one case, statewide statistics in another, and metropolitan statistics in yet another. In the absence of any uniform rule or convention for determining the relevant population from which statistical data may be derived for the purpose of showing a disparate impact, it is possible for courts simply to choose the set of statistics that is most advantageous to the side favored by the judge.

Much of the popular debate over affirmative action focused on the question of whether goals and timetables for the employment of females and minority group members amount in effect to rigid quotas, with supporters for the most part conceding the undesirability of quotas, but throughout the 1970s courts frequently ordered the use of literal racial and gender quotas for Title VII violations, or authorized consent decrees involving the use of such quotas. Section 706(g) of Title VII explicitly authorizes the federal courts to impose remedies for violations. This is hardly a novel mandate; the power of courts to impose judicial remedies has long been recognized as stemming from their traditional authority to grant equitable relief. The concept of equity, however, has changed dramatically since the advent of the Warren Court, and these changes account in large part for the apparent enthusiasm with which courts have embraced group quotas. Thirty years ago equitable relief was by and large applied to specific individuals, focused on specific concrete rights (especially property), was usually exercised in a proscriptive way to block enforcement of an unjust law or action, was largely bounded by precedent, and required an irreparable injury that was immediate and clear.[55] Today all this has changed, but perhaps the most momentous change concerns the frequent substitution of broad social groups (usually defined by racial and gender criteria where civil rights violations are alleged) for specific individuals in the fashioning of equitable relief.[56] Reflecting this trend, courts in the 1970s increasingly treated Title VII violations by employers or labor unions, not as offenses committed against identifiable individual victims, but as offenses perpetrated against the entire group to which the victims putatively belonged. Of course, this is understandable given the salience of the disparate-impact theory in employment discrimination case law. Insofar as disparate-impact theory relies entirely on statistical data to prove Title VII violations, it dispenses with the need to produce individual victims of discrimination.

With no identifiable victims available, courts intent upon providing equitable relief must focus on the entire group that was, so the theory goes, the collective victim of a disparate impact.

This approach stands in marked contrast to the traditional "individual rights" model of jurisprudence, which would limit relief to those specific individuals victimized by discrimination against the group to which they belong, and would limit the *scope* of relief to restoring such individuals to the status they would have had without the discrimination. The "group-rights" model of jurisprudence, of which group-based equity is an integral part, means that when an employer has discriminated against a group (whether intentionally or not), the employer must redress the statistical imbalance presumably caused by the discrimination by preferring members of the maligned group to nonmembers of the group. In most cases the beneficiaries of this kind of relief personally suffered no harm or deprivation at the hands of the particular employer-defendant, and the nonminority group members who were to be systematically disfavored under such an arrangement neither personally engaged in the discriminatory practice at issue nor benefited from its effects.

Even many proponents of group-based equity acknowledge that its quota remedies are generally overbroad, but maintain that identifying individual victims of discrimination is impossible in many situations because, for example, many "victims" will not have applied for employment because of the defendant's reputation for biased hiring. Undoubtedly this assertion is sometimes true, although it seems less plausible when applied to employers whose "bias" consists of nothing more than the use of neutral hiring criteria that happen to produce a disparate racial impact. Moreover, it is curious that many of the individuals and interest groups who make this argument, such as the American Civil Liberties Union, would, in other contexts, be among the first to swear allegiance to the proposition that it is better to let ten guilty people go free than to punish one innocent individual. The analogy is valid if one accepts that for each member of group A who benefits from a racial or gender preference favoring that group, a corresponding member of group B is denied an opportunity—punished, in effect—because of that same racial or gender preference that favors the members of group A. Affirmative action is very much a zero-sum game.

The use of quotas to provide group-based equity tended to occur under judicial auspices even when there was no proven violation of the law. The form that it took was the judicial consent decree, a legal convention that has been described by one political scientist as "an oxymoron if there ever was one—describing the treatment of a defendant who does not admit he is guilty but agrees under compulsion to act as if he were."[57] As a general criticism this is not entirely fair—the consent decree, in which a court agrees to administer the terms of a negotiated settlement between opposing parties to a lawsuit, is surely a useful device for reducing judicial caseloads as well as for saving the time and reducing the litigation expenses of both plaintiff and defendant. Yet in light of administrative regulations and the Title VII case law that prevailed in the 1970s, something about the use of the consent decree in Title VII litigation raises questions. A typical employment discrimination consent decree involves an agreement between a plaintiff and a defendant whereby the plaintiff agrees to drop his complaint alleging unlawful discrimination in exchange for a promise from the defendant to reserve a fixed percentage of all new hires or promotions for members of the group the plaintiff purports to represent. Not only does this potentially lead to a situation in which the plaintiff is encouraged unilaterally to bargain away the rights of innocent third parties (who generally have no direct representation in the process), but the presumption of guilt that attaches to any employer whose employment criteria produce a disparate racial impact, coupled with the extreme difficulty of proving to a court's satisfaction the "job-relatedness" of such criteria, also means that for defendants in a great many Title VII lawsuits the only viable option is to travel the route of negotiated settlement. Viewed in this light, the employment discrimination consent decree seems, as a practical matter, to be coercive, not to mention potentially unjust where the fate of third parties is concerned.

Group Rights and the Constitution

To some, a regime of rights such as the one we have so far described may appear suspiciously dualistic, in that it may seem to establish one set of rights for members of one group while establishing a different set for members of another group. The question might then be asked, Does not such a regime offend the Fourteenth Amendment to the Constitution, which clearly states that no state shall "deny to any person within its jurisdiction the equal protection of the laws"? At first glance perhaps not, because the Fourteenth Amendment is addressed to the several states, and in the Civil Rights Act we are dealing with a federal statute. In 1954, however, the Supreme Court decided that racially discriminatory practices carried out by the federal government—in the case at hand, the maintenance of a segregated public school system in the District of Columbia—violated the Fifth Amendment's due process clause for essentially the same reasons that discrimination practiced by the states was held to violate the Fourteenth Amendment's equal protection clause. Although the Court was careful to point out that "we do not imply that the two [clauses] are always interchangeable phrases,"[58] a plausible argument could be made that a federal statute which, as interpreted by agencies and courts, establishes a dual regime of civil rights is certainly one instance where the two clauses should be treated interchangeably. In any event, there occurred during the 1970s numerous examples of *state* action that resulted in reverse discrimination of the sort experienced by Brian Weber, not the least of which were preferential admissions policies based on race that were adopted by many state university graduate and professional schools. The equal protection clause figures very prominently in any challenge to such policies, as it did in the famous *Bakke* case. Yet here too judges and academic lawyers followed the now-familiar strategy of "showing" the equal protection clause to be so nebulous as to have no readily discernible meaning, and then assigning to it an interpretation according to which conflicts over the allocation of rights are automatically resolved in favor of members of putatively disadvantaged groups.

One of the most influential exponents of this view during the 1970s was Owen Fiss of the Yale Law School. In particular, his article "Groups and the Equal Protection Clause," published in 1976, has become a staple of employment discrimination curricula at many leading law schools, and has been cited with approval in judicial opinions. Fiss wastes no time in asserting the opacity of the equal protection clause; two pages into his article he declares that "the words—no state shall 'deny to any person within its jurisdiction the equal protection of the laws'—do not state an intelligible rule of decision. In that sense the text has no meaning."[59] Apparently Fiss feels no obligation to argue for this position because it is so widely shared among the legal intelligentsia that constitutes his readership. Because of the ambiguity that supposedly inheres in the words of the clause, there has arisen "the need for a mediating principle, and the one chosen by courts and commentators is the antidiscrimination principle."[61] Fiss is careful to emphasize that "the antidiscrimination principle is not the Equal Protection Clause ... it is nothing more than a mediating principle."[61]

The problem with the antidiscrimination principle, in Fiss's view, is that it has proved only partially effective in facilitating "the ideal of equality"[62]—by which he means, not that the laws should apply with equal force to each individual, but rather that they should be applied in ways that promote substantive equality among racial groups. To be sure, creative judges had gone a long way toward realizing the ideal of substantive equality through the mechanism of the antidiscrimination principle:

> At some point in history the word "equal" shifts its location so as to deemphasize the word "protection"—it becomes understood that the Clause guarantees "the protection of equal laws," rather than just the "equal protection of the laws"; but the implications of the original still linger.[63]

Because the implications linger, a new "mediating principle" is called for. Fiss calls his proposed alternative the "group-disadvantaging principle." In brief, he urges that in treating claims that invoke the equal protection clause, courts should assert the primacy of the social group over the individual person. This is necessary because "there are natural classes, or social groups, in American society and blacks are such a group."[64] A collection of individuals becomes a "group," in Fiss's usage, if it satisfies two criteria. First, it must be an *entity*, in the sense that "the group has a distinct existence apart from its members, and also that it has an identity."[65] Secondly, there "is also a condition of *interdependence*. The identity and well-being of the members of the group and the identity and well-being of the group are linked."[66] Further, such a group cannot qualify for a "special position in equal protection theory" unless it possesses two more characteristics, which Fiss thus far ascribes exclusively to blacks:

It must have low socioeconomic and political status, and it must have endured this condition for "an extended period of time."[67]

If each of these criteria is met by a group, it properly becomes the object of a "redistributive strategy," which, according to Fiss, may be regarded as giving "expression to an ethical view against caste, one that would make it undesirable for any social group to occupy a position of subordination for any extended period of time."[68] At this point Fiss raises a pivotal question: "What, it might be asked, is the justification for that vision?" His answer is as follows:

> I am not certain whether it is appropriate to ask this question, to push the inquiry a step further and search for the justification of that ethic. . . . But if this second order inquiry is appropriate, a variety of justifications can be offered. . . . Changes in the hierarchical structure of society—the elimination of caste—might be justified as a means of (a) preserving social peace; (b) maintaining the community as a community, that is, as one cohesive whole; or (c) permitting the fullest development of the individual of the subordinated group who might otherwise look upon the low status of the group as placing a ceiling on their aspirations and achievements.[69]

Leaving aside such questions as whether a "group" is in fact not the same thing as a "caste," or whether social peace is not more easily preserved by *maintaining* hierarchy, the answer given here makes clear that the "vision" Fiss would incorporate into the Fourteenth Amendment is informed by normative values that are precisely the stuff about which political debate in a self-governing society is necessarily concerned. In seeking to allocate to the judiciary the power to decide such quintessentially political questions, Fiss gives little role to the institutions of representative self-government. He seems to sense this, however, and so turns to a familiar argument. Far from making the political system less democratic, judges who follow his prescriptions would actually be improving the quality of American democracy by giving expression to the needs and aspirations of the disadvantaged group which, it is assumed, has little or no representation in the political system as it is presently constituted. Thus,

> [w]hen the product of a political process is a law that hurts blacks, the usual countermajoritarian objection to judicial invalidation—

the objection that denies those "nine men" the right to substitute their view for that of "the people"—has little force. For the judiciary could be viewed as amplifying the voice of the powerless minority; the judiciary is attempting to rectify the injustice of the political process as a method of adjusting competing claims.[70]

Justice Brennan was invoking essentially the same rationale when, speaking for himself and three of his colleagues on the Supreme Court, he suggested in his *Bakke* opinion that the extent to which a person is covered by the equal protection clause should be determined in part by how "well represented" he is "in the political process."[71] Brennan declined to elaborate on this principle in the context of the *Bakke* case, no doubt because he regarded it as self-evident that Bakke, as a white male, was "well represented" by a California Assembly whose elected representatives were themselves predominantly white and male. Later we will have more to say about the belief, apparently held by many within the civil rights elite, that a legislator's race and sex determines the positions he takes on policy issues, and that the positions taken are simply the expression of "interests" relating to race or gender. For present purposes, however, we may turn once again to the invaluable Fiss. Here he explains why the fact that thousands of local and statewide elective offices have been won by black politicians since the passage of the Voting Rights Act has done nothing to ameliorate the supposed political powerlessness of blacks:

> [T]hese black-dominated political agencies—the black city council or the black mayor—must be placed in context. One fact of their context is white domination of those extra-political agencies such as banks, factories, and police, that severely circumscribe the power of the formal political agencies. Another fact is the persistent white domination of the national political agencies, such as the Congress and presidency, agencies that have become the critical loci of political power in American society.[72]

The repeated references to "white domination" of various institutions makes one begin to wonder why whites should not be regarded as a "group" in the sense proposed by Fiss—that is, as an entity whose members are interdependent, and whose individual identity and well-being are linked to the identity and well-being of the group. The reason we are inclined to resist such a notion is that it presupposes a set of distinctly "white" interests with which all white officeholders and businessmen identify and actively seek to promote. Not only would such a state of affairs have precluded passage of the Civil Rights and Voting Rights Acts (unless one resorts to a Marcusean-style "repressive tolerance" argument), but it would hardly explain the continuing popularity and prestige of white national officeholders such as Senators Kennedy, Metzenbaum, and Biden (to name just a few), each of whom would appear to vote consistently against the "white" program (whatever it is imagined to embrace). According to this view, racial interests are paramount in American politics, with traditional categories and distinctions as between, say, Democrats and Republicans, liberals and conservatives, and labor and management relegated to subordinate roles.

Fiss's depiction of blacks as a politically powerless group in need of judicial "representation" fails to take into account the remarkable degree of influence that the organized civil rights community has been able to exert upon the political system.[73] In virtually every respect, the civil rights lobby is an archetype of the kind of political interest group that Douglas and Wildavsky have designated by the term "sect." Their discussion of sects in American political life may fairly be said to have special relevance to the case of the civil rights lobby:

> In the past, the designation "sect" has usually been modified by "powerless" as established forces suppressed it or it rejected the larger society. This is no longer so in America. A distinguishing feature of our time is that sectarian groups can use government to impose restrictive regulations on their enemies instead of the other way around.[74]

Yet for Fiss, and evidently for many others in the legal community, "the injustice of the political process must be corrected, and perhaps as a last resort, that task falls to the judiciary."[75] At what point can it be agreed that judges have succeeded in "correcting" the injustice of the political process? Fiss is understandably vague on this question: "A just political process would be one in which blacks would have 'more' of a voice than they in fact do, but not necessarily one in which they would 'win.'"[76]

As for how groups other than blacks should fare under the equal protection clause, Fiss affirms that "blacks are the prototype of the protected group, but they are not the only group entitled to protection. . . . What the equal protection clause protects is specially disadvantaged groups, not just blacks."[77] Hence, "Jews or women might be entitled to less protection than American Indians, though nonetheless entitled to some protection."[78]

It should be clear by now that in Fiss's hands, the equal protection clause has been transformed into its opposite; the clause is now said to require the *un*equal protection of the laws. Laws or practices should be struck down or upheld depending entirely upon their perceived effect on the putatively disadvantaged group. Thus, "conduct that did discriminate but on the basis of criteria innocent on their face, such as performance on a standardized test for employment or college admission, or geographic proximity for student assignment, could be evaluated from the perspective of whether it had the effect of impairing the status of a specially disadvantaged group."[79] Moreover, the clause's explicit concern for the right of *individuals* to be free from unfair treatment by the state is disallowed:

> I do wish to deny that unfair treatment—such as being judged on the basis of an inappropriate criterion—is the domain of the Equal Protection Clause—even though such unfair treatment may be viewed from the individual perspective as a form of unequal treatment. As a protection for specially disadvantaged groups, the Equal Protection Clause should be viewed as a prohibition against group-disadvantaging practices, not unfair treatment.[80]

Critics of the group rights approach to equal protection jurisprudence have charged that such a regime will lead inexorably to the "balkanization" of American society, as various groups organize and lobby to secure a privileged place at the trough of governmentally dispensed "rights" and entitlements. These fears are only exacerbated by the failure of group rights theoreticians to articulate a formula for determining the specific level of protection various groups are entitled to under the equal protection clause. The group rights theory presupposes a rigid dichotomy between disadvantaged groups and advantaged groups, but it soon becomes clear that this is hard to maintain. For example, black males may be said to be victims of discrimination as blacks, but as males they may also be said to be the beneficiaries of discrimination against women. Indeed, incorporating women into the group rights theory of jurisprudence has proven especially problematic. The following passage, written by the philosopher Hardy Jones, is illustrative. Here Jones attempts to justify reverse discrimination against white males on the grounds that the latter are, in effect, recipients of "stolen goods":

> It might seem that I am committed to the view that "the sins of the fathers be visited on the sons." Now I do not think that sons should be punished for their fathers' sins or even that they should be required to make restitution for them. It is *not* unreasonable, though, that sons sometimes be deprived of certain benefits that rather naturally derive from injustices done by their ancestors. Such deprivation is especially appropriate when they are competing for jobs with persons who have suffered from sins like those generating the benefits. Such benefits are not "due" them. They do not have a "right" to these good things even if they themselves have violated no one's rights. A son who has inherited stolen property should not be jailed for the theft; but he has no right to the goods and may reasonably be expected to give them up. It seems entirely appropriate that they be transferred to the daughter or son of the thief's deceased victim.[81]

There is a serious problem of overinclusiveness inherent in the dichotomy between victims and beneficiaries of past discrimination. For example, some of those whom Jones would call "beneficiaries" of historic injustices may be recent immigrants to the United States, others may be descended from ancestors who, given the opportunity to engage in discrimination, refrained from doing so, and still others may be descended from ancestors who never even had the opportunity to discriminate because they had no meaningful contact with members of the "victim" class. Even putting this problem aside, it is difficult to discern the relevance of the "stolen goods" argument to white women. Although feminists are virtually unanimous in viewing all women as constituting a disadvantaged class of "victims," white women are in fact unlike other putative victims in at least one important respect: Fully one half of their ancestors are, according to the argument, "thieves." The daughter of an affluent white family is no less a "beneficiary" of the "stolen goods" accumulated by her father than is her brother. Jones makes it clear that he would deprive the son of the ill-gotten benefits he derived from his father; he furnishes no rationale for exempting the daughter from the implications of his brand of justice. This is the sort of conundrum that awaits the propounder of dichotomies between advantaged and disadvantaged groups, or between victims and beneficiaries of past discrimination.

In a similar vein, the drive toward a group rights jurisprudence has reintroduced into American life the problem of certifying one's racial or ethnic pedigree in order to qualify for a particular level of legal privilege. At another time and place in American history when race-conscious laws and practices were the norm—the Jim Crow South—the exact composition of a person's racial lineage was a matter of considerable importance, as anyone familiar with the novels of William Faulkner, with their use of quaint anachronisms such as "quadroon" and "octaroon" (to refer to persons with various combinations of white and black ancestors), can attest.[*] One may also recall that the plaintiff in the 1896 case of *Plessy v. Ferguson* originally brought suit because he believed he had erroneously been classified as a Negro, despite his protestations that he was white. Given the direction of civil rights policy and equal protection jurisprudence during the 1970s, it is not surprising that such controversies have resurfaced. In 1985, for example, the Hispanic community in San Francisco became embroiled in a bitter debate over whether Americans of Spanish descent (as opposed to those descended from Mexican, Central American, Cuban, or Puerto Rican immigrants) should qualify for city contracts that had been set aside for minorities.[82] And when the New York City Police Department began promoting officers to the rank of sergeant under a racial quota system, some officers petitioned to have their racial status changed from white to black or Hispanic.[83] If government was teaching that race, ethnicity, and gender are increasingly important determinants of achievement, status, and success, some Americans, at least, were responding in predictable ways.

---

[*]See also C. Vann Woodward, *The Strange Career of Jim Crow* (New York: Oxford Univ. Press, 1974).

Conclusion

We have sketched some of the major regulatory, legal, and doctrinal developments that occurred in the realm of civil rights
policy during the fifteen years preceding the Reagan administration. Whether intended or not, their combined effect as of 1980 had
been to institutionalize what Aaron Wildavsky called the "reverse
sequence" in civil rights.[84] The "original sequence," exemplified
by the text of the Civil Rights Act of 1964 and the congressional
debates that attended its enactment, called first for the establishment of equality before the law. This equality, according to the
traditional formulation, would help secure equality of opportunity, which in turn would promote equality of condition (although
the latter was by no means guaranteed). Almost as soon as the
original sequence was finally codified in law and public policy,
however, legal and political activists began the process of reversing the original sequence, so that now equality of condition was
cast as the categorical imperative of civil rights policy. Equality
before the law was now regarded as a luxury, affordable only in
those instances where legal equality served the paramount goal
of substantive equality. The objective, Wildavsky avers, "is not to
alter the range of inequality of results among individuals, . . . but
to assure that the same distribution of inequality of results obtains
across all relevant groups—whatever that range may be."[85]

The civil rights policies developed and implemented by executive agencies and courts during the 1970s facilitated that objective by substituting a norm of statistical group parity for equal
opportunity, and by making it a crime for employers to "un-
derutilize" groups, rather than to discriminate against individuals, in defiance of both statutes and the Constitution. Indeed, in
their pursuit of group parity, employers were generally *required* to
do the very thing that the Civil Rights Act prohibits—engage in
discrimination against individuals on the basis of their race and
sex. Because of this, Wildavsky concludes that the reverse sequence, far from making equality of opportunity and equality
before the law "more meaningful," as its proponents claim, is actually destructive of both:

> To see why this is so—why equal results drive out equal rights
> rather than fully achieve them, as is commonly asserted—

consider the coercive qualities required to maintain the reverse sequence. How can it be guaranteed that no citizen or group will acquire an unfair (in contemporary discourse, read "unequal") command over resources? Acknowledging that perfect equality of condition is unobtainable and may even be undesirable, attempting nevertheless to attain it justifies regulation of virtually every aspect of life that tends toward substantive inequality, i.e., almost everything. So long as every deviation from equal conditions is regarded as unfair, undemocratic, and therefore, illegitimate, government intervention in the interstices of social life is mandated. In so sweeping a conception of democracy, equality before the law, except for instantaneous votes at the moment of achieving equality of resources, is a fatal impediment.[86]

This passage speaks to one major set of concerns. The other, to which we have alluded throughout this chapter, is that the fundamental changes in the rules of the political system (which, following Wildavsky, we may now think of as the institutionalization of the reverse sequence in civil rights) were brought about not by some broad public consensus as revealed through the normal legislative process, nor by some constitutional command, but rather by a powerful synergism generated by our least representative and least accountable political institutions—the federal bureaucracy and the federal courts.

The unaccountability of these institutions (especially the courts) would make restoring the original sequence a difficult project for any administration. The forward momentum generated by fifteen years of virtually uninterrupted progress toward the establishment of the new regime would be a colossal impediment. But perhaps the greatest single difficulty facing the Reagan administration as it assumed power in 1980 stemmed from the ability of the organized civil rights movement and its influential supporters, notwithstanding the unconventionality of the reverse sequence they so strenuously promoted, to retain a monopoly on the discursive use of that most venerable of phrases—"civil rights."

CHAPTER THREE

Employment Discrimination, the Courts, and the Reagan Justice Department

> The courts have repudiated the administration's policy of backing off on civil rights enforcement.
>
> —Peter Sherwood, quoted in Fred Barbash,
> "The Administration Is Batting Zero on
> Civil Rights in the Supreme Court"

The statement above was made by an ebullient civil rights lawyer following a 1984 decision by the U.S. Supreme Court not to review the case of *Bratton v. Detroit*, in which white officers of the Detroit Police Department, joined by the Civil Rights Division of the Department of Justice, had challenged a voluntarily adopted city policy that established a 50 percent quota for promotion of blacks. The lawyer's reaction was by then both familiar and predictable, reflecting the prevailing view of civil rights activists that any attempt to enforce the civil rights of nonminorities by attacking racial quotas favoring minorities is, *ipso facto*, a "policy of backing off on civil rights enforcement." The *Bratton* case marked the culmination of three years of effort by the Reagan Justice Department to invalidate racial quotas and preference schemes, during which time it had not won a single victory before the Supreme Court.

In this, the first of two chapters in which we will present case studies of the Reagan administration's attempts to reformulate various aspects of civil rights policy, we will analyze six representative employment discrimination cases in which the Justice Department's Civil Rights Division participated as intervenor or *amicus curiae*. No claim is made to portray the totality of the Justice

Department's experience with employment discrimination policy formation and enforcement; the discussion will be limited to selected cases that seem representative of the general effort to reformulate race-conscious civil rights policies, specifically regarding the use of employment quotas and preference schemes based on race.

Reorientation of the Justice Department's Civil Rights Division

Before Reagan's election in 1980, the Civil Rights Division, like the OFCCP and the EEOC, had been a powerful engine in the drive toward a race- and gender-conscious interpretation of the federal civil rights statutes and the Constitution. Although the division, as merely the litigative arm of the federal civil rights enforcement bureaucracy, does not have authority to issue interpretive guidelines and regulations pursuant to statutory law, it nonetheless played an active role in the formulation of civil rights policy throughout the 1970s by consistently urging courts to establish legal precedents that collectively helped to facilitate the transition to a race- and gender-conscious regime of civil rights. As already noted, the division has been described by one prominent civil rights interest group as "the Civil Rights backbone of the federal government, and its activities and policies set the pace not only for other federal departments, but also for state, local, and private agencies."[1]

The salience of the Civil Rights Division was also acknowledged by the Heritage Foundation in its widely circulated 1980 report, *Mandate for Leadership*. The report argued for a "colorblind" approach to civil rights policy and labeled the division a "radicalized" agency. It advised that the new head of the division would have to be willing "to take the heat" for policy changes and to face staff rebellions.[2] Sure enough, by 1982 it was clear that William Bradford Reynolds' outspoken support for the principle of race- and gender-neutrality had earned him the enmity of a large segment of the division's staff. In that year the *National Journal* reported that the Division "is experiencing a barely concealed revolt by many of its 390 employees."[3] Said one division lawyer: "What we see is a conservative administration being activist in the opposite direction. It's this blind ideology—an airtight, rightist view of the world. They're reactionary. It's that simple."[4] "There's a very bad adversary atmosphere of them versus us," said another. "It's really weird. When we—that is, the division—lose in court, all the attorneys go up and down the hall cheering because we feel we really won."[5] Within a year of Reynolds' appointment to head the division, seventy-five attorneys—more than half its complement—had signed a petition opposing Reynolds' policies.[6]

Opposition to the division's efforts under Reynolds was even more intense among members of the organized civil rights lobby. In May 1983, NAACP general counsel Thomas I. Atkins suggested at a hearing of the House Judiciary Subcommittee on Civil and Constitutional Rights that the division be dismantled and its functions assigned to other federal agencies. "Worse than not working, when the Division does work it does so in a harmful manner," he told an interviewer later. "I'm trying to reduce its ability to do harm."[7] Subcommittee chairman Don Edwards (D–Cal.) evidently sympathized with the lobby's frustration. "They don't want to have anything to do with [division attorneys]," he said. "The only reason we have the civil rights laws is for these people, and they're saying that they don't want that kind of protection."[8] To develop an understanding of the specific division actions that led to this remarkable consternation, let us consider the first of our cases.

Connecticut v. Teal: Expanding the Disparate Impact Theory

Connecticut v. Teal was a Title VII case decided by the Supreme Court in June 1982.[9] In light of the circumstances that led to the suit, one may be surprised to learn that it was not a reverse discrimination case on the order of *Bakke* or *Weber*. The state of Connecticut had administered a written examination to employees of its Department of Income Maintenance as the first step in a selection process to determine which employees would be declared eligible for promotion. The mean score on the exam was 70.4 percent. Ordinarily this would have been automatically designated the minimum passing score, but the cutoff point was lowered to 65 to lessen the disparate impact upon black candidates, whose mean score was 6.7 percentage points below that of white candidates.[10] Despite this adjustment, however, only 54.2 percent of the black candidates received passing scores (above 65), compared to a pass rate of 79.5 percent among the white candidates. To compensate further for the still-low pass rate among the blacks, the state employed what the Court of Appeals for the Second Circuit characterized as an affirmative action program "in order to ensure a significant number of minority supervisors."[11] Although 26 blacks and 206 whites received passing scores, of the 46 persons ultimately promoted to supervisory positions, 11 were black and 35 were white, numbers not at all commensurate with the respective pass rates for the two groups.

A plausible argument might have been advanced that the state intentionally discriminated against white candidates on the basis of their race, but this was not the issue raised in *Connecticut v. Teal*. Rather, the suit was brought by four black employees who had scored below 65 on the written exam and were thereby excluded from further consideration in the promotion process. The plaintiffs charged that Connecticut had violated Title VII of the Civil Rights Act (which by this time had been amended by Congress to apply to governmental, as well as private, employers) by requiring, as an absolute condition for consideration for promotion, that applicants pass a test that excluded blacks in disproportionate numbers and that was not job-related. The same provision that the plaintiff in the *Weber* case claimed had been violated by the racial preference plan that had led to his exclusion from his employer's apprenticeship program—Section 703(a) of Title VII—was what was said to have been violated:

> It shall be an unlawful employment practice for an employer ...
> to limit, segregate, or classify his employees or applicants for
> employment in any way which would deprive or tend to deprive any individual of employment opportunities or otherwise
> adversely affect his status as an employee, because of such
> individual's race, color, religion, sex, or national origin.

As a matter of statutory construction, the *Teal* plaintiffs would seem to have had a very poor case. How could they possibly show that in flunking a generally administered, standardized test they had been "deprived" of an employment opportunity *"because of* [their] race, color," and so forth? But given the substantial body of case law based on the disparate-impact theory of employment discrimination developed by the courts in the aftermath of the

Supreme Court's 1971 decision in *Griggs v. Duke Power*, that question was by now irrelevant so far as the plaintiffs in *Teal* were concerned. Or was it? In every previous disparate-impact case, the courts had preoccupied themselves with bottom-line results. The issue was always whether, after a particular hiring or promotion procedure had run its course and the final results were known, women or minority group members had suffered a disparate impact in contravention of the norm of statistical group parity. In *Teal*, however, there was no disparate racial impact at the bottom line. Indeed, with the disparate-impact doctrine firmly established in Title VII case law, officials in Connecticut's Department of Income Maintenance undoubtedly realized that the disparate results of the examination they administered constituted a *prima facie* case of racial discrimination, and that the state might thus be called upon to prove its job-relatedness in court. Rather than undertake such a costly and possibly futile project, they sought to "correct" the test's disparate impact by giving preferential consideration to those blacks who did pass, thereby ensuring that the bottom-line result— the ratio of blacks to whites among those finally awarded promotions—would not be statistically adverse to blacks.

When the state was sued anyway despite these measures, Connecticut's defense was that the bottom-line results of its overall promotion process obviated the disparate impact caused by the examination, and that therefore the state should not be made to prove that its test was job-related. The district court agreed, but the Court of Appeals for the Second Circuit reversed, ruling that where "an identifiable pass-fail barrier denies an employment opportunity to a disproportionately large number of minorities and prevents them from proceeding to the next step in the selection process," that barrier must be shown to be job-related.[12]

When the Supreme Court agreed to review the case, the Civil Rights Division submitted an *amicus curiae* brief in support of Connecticut, thereby reversing the position it had taken in the lower courts during the Carter administration. In its brief, the division called the Court's attention to Section 703(h) of Title VII, which specifically authorizes the use of "professionally developed ability tests" so long as they are not "designed, intended or used to discriminate because of race, color," and the rest. No doubt recognizing that in the *Griggs* case the Court gave short shrift to this provision by asserting that Congress had intended "only to make clear that tests that were *job-related* would be permissible despite their disparate impact,"[13] the division contended that Connecticut's test was not "used to discriminate" because it did not actually deprive disproportionate numbers of blacks of promotions.[14] In effect, the Justice Department was saying that since the Court had required proof of job-relatedness only with respect to those employment practices that yield disparate results, and since in the final accounting there were no disparate results in this instance (except as they may have *favored* blacks), the Court should not require Connecticut to prove that the examination component of its promotion process was job-related.

It is important to note that in so arguing, the Justice Department stopped far short of challenging the validity of Connecticut's second-stage preference under Title VII. Nor did it ask the Court to reverse its *Griggs* ruling. Instead, it asked only that the Court acknowledge that its disparate-impact theory of discrimination is based perforce on statistical comparisons of racial groups (as opposed to particular individuals), and that Connecticut had overcome the disparate impact produced by its test by adopting compensatory procedures to ensure that the overall promotion process would not have a disparate racial impact. A minority of four justices (Powell, Burger, O'Connor, and Rehnquist) agreed with this position, but the majority (Brennan, White, Marshall, Blackmun, and Stevens) ruled that since Section 703(a) "speaks, not in terms of jobs or promotions, but in terms of *limitations* and *classifications* that would tend to deprive any individual of employment *opportunities*,"[15] Connecticut's test must meet the job-relatedness requirement because it served as a "limitation" that denied the plaintiffs, as individuals, the "opportunity" to compete equally for promotions. "The suggestion that disparate impact should be measured only at the bottom line ignores the fact that Title VII guarantees these individual respondents the *opportunity* to compete equally with white workers on the basis of job-related criteria," Justice Brennan declared in his opinion for the Court. (Notice how the norm of statistical group parity operates here: Brennan suggests that if an employment criterion, such as Connecticut's test, produces a disparate racial impact that is adverse to blacks as a group, then it follows that those blacks—but only those blacks—who performed poorly on the test were denied "the opportunity to compete equally" for promotions. In contrast, the numerous whites who failed the same test presumably were not denied an opportunity to compete equally for promotions, because whites as a group fared relatively well.)

Brennan's opinion for the Court is particularly noteworthy for its uncharacteristic solicitude for the civil rights of individuals.* His emphasis on Title VII's concern for individuals, however, seems misplaced within the context of the disparate-impact theory of discrimination (to which Brennan wholeheartedly subscribes). Indeed, this was the gravamen of Justice Powell's dissent, in which he was joined by three of his colleagues. Powell accused the majority of having "confuse[d] the individualistic aim of Title VII with the methods of proof by which Title VII rights may be vindicated."[16] He continued:

> The respondents, as individuals, are entitled to full personal protection of Title VII. But having undertaken to prove a violation of their rights by reference to group figures, respondents cannot deny petitioners the opportunity to rebut their evidence by introducing figures of the same kind. Having pleaded a disparate impact case, the plaintiff cannot deny the defendant the opportunity to show that there was no disparate impact.[17]

These words, which speak not to the legality or desirability of race-conscious rules of adjudication but rather to the need for a consistent application of doctrinal principles, absolutely failed to impress the Court's majority.

For the Civil Rights Division, the *Teal* decision was a total loss. Although the Court's affirming of an apparently victim-specific remedy may seem on a superficial level to comport with Assistant Attorney General Reynolds' stated objective of reorienting civil rights policies toward the individual and away from the group, the decision actually blends those features of each approach that are most advantageous to plaintiffs in cases such as *Teal*. The decision

---

*See Opinion of Justice Brennan. "Title VII does not permit the victim of a facially discriminatory policy to be told that he has not been wronged because other persons of his or her race or sex were hired. That answer is no more satisfactory when it is given to victims of a policy that is facially neutral but practically discriminatory. Every *individual* employee is protected against both discriminatory treatment and 'practices that are fair in form but discriminatory in operation.'" (Emphasis in original.) 457 U.S. 440, 455–456.

thus stands as a model of result-oriented jurisprudence. Its effect would seem to be to expand the scope of the disparate-impact theory well beyond the boundaries originally established in *Griggs*. Under Teal, disparate results in *any particular component* of an employment practice establishes a *prima facie* case of discrimination. Employers would no longer be able to adjust for the racially disparate outcomes produced in one stage of an employment procedure by affording preferential treatment to members of adversely affected minority groups in subsequent stages. In light of this further judicial enlargement of the meaning of "discrimination," it seemed certain that employers would have an even greater incentive than before to eliminate standardized testing, once regarded as the cornerstone of merit employment procedures.

Interestingly, the Washington Council of Lawyers, a self-proclaimed "public interest bar association," cited the "unequivocal rejection by the Supreme Court of the [Civil Rights] Division's position" in the *Teal* case as "further evidence that the division has abandoned vigorous enforcement of Title VII."[18] In reality, the Division lost precisely because it *did* seek to enforce Title VII as interpreted in *Griggs* and its progeny. Evidently, in the opinion of some civil rights activists, attempts merely to enforce the requirements of *existing* case law are not sufficient to constitute "vigorous enforcement of Title VII"; rather, the division's proper function must be to assist the organized civil rights lobby in its continuing drive to extend the boundaries of current race-conscious civil rights doctrine.

Williams v. New Orleans:
Enacting Racial Preferences via the Consent Decree

Williams v. New Orleans,[19] decided by the Court of Appeals for the Fifth Circuit in April 1984, concerned a consent decree negotiated between the New Orleans Police Department (NOPD) and a class of black plaintiffs, some of whom had applied for positions with the department and some of whom were members of the force. The plaintiffs earlier had complained of discriminatory policies in the selection, training, and promotion of city police officers. Rather than go to trial, however, the parties agreed, in October 1981, to submit a proposed consent decree to the district court for its approval.

According to the district court, the thirty-three-page proposed decree governed "virtually every phase of an officer's employment by the New Orleans Police Department."[20] Some of its more noteworthy provisions included the assignment of "buddies" to guide black applicants through the application process; new entry level procedures to ensure that the proportion of blacks who graduated from the police academy was no lower than the proportion of blacks who passed the entry level examination; the elimination of all general intelligence tests; the creation of forty-four new supervisory positions immediately and the appointment of black officers to all forty-four positions; the subsequent promotion of one black officer for every white officer promoted until blacks constituted 50 percent of all ranks within the NOPD; a requirement that any black officer who failed to complete the probationary period following promotion would be replaced by another black officer; and the automatic invalidation of any test item having a "statistically significant adverse impact against blacks."[21]

Such is the stuff of the modern employment discrimination consent decree. The officials of the New Orleans Police Department were only too happy to agree to these terms, but the department's rank and file were not. Objections to the decree were filed with the district court by roughly three-fourths of the officers, including associations of Hispanic and female officers.[22] The district court judge, Morey L. Sear, responded to these objections by withholding approval of the decree, indicating, however, that the decree was satisfactory in every respect save one: the provision requiring black and white officers to be promoted on a one-to-one basis until blacks constituted 50 percent of all ranks within the NOPD. That provision, said Judge Sear, exceeded the court's remedial objectives and seriously jeopardized the career interests of nonblack officers.[23] The parties were encouraged to modify the decree accordingly and resubmit it for the court's approval. The plaintiffs, however, appealed this decision on grounds that the district court had abused its discretion in conditioning its approval of the decree on the deletion of the promotion quota, and a panel of the Fifth Circuit agreed. The case was remanded to the district court with instructions for Judge Sear to sign the decree.

At this point the Justice Department formally intervened with a request for a rehearing by the full appellate court; the Civil Rights Division would use the occasion to argue its belief that wholesale relief to members of an entire racial class—without regard to whether each individual member of the class was an actual victim of discrimination—is never justified under Title VII. The division based its contention on the last sentence of Section 706(g) of Title VII, which reads as follows:

> No order of the court shall require the admission or reinstatement of an individual as a member of a union, or the hiring, reinstatement, or promotion of an individual as an employee, or the payment to him of any back pay, if such individual was refused employment or advancement or was suspended or discharged for any reason other than discrimination on account of race, color, religion, sex, or national origin. . . .

Like every other provision in Title VII, this one speaks in terms of *individuals*, and it specifically enjoins courts from ordering the hiring or promotion of any individual unless his original failure to be hired or promoted was due to discrimination. Does this mean that a court could not authorize a consent decree requiring the promotion of a class of individuals, through the mechanism of a racial quota, in the absence of probative evidence that the employer in question had practiced discrimination against each member of the plaintiff class? The Civil Rights Division contended that it does.

The Fifth Circuit's response was to brush this pivotal question aside, curtly observing that "[t]his court has long upheld the use of affirmative action in consent decrees under Title VII and has not required that relief be limited to actual victims of discrimination."[24] Moreover, "the use of quotas or goals under Title VII without regard to specific victims as one means to remedy past discrimination has been upheld regularly throughout the federal courts of appeal."[25] This, of course, could hardly have come as a revelation to the lawyers in the Civil Rights Division or to students of Title VII jurisprudence. What had been asked for was a reexamination of the issue in light of the circumstances presented by *Williams*. The court's majority would have none of this, declaring summarily that "[t]he question of whether affirmative action provisions are permissible as a general remedy under Title VII is not an issue in this case."[26] The majority then proceeded to the narrower question of whether the district court had abused its discretion. The district court's ruling was upheld (resulting in the deletion of the one-to-one promotion quota) on the grounds that the district court showed proper concern for the fate of "the numerous intervening parties whose interests would have been affected by the decree."[27] The court thus recognized the unfairness of the decree, but not according to some principled rationale; by casting its approval of the district court ruling in terms of judicial discretion and the need to "balance" competing interests, the court seemed in effect to say that discrimination against whites to help blacks is appropriate under Title VII, provided there isn't too much of it! In any event, it is clear that the Civil Rights Division had failed in its attempt to overturn judicial recourse to broad remedial racial quotas.

Only four (Higginbotham, Garwood, Jolly, and Gee) of the Fifth Circuit's thirteen members found merit in the division's stand against affirmative action quotas. Writing for three members of this dissident minority, Judge Patrick Higginbotham recalled the legislative history of Title VII, especially Senator Humphrey's remark that

> there is nothing in [Title VII] that will give any power to any court to require hiring, firing, or promotion of employees in order to meet a certain racial "quota" or to achieve a certain racial balance—That bugaboo has been brought up a dozen times but it is nonexistent.[28]

Although acknowledging that the Supreme Court had upheld the use of racial preference in promotion in its *Weber* decision, Higginbotham distinguished *Williams* from *Weber* by noting that "the *Weber* Court decided only that Congress did not intend to limit traditional business freedom to such a degree as to prohibit all voluntary, race-conscious affirmative action."[29] *Williams* posed a rather different question—whether requiring a public agency to afford preferential treatment to members of one race until a racial quota is achieved is a permissible judicially imposed remedy under Title VII. According to Higginbotham, "The legislative history of Title VII answers this question in clear terms. Such a practice cannot be required." He then struck at the heart of the issue:

> A quota which injures persons not participating in accused segregation patterns to the benefit of persons who were not its victims

is responsive to a wrong defined in terms of a failed social order—
a judicially envisioned distribution of jobs among races, ethnic
groups, and sexes. Such social ordering is a peculiar use of judicial
power because judicial power to resolve disputes has traditionally
and constitutionally been confined in the main to disputes whose
dimensions are drawn by adverse parties.[30]

Higginbotham was correct in noting the peculiarity of judicially imposed "social ordering" within the broad historical context of Anglo-American jurisprudence. Yet, as noted in Chapter 2,
the invention of group-based equity by late twentieth century ju-
rists had seriously vitiated the traditional injunction that the "judicial power to resolve disputes" be "confined in the main to
disputes whose dimensions are drawn by adverse parties." The
sweeping, group-oriented equitable relief that the Fifth Circuit
proposed to uphold in *Williams* made sense only if one defined
the "adverse parties" as entire racial groups. This was both understood and deplored by Higginbotham:

> The principal failing of the proposed quota is that it regards all
> members of the black race as a single class, rather than recognizing
> that the group is composed of individuals, some of whom have
> suffered the invidious effects of past discrimination and some of
> whom have not. I have no objection, of course, to grouping those
> individuals who have suffered some wrong and now prosecute
> [sic] their case on a group basis. . . . What I cannot accept is the
> notion that "the black race" is an independent legal entity and that
> relief for past discrimination against black persons should take the
> form of special advantages granted in the future to "the black
> race." Races, per se, are not proper parties to a court action.[31]

This, as we have noted, was the essence of the Justice Department's position as well. A quite different view was expressed in a
separate opinion written by Judge John Minor Wisdom and joined
by five of his colleagues (Brown, Politz, Randall, Tate, and Johnson).
While concurring in the court's rejection of the Civil Rights
Division's per se attack on promotion quotas, Wisdom dissented
from its holding that the district court had acted properly in dis-
allowing the particular promotion quota at issue in *Williams*. His
opinion is of particular interest because, although none of the
other opinions written in regard to the case addressed constitutional

issues, Wisdom's does. It is not surprising, then, that his long opinion is liberally sprinkled with citations to articles written by leading professors of constitutional law, including the redoubtable Owen Fiss. These sources are used mostly to support a group rights "interpretation" of the Fourteenth Amendment's equal protection clause, consonant with the position espoused by Fiss which we considered in Chapter 2.

Wisdom does not, however, go so far as to explicitly adopt Fiss's "group-disadvantaging principle" to the exclusion of the more orthodox "antidiscrimination principle." Yet because he apparently sees adherence to the antidiscrimination principle as leading necessarily to injustice, at least at the present time, the effect is much the same as if Wisdom had adopted the group-disadvantaging principle. He wrote, for example, that

> the Constitution calls for equal treatment under the law, and in light of the pervasive past discriminatory practices and the present effects of these practices, in many cases *this goal* can be achieved only by taking active, affirmative steps to remove the effects of prior inequality.[32]

By this reasoning, legal rules and principles are understood not as immediate injunctions to be obeyed and enforced in the here and now, but rather as prospective "goals" that can realistically be met only after an indeterminate period during which judges must authorize various race-conscious measures designed to ensure that the goal of nondiscrimination may someday be realized. Or, to use Judge Higginbotham's terms, the goal of equal treatment under the law must not conflict with "a judicially envisioned distribution of jobs among races, ethnic groups, and sexes." So long as it does, the goal of equal treatment must be deferred. This view, summed up in Justice Blackmun's dictum that "to get beyond racism, we must first take account of race . . . [a]nd in order to treat some persons equally, we must treat them differently," had by 1980 become quite common throughout the federal judiciary, and although it appears on the surface not to be as radical a doctrine as Fiss's overt repudiation of the antidiscrimination principle, it does tend in practice to produce the same kind of results.

Judge Wisdom was not content to rely solely on the equal protection clause to advance his argument that "[t]he Constitution is race-conscious."[33] His signal contribution in support of that conclusion was to aver that the Thirteenth Amendment (which abolished slavery) offers a constitutional justification for race-conscious affirmative action. His contention is based on the first Justice Harlan's *dissenting* opinion in the *Civil Rights Cases*, proclaiming that "the Thirteenth Amendment may be exerted— for the eradication, not simply of the institution [of slavery], but of its badges and incidents. . . . "[34] Thus, concludes Wisdom, the "underrepresentation of blacks on the [New Orleans police] force since 1898, or perhaps since 1847–77, is a badge of slavery: it is a sign readily visible in the community that attaches a stigma upon the black race."[35]

Here is what the Thirteenth Amendment says in full:

Section 1. Neither slavery nor involuntary servitude, except as a punishment for crime whereof the party shall have been duly convicted, shall exist within the United States, or any place subject to their jurisdiction.

Section 2. Congress shall have power to enforce this article by appropriate legislation.

The Wisdom opinion would thus seem to transcend even the mode of constitutional adjudication conventionally denoted by the term "judicial activism." With the obvious exception of the U.S. Supreme Court and the possible exception of the Court of Appeals for the District of Columbia Circuit, the Fifth Circuit is probably the most influential court in the country with respect to civil rights issues, encompassing as it does much of the deep South. That six of thirteen judges on that court could subscribe to such an extraordinary (even by contemporary standards) reading of the Constitution was a telling indication of the extent to which some judges were prepared to go to promote race-conscious civil rights policies. Indeed, from the Civil Rights Division's point of view, the Wisdom opinion—even though it failed by one vote to carry the day—might have seemed even more portentous than the majority's rejection of its attack on racial quotas. How, after all, could a fundamental reformulation of civil rights doctrine be achieved through the courts when a substantial portion of the most influential appellate court judges were apparently committed to expanding race-conscious civil rights doctrine well beyond existing boundaries?

Firefighters v. Stotts: A Tentative Victory for Race Neutrality

Although before 1980 the Supreme Court had upheld the voluntary use by private employers of racial preferences in job hiring and promotions, it had yet to rule on the question of whether racial criteria could be used to determine job layoffs during periods of economic distress. Here again, Congress had anticipated the emergence of this issue during the debates that preceded the enactment of the 1964 Civil Rights Act, and the results of its deliberations were stated in the form of Sections 706(g) and 703(h). We have already had occasion to quote from the relevant provisions of the former section, the effect of which was to prohibit courts from ordering, *inter alia*, "the hiring, reinstatement, or promotion of an individual as an employee . . . if such individual was refused admission . . . for any reason other than discrimination on account of race, color," and the rest. Section 703(h) provides:

> Notwithstanding any other provision of this subchapter, it shall not be an unlawful employment practice for an employer to apply different standards of compensation, or different terms, conditions, or privileges of employment pursuant to a bona fide seniority or merit system . . . provided that such differences are not the result of an intention to discriminate because of race, color, religion, sex, or national origin. . . .

During the early 1980s, as the national economy went into recession, many unionized workers across the country were laid off by their employers on the basis of seniority, generally in accordance with seniority-based layoff procedures that had been written into collective bargaining agreements between unions and employers. The use of seniority as a criterion for determining layoffs reflected the widely held belief that employers as well as fellow workers should be especially sensitive to the plight of older workers, inasmuch as they typically have greater financial commitments and less job mobility than their less senior counterparts. Moreover, seniority effectively displaced personal favoritism, nepotism, and ethnic or racial prejudice as grounds for determining layoffs. In the early 1980s, however, many employers, particularly in the public sector, were operating under Title VII consent decrees that required them to exercise racial preference for minorities in hiring and promotion, and it soon became clear that if widespread seniority-based layoffs went into effect, the "gains of affirmative action" would rapidly be eroded as recently hired members of the preferred groups succumbed to the rule of "last hired, first fired."

In a number of such instances the original plaintiffs went back to court, urging that existing employment discrimination consent decrees be amended to apply race-conscious principles to layoffs as well as to hiring and promotion. Despite the plain language of Section 706(g), and especially 703(h), many courts promptly obliged. When, for example, the City of Boston found itself confronted with fiscal problems of so serious a magnitude that 1,300 Boston schoolteachers had to be laid off, a federal judicial order was issued forbidding any reduction in the minority share of school employment.[36] The result was that tenured white teachers with up to fifteen years of service were laid off, while the school board continued to hire new black teachers. Three years later there were still over 400 white teachers laid off in Boston; for all intents and purposes they had lost their jobs in the cause of racial equality.[37]

Such decisions represented significant departures from the letter and spirit of Section 703(h), but in the absence of a definitive Supreme Court ruling upholding racially determined layoffs it would have been premature to conclude that the conventional principles governing job layoffs had been permanently supplanted by the tenets of race-conscious civil rights doctrine. In 1983, however, the Court agreed to review *Firefighters Local No. 1784 v. Stotts*,[38] a case that presented essentially the same basic question that was at issue in the Boston schoolteachers case, but under far less prepossessing circumstances for a momentous legal engagement. (Inexplicably, the Supreme Court had *twice* refused to review the Boston case.[39]) The case involved a clash between black firefighters, hired by the City of Memphis under a consent decree, and white firefighters with seniority rights under their labor agreement. The consent decree had established racial hiring and promotion quotas within the fire department pursuant to two separate lawsuits brought against the city. The first, which challenged the city's overall employment practices, was brought by the federal government and ended with a 1974 consent decree (with no admission of liability) that established the long-term goal of a racially proportionate workforce in the fire department, to be pursued through an interim quota requiring that 50 percent of new hires be black. The second suit was a class action brought by the respondent Carl Stotts attacking the hiring and promotion practices of the fire department alone. This case was settled in 1980 by yet another consent decree, which reiterated the long-term employment goal and the 50 percent hiring quota for blacks, but added a 20 percent promotion quota as well. It also contained a directive that eighteen named black firefighters be given immediate promotion.[40]

The present case, which could be called "*Stotts II*," arose in the spring of 1981, when fiscal difficulties caused the city to begin a program of layoffs. The city's established personnel policy, detailed in a memorandum of understanding with the firefighters' union, announced that layoffs would occur according to a last-hired, first-fired schedule.[41] Had the city proceeded on this basis (as it had proposed to do), the result would have been a layoff of twenty-five whites (out of 497) and fifteen blacks (out of eighty-five), with all the latter to be drawn from the eighteen new hires employed under the 1980 decree, as well as the demotion of fourteen of the eighteen named blacks who had been promoted under that decree. The upshot would have been a reduction in black employment in the fire department from an 11 percent to a 10 percent share.[42] When the class represented by Stotts sought an injunction against the discharge of the fifteen blacks, the district judge, relying on the consent decree, forbade the city to apply its seniority policy in a way that would reduce the proportional representation of blacks in the fire department. The city responded by ordering the fire department to execute its layoffs by dismissing senior white firefighters.[43] On appeal, the Court of Appeals for the Sixth Circuit affirmed, concluding that the district court's modification of the original consent decree was permissible under general contract principles because the city had "contracted" to provide "a substantial increase in the number of minorities in supervisory positions" and the layoffs would breach that contract.[44]

Although *Stotts* clearly presented fundamental issues under Title VII every bit as profound as those presented by the Boston

schoolteachers and similar cases, by the time the case reached the
Supreme Court (arguments were heard on December 6, 1983), it
had begun to take on the appearance of a tempest in a teapot. For
one thing, because of changes in the city's layoff schedule (the
fiscal crisis in Memphis evidently proved to be not as grave as had
initially been forecast), only three additional whites were laid off
by the fire department, and these were recalled less than a month
later (although each lost roughly $1,200 in back pay, less unem-
ployment insurance benefits).[45] Moreover, it so happened that all
six of the firefighters actually affected by the judicial order—the
three "senior" whites who were laid off and the three "junior"
blacks who were retained—were all hired on the same day, less
than two years earlier. The reason the blacks ranked below the
whites on the seniority list was that the first letter in their last
names came later in the alphabet, and the Memphis seniority system used alphabetical priority as its tie-breaking device.[46] Furthermore, the modified consent decree was cast as a temporary
restraining order, addressed specifically to the layoffs scheduled
for June 1981, rather than as a permanent injunction, so it was by
no means certain that the order would apply to future layoffs.[47]

The brevity of the layoffs and demotions, the small amount of
money involved, and especially the apparent evanescence of the
judicial order under review combined to make for a plausible argument that the *Stotts* case was "moot," and therefore unfit for the
exercise of judicial power. The mootness issue provided a convenient pretext for those members of the Court who, on the basis of
their votes in previous cases involving challenges to race-
conscious civil rights doctrine, would have been most inclined to
defend the modified consent decree at issue in *Stotts*. Rather than
issue a judgment on the merits of the case, which would have
required some effort to reconcile Section 703(h) with the terms of
the modified consent decree, Justices Brennan, Marshall, and
Blackmun could argue that the decision of the Court of Appeals
should be permitted to stand on grounds of mootness.

For their part, the remaining six justices had little difficulty
rebutting the mootness argument, and although their analysis
"was by no means free of difficulty," according to a pair of legal
scholars who studied the case, "the majority did not stray indefen-
sibly beyond the bounds of mootness doctrine in finding *Stotts* fit
for decision."[48] Indeed, the rationale for finding the case justiciable

that was propounded by Justice White in his opinion for the Court does seem persuasive, if not compelling:

> Undoubtedly, not much money and seniority are involved, but the money and seniority at stake does not determine mootness. As long as the parties have a concrete interest in the outcome of the litigation, the case is not moot notwithstanding the size of the dispute. [Citation omitted.] Moreover, a month's pay is not a negligible item for those affected by the injunction, and the loss of a month's competitive seniority may later determine who gets a promotion, who is entitled to bid for transfers or who is first laid off if there is another reduction in force. These are matters of substance, it seems to us, and enough so to foreclose any claims of mootness.[49]

Turning to the merits of the case, the Court averred that "the issue at the heart of this case is whether the District Court exceeded its powers in entering an injunction requiring white employees to be laid off, when the otherwise applicable seniority system would have called for the layoff of black employees with less seniority."[50] The Court then proceeded to explain its reasons for finding that the district court's injunction was improper. First, as one might have expected, the Court assigned much importance to the language of Section 703(h) protecting bona fide seniority systems, declaring that "it is inappropriate to deny an innocent employee the benefits of his seniority in order to provide a remedy in a pattern or practice suit such as this."[51] (A "pattern or practice" suit, we should note, is one in which statistical evidence is adduced to demonstrate a continuous adverse effect on the employment or promotion prospects of a particular minority group. Title VII suits predicated upon the disparate impact theory of employment discrimination are thus a major subspecies of the "pattern or practice" suit. In Title VII case law, pattern or practice suits are distinguished from suits alleging specific harm to identifiable victims.) It also took up the vexing issue, inherent in the very nature of consent decrees, of the extent to which the rights or legitimate interests of unrepresented third parties may have been abrogated by the terms of the decree. Thus, the Court held that

> it must be remembered that neither the Union nor the nonminority employees were parties to the suit when the 1980 decree

was entered. Hence the entry of that decree cannot be said to indicate any agreement by them to any of its terms. Absent the presence of the Union or the non-minority employees and an opportunity for them to agree or disagree with any provisions of the decree that might encroach on their rights, it seems unlikely that the City would purport to bargain away non-minority rights under the then-existing seniority system. We therefore conclude that the injunction does not merely enforce the agreement of the parties as reflected in the consent decree. If the injunction is to stand, it must be justified on some other basis.[52]

The conclusion expressed by the final two sentences of this passage stated a holding that was important in its own right. Its apparent effect was to announce that the purpose of a consent decree should be conceived narrowly and precisely, so as to preclude the possibility that as circumstances change following the negotiation of a decree, one of its parties could simply appeal to a sympathetic judge to modify or amend the original decree in whatever way is deemed necessary to effect the decree's "larger" purpose. The prevalence of this kind of open-ended consent decree during the 1970s had in some instances served to confer upon judges *de facto* authority for administering large and complex social institutions, including prisons, state mental hospitals, and public school districts. The majority's categorical rejection of the open-ended consent decree may thus in itself have been regarded as a minor victory for advocates of a race-neutral regime of civil rights, given the prominent role of activist judges in helping to establish and expand race-conscious civil rights doctrine.

This, combined with the Supreme Court's refusal to abide the incompatibility of the district court's injunction with the layoff provisions contained in Section 703(h), signaled the Civil Rights Division's first victory before the Supreme Court. In the context of job layoffs, the Court unequivocally endorsed Assistant Attorney General Reynolds' expressed belief that "make-whole" relief is only appropriate to individual victims of proven discrimination:

If individual members of a plaintiff class demonstrate that they have been actual victims of the discriminatory practice, they may be awarded competitive seniority and given their rightful place on the seniority roster. [However, it is also] clear that mere membership in the disadvantaged class is insufficient to warrant a seniority award; each individual must prove that the discriminatory practice has had an impact on him. Even when an individual shows that the discriminatory practice has had an impact on him, he is not automatically entitled to have a nonminority employee laid off to make room for him.[53]

The Court went on to note that in *Stotts* there had been "no finding that any of the blacks protected from layoff had been a victim of discrimination and no award of competitive seniority to any of them."[54]

The Court might well have ceased its inquiry at this point, and in light of its dismal experience before the federal appellate courts generally, the Civil Rights Division (or at least its leadership) would no doubt have been pleased at having scored its first Supreme Court victory. Justice White's majority opinion continued, however. Invoking Section 706(g), it went on at some length to cast doubt on the validity, not merely of classwide racial preference schemes in the context of layoffs, but with regard to hiring and promotion as well. Elaborating on "the policy behind Section 706(g) of Title VII, which affects the remedies available in Title VII litigation," White acknowledged that

[t]hat policy, which is to provide make-whole relief only to those who have been actual victims of illegal discrimination, was repeatedly expressed by the sponsors of the Act during the congressional debates.[55]

White followed this statement with a recitation of illustrative oral testimony and interpretive memoranda that were put forward by Senators Humphrey, Clark, and Case (see Chapter 2), all disclaiming any intent to authorize courts or administrative agencies to grant any form of preferential treatment to "anyone who was not discriminated against in violation of [Title VII]."[56] The Court's opinion concluded with an observation that "[t]he Court of Appeals holding that the District Court's order was permissible as a valid Title VII remedial order ignores not only our ruling in *Teamsters* [a case decided in 1977, which also involved a Title VII challenge to a bona fide seniority system] *but the policy behind Section 706(g) as well.*"[57]

Was the Court serving notice of a shift to a more "interpretivist" mode of adjudicating Title VII claims, according to which broad, race-conscious remedies in "pattern or practice" cases would be disallowed owing to the prohibitory language of the title itself and its principal congressional sponsors? It must be noted that although the Court had invalidated the modified consent decree by a vote of 6 to 3, only five of the six justices who voted with the majority joined in White's opinion for the Court.* Justice Stevens filed a separate opinion that concurred in the judgment, but which labeled the Court's discussion of Title VII "wholly advisory." Still, a narrow majority had apparently expressed its agreement with the stated position of Assistant Attorney General Reynolds and the Civil Rights Division. Because the Court's actual decision pertained only to the parties in *Stotts*, however, one could not say with any degree of certainty what, if any, implications the Court's opinion might have for race-conscious affirmative action in general.

Nevertheless, appearing to adopt what Martin Shapiro once called "the typical lawyers' strategy of telling judges they have been doing something in the hope that this will embolden them to actually do it,"[58] Reynolds, obviously elated by the decision, described it as an "unequivocal" statement that court-ordered or court-enforced racial quotas of any kind were illegal under Title VII.[59] "I said some time ago that civil rights was at a crossroads; that we would either take the path of race-conscious remedies . . . or the high road of race neutrality," he said. "The Court has moved us off the crossroads and propelled us down the path we have been urging. It is an exhilarating decision."[60] Within four months following the decision of the case on June 12, 1984, the Civil Rights Division had employed it in the service of new challenges to no fewer than fifty-one existing consent decrees that had settled previous employment discrimination cases in a variety of cities, counties, school districts, and state agencies. Most of those decrees involved racial quotas for hiring and promotion rather than layoffs.[61] Some differed from the decree at issue in *Stotts* in that there had been a prior judicial finding of discrimination on the part of the employer. They all resembled the *Stotts* decree in the critical respect that they afforded preferential treatment to persons who had not themselves suffered any discrimination at the hands of

---

*In addition to White, the others were Burger, Powell, Rehnquist, and O'Connor.

the employer, and all had the ineluctable effect of systematically disfavoring innocent members of nonminority groups.

By February 1985, district and appellate court decisions had been handed down in six important cases, each of which involved challenges to the use of race-conscious employment criteria, though not necessarily as mandated by judicial orders. In each case plaintiffs had urged judges to adopt a broad reading of the Supreme Court's *Stotts* opinion, consistent with that of the Civil Rights Division. In each case the division's position was rejected. The Court of Appeals for the Third Circuit upheld the use of quotas to promote "racial balance" in the assignment of school-teachers in Philadelphia, contending that the *Stotts* decision was "inapplicable" because there was "no requirement of race-conscious layoffs."[62] A federal district judge in South Bend, Indiana, upheld a section of a teachers' contract providing that no blacks would be laid off after concluding that the *Stotts* decision applied to "court-imposed affirmative action programs," but not to the South Bend plan, because the latter had been voluntarily adopted.[63] The Court of Appeals for the Sixth Circuit rejected a suit brought by thirty-eight white men challenging a racial quota system for hiring firefighters in Detroit, on the grounds that the fire department had a history of racial discrimination, that the plan was adopted voluntarily, and that no employees were deprived of seniority rights.[64]

A district judge in Detroit upheld a voluntary promotion quota designed to ensure that white and black police officers would be promoted in equal numbers. The judge wrote that the *Stotts* ruling had not "substantially changed the legal standards under which this case must be decided."[65] The Court of Appeals for the Ninth Circuit upheld an affirmative action plan adopted by the transportation agency of Santa Clara County, California, even though it resulted in the promotion of a woman who had a lower examination score than a male employee seeking the same job. The court declared that the "plan was a lawful attempt to break down entrenched patterns of discrimination."[66] Finally, the Court of Appeals for the Sixth Circuit upheld a contract provision limiting the number of black teachers who would be laid off in Jackson, Michigan. The court decided that it was permissible because blacks had been "chronically underrepresented" on the teaching staff. Moreover, the court found *Stotts* irrelevant because the layoff provision stemmed not from a court order but from "voluntary decisions in the collective bargaining process."[67]

The Supreme Court's discussion of the policy behind Section 706(g) may indeed have been "wholly advisory," as Justice Stevens suggested, but, if so, that "advice" had been resoundingly and uniformly rejected by the lower courts.

Wygant v. Jackson Board of Education: A Retreat from the Implications of Stotts?

Of the lower court decisions mentioned above, the Supreme Court had by the end of its 1986 term agreed to review only one—the decision upholding race-based layoffs of schoolteachers in Jackson, Michigan. As noted, the case differed from *Stotts* in that the challenged layoff procedure was provided for in a collective bargaining agreement rather than imposed by judicial order. On the other hand, it was similar to *Stotts* in that no prior judicial finding of discrimination against minorities by the employer had ever been made. Indeed, unlike *Stotts*, a court had inquired fully into the question of prior discrimination and concluded categorically that "there is no history of overt past discrimination by the parties to this [labor] contract."[68] There thus was a definitive judicial finding of non-discrimination on the part of the Jackson School Board. This explains why the Sixth Circuit, in upholding the race-based layoff provision, predicated its decision on the notion that blacks had been "chronically underrepresented" on the teaching staff, rather than subject to any form of actual discrimination. There was one more respect in which *Wygant* differed from *Stotts*, and for that matter from all previous court rulings and administrative regulations designed to correct minority group underrepresentation: The extent to which minority group members were said to be adequately represented on the Jackson teaching staff was determined not by comparing the percentage of currently employed minority *teachers* with the percentage of qualified minorities in the relevant labor pool (however geographically delimited), but rather by comparing the percentage of currently employed minority teachers with the percentage of minority *students* currently enrolled in the Jackson public schools.

This last point is of critical importance, because if the conventional means of determining minority group underrepresentation had prevailed in the Jackson School District, blacks might conceivably have been considered *overrepresented*. Consider that in 1980–81, when the white plaintiff Wendy Wygant was being laid off for the seventh time to protect the jobs of less-senior minority teachers, minorities constituted 13.5 percent of the teachers in the Jackson schools while constituting only 9.7 percent of the population of Michigan.[69]* Nevertheless, the collective bargaining agreement between the board and the Jackson Education Association provided that in the event of layoffs "teachers with the most seniority in the district shall be retained, except that at no time will there be a greater percentage of minority personnel laid off than the current percentage of minority personnel employed at the time of the layoff."[70] Because black students in the district exceeded 13.5 percent and their numbers were likely to grow steadily into the foreseeable future, the effect of this rule was to create a contractual ratchet, whereby the percentage of minority teachers would be gradually increased (through the use of hiring quotas, which were not an issue in the case), but could never be reduced.[71]

When suit was brought, the school board contended, and the lower courts agreed, that it was appropriate for the school board to devise measures that would ensure that the percentage of minority teachers would be commensurate with the percentage of minority students, because the minority teachers' utility as "role models" for minority students would help combat the effects of societal discrimination. In the words of the district court:

> [I]n the setting of this case, it is appropriate to compare the percentage of minority teachers to the percentage of minority students in the student body, rather than with the percentage of minorities in the relevant labor market. It is appropriate because teaching is more than just a job. Teachers are role models for their students. This is vitally important because societal discrimination has often deprived minority children of other role models.[72]

---

*Although established precedents furnish little guidance as to the appropriate population group for purposes of comparison, an argument could be made that since "qualified" teachers must by definition be certified by a state licensing authority, the state of Michigan, rather than the City of Jackson or the United States as a whole, is the relevant population group with which to compare the percentage of minority teachers employed in the Jackson schools.

The Court of Appeals for the Sixth Circuit, in affirming the judgment of the district court, adopted essentially this same reasoning and language. Both courts, however, had resorted to making peremptory assertions regarding social science controversies about which there is considerable disagreement among scholars. The utility of "same-race role models" has been much discussed in the scholarly literature, yet no consensus as to their relative effectiveness has thus far emerged.[*]

Even assuming, however, that same-race role models are helpful in alleviating the effects of "societal discrimination," the Supreme Court would have to decide whether the burden imposed on senior white teachers by race-based layoffs could be justified under the Fourteenth Amendment's equal protection clause. (Unlike the plaintiffs in *Stotts*, who challenged a judicial order made pursuant to a Title VII lawsuit, the plaintiffs in *Wygant* invoked the equal protection clause as the basis for their attack on a voluntary action undertaken by a public employer.) Since announcing its decision in the 1944 case of *Korematsu v. United States*,[73] the Court has applied a standard of "rigid" or "strict" scrutiny when reviewing state laws and policies that establish racial categories. Although in the *Bakke* case four justices argued for the use of a more lenient standard of review in cases involving challenges to race-conscious affirmative action policies (where the discrimination that occurs is said to be "benign"), a majority has consistently held that whenever government policies classify people according to race and thereby treat them differently, such classifications are "inherently suspect." Once the existence of a suspect classification has been established, it is afforded strict scrutiny, which means, first, that the government must show that the law or policy under review serves a *compelling* state purpose; and, second, that the suspect instrument used to accomplish the compelling purpose is *narrowly tailored*, meaning that there exists no alternative instrument that is less burdensome or intrusive.

The Sixth Circuit had refused to apply the "strict scrutiny" standard of review, applying instead the far less stringent "rea-

---

[*]For an example of a study that failed to discover any positive correlation between same-race role models and student performance, see M. W. Clague, "Voluntary Affirmative Action Plans in Public Education: Matching Faculty Race to Student Race," *Journal of Law and Education*, Vol. 14, No. 3 (July 1985).

sonableness" test that the Supreme Court has used in reviewing legislative acts said to discriminate on grounds other than race, religion, or sex. As noted, however, the Supreme Court had never departed from its practice of applying strict scrutiny to policies containing racial classifications, and so seldom in the Court's recent history had a racial classification survived strict scrutiny that it had become axiomatic among constitutional lawyers that as employed by the Court, this standard of review was generally "strict in theory but fatal in fact."[*] Hence, by a 5 to 4 vote, the Court in *Wygant* did reverse the Court of Appeals on the grounds that maintaining same-race role models for the benefit of minority students did not constitute a compelling state interest, and that, moreover, the means used to achieve the school board's objective was "not sufficiently narrowly tailored." Writing for a plurality of the Court, Justice Powell observed that

> [o]ther less intrusive means of accomplishing similar purposes—such as the adoption of hiring goals—are available. For these reasons, the board's selection of layoffs as the means to accomplish even a valid purpose cannot satisfy the demands of the equal protection clause.[74]

The Civil Rights Division had sided with the plaintiffs in the case, urging the Supreme Court to adopt the same victim-specific approach to race-conscious remedies for proven civil rights violations under the Constitution that Reynolds claimed the Court had endorsed with respect to statutory violations in *Stotts*. The plurality (Powell, Rehnquist, and Burger, with O'Connor and White concurring separately) did affirm that race-conscious measures

---

[*]A notable exception to this rule occurred in *Bakke*. There, Justice Powell, whose lone opinion spoke for an otherwise divided Court, suggested that if a medical school were to use race "as one factor" in its admissions process in order to promote diversity within its student body, such use of racial criteria would be upheld as serving a compelling state interest. Moreover, four justices endorsed Justice Brennan's position that an "intermediate" level of scrutiny was appropriate in deciding challenges to affirmative action racial preference schemes. Furthermore, something less than strict scrutiny seems to have been used in *Fullilove v. Klutznick*, 448 U.S. 448 (1980), in which the Court upheld the use of racial preference in awarding government-funded construction contracts.

could not be justified in the absence of proof of discrimination by the entity to which the measures pertained. Hence, wrote Powell,

> [t]his Court never has held that societal discrimination alone is sufficient to justify a racial classification. Rather, the Court has insisted upon some showing of prior discrimination by the governmental unit involved before allowing limited use of racial classifications in order to remedy such discrimination.[75]

What of the victim-specific approach to remedial action that the Civil Rights Division had advocated and that the Court seemingly adopted in the *Stotts* case in its discussion of "the policy behind Section 706(g)"?

The answer to this question was adumbrated by Powell's reference to "hiring goals" as an apparently acceptable means of redressing past discrimination, and was finally confirmed (albeit obliquely) by the Court's treatment of a related issue raised by the Civil Rights Division. The division argued that before remedies for civil rights violations could be enacted, an independent administrative agency, legislative body, or court must initially have determined that the public employer proposing to effect such remedies had itself been guilty of previous discrimination. The plurality clearly held that race-conscious remedies were not permissible in the absence of previous discrimination by the public employer affected by such remedies, but it just as clearly rejected the division's contention that the enactment of race-conscious remedies must be preceded by a "contemporaneous" independent finding of prior discrimination. In other words, "voluntary" race-conscious affirmative action was allowable under the equal protection clause so long as it purported to remedy some concrete act(s) of discrimination for which the employer was directly responsible. Direct evidence of such discrimination, however, would be required only in the event that the affirmative action policies were challenged by nonminority employees in court. In Powell's words,

> a public employer like the Board must ensure that, before it embarks on an affirmative action program, it has convincing evidence that remedial action is warranted. That is, it must have

sufficient evidence to justify the conclusion that there has been prior discrimination.

Evidentiary support for the conclusion that remedial action is warranted becomes crucial when the remedial program is challenged in court by nonminority employees.[76]

Justice O'Connor made the same point somewhat more emphatically:

The imposition of a requirement that public employers make [formal] findings that they have engaged in illegal discrimination before they engage in affirmative action programs would severely undermine public employers' incentive to meet voluntarily their civil rights obligations. . . . This conclusion is consistent with our previous decisions recognizing the States' ability to take voluntary race-conscious action to achieve compliance with the law even in the absence of a specific finding of past discrimination.[77]

The difficulty with O'Connor's reasoning is that she treats "public employers" as if they were static entities, capable of recognizing and admitting "their" past mistakes and of taking steps to rectify them. Notwithstanding civil service reforms designed to make public employers less responsive to partisan political pressures, however, public employers are in fact often affected by the political or ideological agendas of elected politicians. A new administration, be it at the state, county, municipal, or board level, could easily claim that the previous administration had discriminated against certain discrete groups as a way of justifying preferential treatment for those groups under the new administration. If the groups in question happen to be the same groups that were instrumental in electing the new administration to office, the new administration will have discovered a particularly convenient (and apparently legal) method of rewarding its supporters by means of what amounts to an innovative form of patronage. This, of course, is a worst-case scenario, and yet is surely not so fanciful that it ought not be considered in juxtaposition with O'Connor's "best-case" assumptions.

Expanding upon O'Connor's theme, Justice Marshall, in a dissent that was joined by Justices Brennan and Blackmun, wrote that

[t]he real irony of the argument urging mandatory, formal findings of discrimination lies in its complete disregard for a long-standing goal of civil rights reform, that of integrating schools

without taking every school system to court. . . . It would defy
equity to penalize those who achieve harmony from discord, as
it would deny wisdom to impose on society the needless cost of
superfluous litigation.[78]

It scarcely needs saying that from the standpoint of innocent
third parties whose seniority rights have been abrogated by those
who strive to "achieve harmony from discord," litigation to determine whether race-conscious remedies were truly warranted
would hardly seem "superfluous." Under the rule apparently subscribed to by at least seven members of the Court (Justices White
and Stevens did not address the issue), a doctrinaire or politically
motivated public employer could unilaterally decide to adopt
race-conscious employment policies, and initially, at least, it need
satisfy no one but its own decision makers that the plan could be
justified as remedial. Only if suit is brought (a suit, incidentally,
that will certainly entail no small amount of time or monetary
expense) will the public employer be required to divulge its reasons for believing that race-conscious measures are justified. Even
here, the burden of plaintiffs, according to Justice O'Connor, ought
to be substantial:

> [A]s the Court suggests, the institution of such a challenge does
> not automatically impose upon the public employer the burden
> of convincing the court of its liability for prior unlawful discrim-
> ination; nor does it mean that the court must make an actual
> finding of prior discrimination based on the employer's proof
> before the employer's affirmative action plan will be upheld. In
> "reverse discrimination" suits, as in any other suit, it is the plain-
> tiffs who must bear the burden of demonstrating that their rights
> have been violated [sic*]. . . . For instance, in the example posed
> above, the nonminority teachers could easily demonstrate that
> the purpose and effect of the plan is to impose a race-based
> classification. But when the Board introduces its statistical proof
> as evidence of its remedial purpose, thereby supplying the court
> with the means for determining that the Board had a firm basis

---

*As discussed in Chapter 2, the disparate-impact theory of employment discrim-
ination holds that once a showing of a discriminatory effect is made, it is the
defendant who automatically assumes the burden of rebutting the inference of
unlawful discrimination.

for concluding that remedial action was appropriate, it is incumbent upon the nonminority teachers to prove their case; they continue to bear the ultimate burden of persuading the Court that the Board's evidence did not support an inference of prior discrimination and thus a remedial purpose, or that the plan instituted on the basis of this evidence was not sufficiently "narrowly tailored." Only by meeting this burden could the plaintiffs establish a violation of their constitutional rights, and thereby defeat the presumption that the Board's assertedly remedial action based on the statistical evidence was justified.[79]

A striking feature of this detailed pronouncement is the remarkable degree to which it departs from the historic application of "strict scrutiny" to government policies making use of racial classification. In O'Connor's formulation, a racial classification that purports to serve a "remedial purpose" is automatically presumed to be constitutionally permissible unless that presumption is effectively rebutted by those alleging an equal protection violation.

As for the Civil Rights Division's victim-specific approach to remedying civil rights violations, it follows that if public employers can justify, when challenged in court, their race-conscious employment policies by reference to "statistical evidence" (explicitly approved by O'Connor and, it seems reasonable to infer from their endorsement of numerical hiring goals, by Powell, Burger, and Rehnquist as well), then even the plurality that struck down the Jackson layoff plan would permit nonvictims to be among the principal beneficiaries of racial preferences. As if to emphasize this point, O'Connor declared that

the Court has forged a degree of unanimity; it is agreed that a plan need not be limited to the remedying of specific instances of identified discrimination for it to be deemed sufficiently "narrowly tailored," or "substantially related," to the correction of prior discrimination by the state actor.[80]

Recognizing that a corollary of racial preference for nonvictims is "reverse" discrimination against innocent persons, Justice Powell asserted that "[a]s part of this Nation's dedication to eradicating racial discrimination, innocent persons may be called upon to bear some of the burden of the remedy."[81] Parenthetically, we may note that it is this sort of sweeping moral catechism that, when substituted for the application of explicit, readily intelligible legal rules (in this case, the antidiscrimination mandate implicit in the equal protection clause), is the hallmark of modern judicial activism. Powell offers no formula for determining the proper allocation of the burden among particular innocent individuals; no method for predicting which of them "may be called upon," and under what circumstances. Because the plurality did not need to rely upon this particular pronouncement in its disposition of the case, Powell's words are mere dicta. They served to indicate forcefully, however, that the Court's decision in *Stotts* had in no way signaled the decisive shift in the Court's thinking that Assistant Attorney General Reynolds had imputed to it.

The *Wygant* Dissent: Toward a Racially Proportionate Distribution of Hardship

Our discussion of *Wygant* has thus far focused mostly on the plurality and concurring opinions. If these did little to vindicate the Civil Rights Division's interpretation of *Stotts*, the two dissenting opinions were especially revealing of the increasing extent to which the group rights approach to equal protection jurisprudence had become entrenched among the Court's three most liberal members. These justices—Brennan, Marshall, and Blackmun—joined in an opinion written by Justice Marshall that was remarkable not so much for the decision it recommended (upholding the school board's race-based layoff scheme) as for the way in which it framed the issues of the case. To Marshall, the plaintiffs were not autonomous individuals who had lost their jobs solely because of their color; rather, they were those members of the white race who had the least seniority, and therefore properly bore the brunt of their race's fair share of the hardship imposed by unavoidable layoffs. The race-based layoff provision in the teachers' contract, wrote Marshall,

> avoided placing the entire burden of layoffs on either the white teachers as a group or the minority teachers as a group. Instead, each group would shoulder a portion of that burden equal to its portion of the faculty. Thus, the overall percentage of minorities on the faculty would remain constant.[82]

In Marshall's analysis the plaintiffs became veritable representatives of the white race, or rather, of "the white teachers as a group," responsible for fulfilling the group's putative obligations. "To petitioners, at the bottom of the seniority scale among white teachers," he observed, "fell the lot of bearing the white group's proportionate share of layoffs that became necessary in 1982."[83] The idea that each racial group should bear a "proportionate share" of layoffs is wholly consistent with the norm of statistical group parity. If the range of social goods and benefits (such as a lucrative job or admission to a prestigious professional school) are to be distributed in equal proportions from one group to the next, then so too should the range of life's burdens and hardships. Thus Marshall is led to conclude that the layoff provision in the Jackson teachers' contract is by no means "not sufficiently tailored." Rather, it is "a narrow provision because it allocates the impact of unavoidable burden proportionately between two racial groups."[84] Furthermore, "it places no absolute burden or benefit on one race, and, *within the confines of constant minority proportions*, it preserves the hierarchy of seniority in the selection of individuals for layoff."[85] That is to say, the provision preserves the hierarchy of seniority, but along racially segregated lines; each group is conceived as having its own exclusive hierarchy of seniority.

Marshall had clearly broken new ground here. His innovation lies in his extension of the concept of group rights to group responsibility. Responsibility for bearing the hardships and suffering that regularly befall "society"—such as, in the present example, the social and economic dislocations that result from fiscal insolvency—should in fairness be distributed proportionately among racial groups. Notwithstanding the equal protection clause's requirement of equal treatment for individual persons, Marshall teaches that it is constitutionally permissible for governments to hold an individual responsible for his race's proportionate share of society's burdens. When reflecting on the overt race-consciousness that evidently informs Marshall's jurisprudence, it is important to bear in mind that Marshall is not attempting here to fashion a remedy for some real or imagined violation of statutory or constitutional law. Rather, he is recommending it as a quite normal structural arrangement for allocating hardship under any circumstances.

From a comparative perspective it is easy to discern the profoundly traditionalistic—perhaps even feudal—character of the system here constructed, for although it evokes an ethos quite foreign to the modern, individualistic legal-rational culture of the West, it is common in traditional societies for social obligations and responsibilities to be allocated among individuals on the basis of their membership in the relevant clan, tribe, race, or caste.

The Sheet Metal Workers Association Case: Repudiation of *Stotts* and "the Policy behind Section 706(g)"

That the Court in *Wygant* seemed to be retreating from the broad attack on racial quotas and preference schemes which it had apparently launched in *Stotts* was amply confirmed on July 2, 1986, when the Court handed down decisions in two more cases in which the Justice Department challenged the legality of race-conscious affirmative action doctrine. In the first case, *Local 28 of the Sheet Metal Workers' International Association v. Equal Employment Opportunity Commission*,[86] six members of the Court (Brennan, Marshall, Blackmun, Stevens, Powell, and White) held that "a district court may, in appropriate circumstances, order preferential relief benefiting individuals who are not the actual victims of discrimination as a remedy for violations of Title VII."[87] Five of these justices (all but White) agreed that the present case established "appropriate circumstances" for awarding racial classwide relief in the form of preferential treatment for blacks.

As always, the Court was obliged to give at least the appearance that it was taking seriously the language of Section 706(g) and its pivotal admonition to judges:

> No order of the court shall require the admission or reinstatement of an individual as a member of a union . . . if such individual was refused admission, suspended, or expelled, or was refused employment or advancement or was suspended or discharged for any reason other than discrimination on account of race, color, religion, sex, or national origin in violation of . . . this title.

In his plurality opinion, Justice Brennan, countering familiar arguments made by both the Sheet Metal Workers' Association and the Solicitor General, declared that "[t]he sentence on its face addresses only the situation where a plaintiff demonstrates that a union (or an employer) has engaged in unlawful discrimination, but the union can show that a particular individual would have been refused admission even in the absence of discrimination, for example because the individual was unqualified. In these circumstances, Section 706(g) confirms that a court could not order the union to admit the unqualified individual."[88]

The Supreme Court thus took the position that Congress intended to prohibit courts from granting relief to "unqualified" persons who have been subjected to racially discriminatory policies, but that Congress never addressed the question of whether courts could grant relief to persons who are qualified but who never suffered personally from the union's or employer's discriminatory policy—persons who, for all that is known, may not even have been part of the labor force at the time the alleged discrimination took place. The Supreme Court could therefore uphold a district court ruling that had ordered the New York City–based union local to meet a 29.23 percent nonwhite-membership quota by August 31, 1987. The Court also upheld the lower court's creation of an "Employment, Training, Education, and Recruitment Fund" to "be used for the purpose of remedying discrimination."[89] The fund, which was to be paid for by the union's membership, "paid for nonwhite union members to serve as liaisons to vocational and technical schools with sheet metal jobs for qualified nonwhite youths, and extended financial assistance to needy apprentices, giving them the benefits that had traditionally been available to white apprentices from family and friends."[90]

By treating the racial quota as a remedy for past discrimination, the Court was able to sidestep Title VII's explicit disavowal of any interpretation that would regard it as an instrument for enforcing substantive group parity, although the Court's attempt to explain away the relevance of the last sentence of Section 706(g) may strike some as less than convincing, especially in light of the Court's discussion of it in *Stotts*. The particular circumstances of the case, however, make clear that, as we have already suggested, the Court's refusal to accede to the proposition that remedies should only be available to actual victims derives from the justices' awareness—never explicitly articulated—that to adopt such a rule would be to alter radically the legal meaning of the very wrong to which the remedy is addressed— "discrimination."

We have argued that group-based relief makes sense only if the wrong which it purports to remedy is understood as the absence of group parity—that is, a state of affairs in which wealth-producing social goods, such as jobs and places in apprenticeship programs and professional schools, are distributed unevenly among the relevant groups. It is evident that the Court's opinion in the *Sheet Metal Workers* case follows this approach, not least because each of the justices who voted with the majority stressed that group-based relief was in order precisely because the union was supposed to have practiced "egregious" discrimination. Indeed, in announcing the rule of decision that governed the Court's judgment, Justice Brennan wrote that "[s]pecifically, we hold that such relief may be appropriate where an employer or labor union has engaged in persistent or egregious discrimination, or where necessary to dissipate the lingering effects of pervasive discrimination."[91] The district court, too, had characterized the union's discriminatory practices as "egregious," and had held the *Stotts* ruling inapposite because "this case, unlike *Stotts*, involved intentional discrimination."[92]

Remember that in the *Weber* case the Court ruled that a private employer could voluntarily engage in race-conscious affirmative action on the theory that Title VII's prohibition of racial discrimination was not intended by Congress to interfere with "traditional business freedom" if used to practice "benign" discrimination. Therefore, private employers need not justify their voluntarily adopted racial preference schemes as "remedies" for past discrimination against minorities. The *Weber* ruling, however, did not directly apply to private employers or unions who were compelled by court order to adopt race-conscious procedures for dealing with prospective employees or members. Local 28 of the Sheet Metal Workers Association, to its chagrin, had been placed under just such an arrangement, and hence the court-ordered affirmative action plan under which it was forced to operate could be sustained only if supported by evidence that the union had discriminated. The Court was thus at pains to emphasize the extraordinary character of the discrimination previously practiced by the union—it was "intentional" and "egregious." In such cases (but presumably not in others where the putative discrimination was less than "egregious") race-conscious affirmative action was found to be an appropriate remedy.

It is important to ask what constitutes intentional, egregious discrimination. Reflection on this question from a common-sense perspective might yield an answer such as the following: Intentional, egregious discrimination would, in the extreme case, be exemplified by an employer who publicly announced that he would refuse to accept applications for employment from persons who belong to particular groups, as when factories in Northeastern industrial cities during the nineteenth century displayed signs bearing such messages as "Now Hiring: No Irish Need Apply."[93] A less extreme example, utilizing a more practicable method given the enactment of modern civil rights legislation, would be to accept applications for employment or union membership without regard to the applicant's race, but to favor members of one group over members of another during the selection process, even where, on the basis of neutral hiring criteria, the disfavored individuals present credentials or qualifications superior to those of the favored individuals. It is difficult, from a common-sense perspective, to imagine another form of discrimination that would qualify as "egregious," or even, perhaps, as "intentional."

As it happens, Local 28 did use neutral criteria for determining admission to its apprenticeship program; applicants had to possess a high school diploma and score high, relative to other applicants, on a competitive entrance examination. Thus, for Local 28 to have been found guilty of practicing "egregious" discrimination against nonwhites, one might have expected that one or more nonwhite applicants for admission to the local, despite having both a high school diploma and a relatively high score on the examination, were nevertheless passed over in favor of white applicants who lacked one or both of these attributes. In fact, no such unsuccessful nonwhite applicant was produced during the course of the litigation. Instead, the doctrinal legacy of *Griggs* and its progeny displaced the common-sense understanding of what "egregious discrimination" might entail. Hence,

> the [district] court found that petitioners had adopted discriminatory procedures and standards for admission into the apprenticeship program. The court examined some of the factors used to select apprentices, including the entrance examination

and high school diploma requirement, and determined that these criteria had an adverse discriminatory impact on nonwhites, and were not related to job performance. The court also observed that petitioners had used union funds to subsidize special training sessions for friends and relatives of union members taking the apprenticeship examination.[94]

It is not too much to say that the Supreme Court's uncritical acceptance of the district court's equation of disparate impact and "egregious discrimination" necessarily determined the outcome of the case. It would be impossible to redress a wrong defined in terms of adverse group impact by permitting relief only to actual victims of discrimination, because the wrong by its very nature was suffered by the group as a collective entity rather than by any of its particular members.

The logic of disparate impact is also evident in the Court's agreement with the notion that the use of union funds to subsidize "special training sessions for friends and relatives of union members taking the apprenticeship examination" was discriminatory, and by its approval of the district court's creation of a union-subsidized fund for the sole benefit of nonwhite applicants, "for the purpose of remedying discrimination." To be sure, whenever a union whose membership is drawn predominantly from one group engages in nepotistic recruitment and training practices, there is bound to be an adverse impact on members of other groups. That, however, is only because nepotism has an adverse impact on all prospective applicants—white or otherwise—who are not fortunate enough to have a friend or relative among the union's current membership. It is typical of group-based equity to regard nepotism, whose disfavored "victims" actually comprise all those who are not friends or relatives of incumbents, as disfavoring only the racial or ethnic group that is statistically under-represented. Thus, one effect of the district court's remedy was the creation of a second class of specially "advantaged" applicants against whom nonminority applicants unrelated by kith or kin to any of the union's incumbents must compete for scarce positions. One could say of such applicants that they were now doubly disadvantaged in the competition for union apprenticeships, being disfavored on the one hand because of their lack of "connections" and on the other hand because of their race.

Local No. 93, International Association of Firefighters v.
City of Cleveland

The other case decided by the Supreme Court on July 2, 1986 involved circumstances nearly identical to those of the *Williams* case
considered above. The issue before the Court was similar to the issue
decided in the *Sheet Metal Workers* case, but with a twist: The Court
was asked to consider whether Section 706(g) of Title VII "precludes
the entry of a consent decree which provides relief that may benefit
individuals who were not the actual victims of the defendant's discriminatory practices."[95] Here again, "discriminatory practices"
were alleged to include such items as "the written examination used
for making promotions . . . "[96] Due to the nature of the consent decree
settlement process, however, these allegations were never proved in
court. As was suggested by the lawyer for the City of Cleveland in
oral arguments before the Court, the city's previous experience had
provided it with ample incentive to settle the lawsuit, brought by a
group of black firefighters who called themselves the Vanguards, as
quickly and painlessly as possible:

> [W]hen this case was filed in 1980, the City of Cleveland had eight
> years at that point of litigating these types of cases, and eight
> years of having judges rule against the City of Cleveland.
>   You don't have to beat us on the head. We finally learned what
> we had to do and what we had to try to do to comply with the
> law, and it was the intent of the city to comply with the law fully.[97]

Thus the city eagerly entered negotiations with the Vanguards to
avoid another round of futile litigation.

In November 1981, the two parties submitted to the district
court a proposed consent decree, the features of which were delineated by Justice Brennan in his opinion for the Court:

> The first step required that a fixed number of already planned
> promotions be reserved for minorities: specifically, 16 of 40
> planned promotions to Lieutenant, 3 of 20 planned promotions
> to Captain, 2 of 10 planned promotions to Battalion Chief, and
> 1 of 3 planned promotions to Assistant Chief were to be made
> to minority firefighters. . . . The second step involved the estab-
> lishment of "appropriate minority promotion goal[s]," . . . for
> the ranks of Lieutenant, Captain, and Battalion Chief. The

proposal also required the City to forgo using seniority points as a factor in making promotions. . . . The plan was to remain in effect for 9 years, and could be extended upon mutual application of the parties for an additional 6-year period.[98]

The city, in fact, was so eager to reach an accommodation with the Vanguards that it negotiated without ever consulting the local firefighters' union, whose members obviously stood to be strongly affected by the decree's provisions. Upon learning of this, the district judge declared himself to be "appalled that these negotiations leading to this consent decree did not include the intervenors . . . ,"[99] and thus refused to consider it until the firefighters' union was brought into the discussions.

There followed negotiations that resulted in first one modified version of the original proposed decree, and then another, but both were opposed by representatives of Local 93. The second modified decree, which was eventually approved by the district court judge, was rejected by the union's membership by a vote of 660 to 89.[100] That decree

required that the city immediately make 66 promotions to Lieutenant, 32 promotions to Captain, 16 promotions to Battalion Chief and 4 promotions to Assistant Chief. These promotions were to be based on a promotional examination that had been administered during the litigation. The 66 initial promotions to Lieutenant were to be evenly split between minority and non-minority firefighters. However, since only 10 minorities had qualified for the 52 upper-level positions, the proposed decree provided that all 10 should be promoted. The decree further required promotional examinations to be administered in June 1984 and December 1985. Promotions from the lists produced by these examinations were to be made in accordance with specified promotional "goals" that were expressed in terms of percentages and were different for each rank. The list from the 1985 examinations would remain in effect for two years, after which time the decree would expire.[101]

Did such an arrangement, which clearly benefited persons who were not themselves victims even of alleged, much less proven, discrimination, violate Title VII, specifically the final sentence of Section 706(g)?

In the *Sheet Metal Workers* case, the Court ruled that racial class-wide "relief" could be granted by courts in "appropriate cases," such as those involving "egregious" or "intentional" discrimination. The allegations of discriminations had never been litigated in the present case, and hence there was no record from which the Court could determine whether sufficiently egregious discrimination had occurred. Resolute in its desire to uphold race-conscious civil rights doctrine, however, the Court devised an ingenious, if legally questionable, solution to this problem: It held that "whether or not Section 706(g) precludes a court from imposing certain forms of race-conscious relief after trial, that provision does not apply to relief awarded in a consent decree."[102] In other words, the final sentence of Section 706(g), which begins with the words, "No order of the court shall require . . . ," has no bearing on consent decrees because such instruments are not "orders of courts."

From a legal standpoint, this was a bizarre holding for a number of reasons. Most importantly, the decision seemed to overrule *Stotts*, which just two terms earlier had decided that Section 706(g) was applicable to a judicial order that modified an existing consent decree. To reconcile the *Cleveland Firefighters* ruling with that issued in *Stotts*, one would have to find plausible the notion that a *modified* consent decree constitutes an "order of the court" within the meaning of Section 706(g), but that a consent decree in its original form does not. Moreover, the ruling was at odds with major precedents which had established unequivocally that consent decrees were indeed judicial orders, rather than "contracts," as Justice Brennan contended, because the authority of courts to enforce them is rooted in the nexus between the decree and the statute that it is ultimately intended to enforce. Thus the Court in *Stotts* found it useful to quote language from the Court's opinion in the 1961 case of *Railway Employers v. Wright*, to wit,

"[T]he District Court's authority to adopt a consent decree comes only from the statute which the decree is intended to enforce," not from the parties' consent to the decree.[103]

Although Brennan cited a leading academic authority on federal practice as support for his position, he omitted, as Justice Rehnquist noted in dissent, a key sentence from the passage he quoted:

> But the fact remains that judgment is not an *inter partes* contract; the Court is not properly a recorder of contracts, but is an organ of government constituted to make judicial decisions and when it has rendered a consent judgment it has made anadjudication.[104]

It is thus their capacity as instruments of adjudication, whose legitimacy is derived from statutory law, that has caused consent decrees traditionally to be regarded as "orders of the court."

Even if it were reasonable to insist that consent decrees are mere "contracts," it must be acknowledged that no contract is legally enforceable unless all those affected by it have initially agreed to its terms. The Cleveland consent decree, however, was approved despite the objections of Local 93. Brennan's solution here was simply to deny that the union was in any way affected by the decree:

> [T]he consent decree entered here does *not* bind Local 93 to do or not to do anything. It imposes no legal duties or obligations on the Union at all; only the parties to the decree can be held in contempt of court for failure to comply with its terms.[105]

Justice Rehnquist observed in his dissent that this statement

> verges on the pharisiacal; the decree does bind the City of Cleveland to give preferential promotions to minority firemen who have not been shown to be the victims of discrimination in such a way that nonminority union members who would otherwise have received these promotions are obviously injured.[106]

However shaky the Court's rationale may have been from a purely legal standpoint, there is no denying its utility as a political expedient. The Court's opinion not only enabled it to reach the result that it desired in the particular case at hand, but it also served to stymie the Justice Department in the pursuit of its broader agenda. We noted earlier that following the *Stotts* ruling the Civil Rights Division had moved to overturn fifty-one existing affirmative action consent decrees around the country on the grounds that their terms were impermissible under Section 706(g). Most of these motions were still pending by the time the *Sheet Metal Workers* and *Cleveland Firefighters* cases were handed down.

Because it applied narrowly to judicially fashioned "remedies" for proven instances of "discrimination," the Court's decision in the former case would probably have had little effect on the effort to overturn the decrees. But by deciding in *Cleveland Firefighters* that Section 706(g) has absolutely no bearing on consent decrees, the Court succeeded in pulling the rug out from under the Justice Department—the very same rug, incidentally, that the Court itself had furnished in *Stotts*. It is difficult to imagine that this consideration was not a factor in the Court's decision. It would appear that Supreme Court justices, far from "following the election returns," sometimes seek actively to confound executive initiatives with which they disagree, even when the initiatives are grounded in the prior decisions of those very same justices.

As would be expected, the Civil Rights Division tried to put the best possible face on the July 2 decisions. Calling the rulings "disappointing" and "extremely unfortunate," Assistant Attorney General Reynolds nonetheless emphasized language in the Court's opinion suggesting that racial preferences are the "least preferred" remedy, to be used only under extraordinary circumstances.[107] There were immediate signs, however, that employers and the press took these perfunctory caveats no more seriously than the Court did. For instance, two days after the rulings were handed down the *New York Times* ran a story in its "Business Day" section under the headline, "Minority Hiring Ruling Puts Concerns on Notice." Given its title, one might have expected the article to explain the limitations that the Court had seemingly placed on the use of racial preference in hiring and promotion. Instead, readers were informed that the decisions "do send a warning to companies that have been lax, according to experts and executives. . . . [F]or the 'substantial' number of companies that have 'downgraded the importance of their affirmative action programs' during the Reagan Administration," the article continued, "the decision is a 'clear warning that they must take affirmative action seriously again,' according to D. Quinn Mills of the Harvard Business School."[108] In reality, of course, the decisions in no way pertained to the voluntary "affirmative action programs" of private companies, and so hardly constituted a "warning" to the business community, clear or otherwise. Yet already the decision was being received as such, in part because of the mediating influence of partisan "experts."

Conclusion

The politics of civil rights is dominated by magic words—some positive, such as "equal opportunity," and some negative, such as "discrimination." The cases examined here suggest that this is no less true of the most rarefied juridical discourse on the subject than it is of popular soapbox oratory. In either forum emotionally freighted words and phrases are invoked, with little or no attention to what they might actually mean, to give judicially enacted race-conscious social policy an aura of legitimacy.

The magic words that make up the rhetoric of civil rights are compelling in part because of their abstract connotations—justice and equity in the case of "equal opportunity," meanness and bigotry in the case of "discrimination"—but also because their use has been associated historically with the experience of oppressed groups. In the past, the measure of a group's oppression consisted in the mix of public laws and private practices intended deliberately to exclude, isolate, and subjugate that group. In the 1970s and 1980s the measure of a group's oppression was, at least in certain influential circles, transformed; a group was considered to be oppressed to the extent that it lacked parity with other groups. The Constitution and the civil rights statutes could be used effectively to combat the original form of oppression, but they were, if taken literally, wholly unresponsive to the revised version. Hence the need, for those who would use public law to correct substantive disparities among groups, to continue to define their mission as "remedying discrimination."

A judiciary in pursuit of a mission such as this one will thus quite naturally want to use its remedial authority to promote redistribution along group lines. The tendency will nearly always be to take from the "advantaged" group and give to the "disadvantaged" group. Hence the most blatant and direct forms of intentional discrimination will be countenanced if practiced against members of the advantaged group for the purpose of "remedying" even the most tenuous claims of discrimination brought by members of the disadvantaged group. This stance explains the remarkable asymmetry in the courts' treatment of issues involving discrimination against minorities as against issues involving discrimination against nonminorities.

The generally euphoric response by the influential news media to the *Sheet Metal Workers* and *Cleveland Firefighters* decisions illustrated well the emotive force behind the rhetoric of civil rights. "Contrary to the legal arguments of the Justice Department, the [Supreme] Court insists that victory over discrimination cannot yet be declared," announced the *New York Times* in a lead editorial. "Nor may government pretend that its remedial task is done."[109] In its enthusiasm, the *Times* could not resist attributing to the Court a position it did not, and which perforce it could not, take: "[T]he high court has resoundingly rejected the Administration's arguments that race-conscious affirmative action to redress discrimination is itself discriminatory against whites."[110] The Court, of course, suggested to the contrary that discrimination against whites was an acceptable by-product of race-conscious affirmative action. The *Times'* eagerness to pretend otherwise perhaps betrays a visceral aversion to discrimination even when practiced against nonminorities. The Justice Department might well have aided its cause by focusing debate on the meaning of "discrimination" instead of on the appropriate form of relief.

Understanding the nature of a wrong is critical to defining the nature and scope of its remedy. The cases examined here demonstrate just how vague and subjective is our current understanding of "discrimination" and its antonym, "equal opportunity." As used in contemporary discourse they are provocative catch-phrases that serve to legitimate the bureaucratic and judicial administration of group parity. Another such phrase, as we shall discover in Chapter 4, is "school desegregation."

RACE AND THE SCHOOLS

Where once it was said to be unequal, and therefore unconstitutional, to send certain children to certain schools,
solely because of their race or color, it is now held to be a
requirement, an "affirmative" requirement, of that same
equality.

—Harry V. Jaffa,
The Conditions of Freedom

Americans must choose between standard, apparently desirable modes of policy choice and enactment, and the goal
of eradicating racism. If whites cannot bring themselves to
give up the advantages that America's racial and class
practices give them, they must permit elites to make that
choice for them.

—Jennifer L. Hochschild,
The New American Dilemma:
Liberal Democracy and School Desegregation

Thus far in our discussion we have seen how constitutional and
statutory language was manipulated in the service of that foremost goal of the modern civil rights movement, the creation of
statistical parity among racial groups. Statistical disparities
among groups in employment were automatically equated with
discrimination; hence, any such disparities could be treated by
courts and agencies as wrongs in need of a suitable remedy. Since
the wrong all too often had no demonstrable connection to discrimination as it is commonly understood, the remedy could

rarely take the form of a simple injunction against discrimination. Instead, new procedures for hiring, promoting, and discharging workers were required, designed to ensure that the goal of statistical group parity would be approached, if not actually realized in all situations.

Parallels to School Desegregation

Throughout the 1970s, the same integrationist ideal that became, in effect, the law of the land in the realm of employment also became the principle according to which children were assigned to public schools. Just as the constitutional and statutory prohibitions against discrimination were transformed by judges and agency officials into a positive governmental obligation to enforce statistical group parity, so too were similar prohibitions against government-compelled racial segregation in public school districts transformed into a governmental obligation to impose statistical racial balance in the public schools. This project, which has been more than adequately described and analyzed elsewhere,* was carried out by the Supreme Court under the aegis of the equal protection clause and the historic precedent set in *Brown v. Board of Education*,[1] the 1954 case in which the Court first established that the equal protection of the laws precluded state-enforced, or *de jure*, racial separation in the assignment of children to public schools. The most controversial episode in the movement to impose racial balance in the schools occurred in 1971, when for the first time the Court upheld judicial orders requiring the busing of students to schools located beyond those closest to their homes, in order to achieve racial balance in other, more distant schools.

Beyond the practical objections voiced by many parents about the practice of busing itself—the often substantial amount of time it subtracted from arguably more worthwhile activities, and concerns relating to school-bus safety—racial busing represented to many an inexcusable incursion by government into the sphere of individual liberty for what seemed a rather frivolous purpose—so that black and white children could sit together in the same class-

---

*See Lino A. Graglia, *Disaster by Decree: The Supreme Court Decisions on Race and the Schools* (Ithaca: Cornell Univ. Press, 1976).

rooms. The assignment and transportation of students to achieve racial balance had all the trappings of a classic violation of the Kantian injunction against treating individuals as means to an end: black and white children were moved about like so many differently colored ceramic tiles, systematically arranged to form a pleasing mosaic.

Of course, it could hardly be maintained that the more radical of the integrationists were motivated by mere aesthetic considerations. Such people saw compulsory busing as a tool that could be used to force whites to "give up the advantages that America's racial and class practices give them," in the quasi-Marxian formulation employed by Jennifer Hochschild, quoted in the epigraph. The moderate integrationist position, on the other hand, took its bearings not so much from class analysis as from the belief that bringing together people of diverse backgrounds at an early age (the earlier the better, in the opinion of many) offered the best hope for fostering racial understanding and harmony in the next generation of Americans. By beginning with children, went the theory, the integrationist movement could help to immunize children from the pernicious effects of the racial prejudice and stereotyping they were bound to confront as they grew older. Moreover, school racial integration would ensure that what was solemnly referred to as "the promise of *Brown*" would be realized in fact—that black children and white children would be guaranteed a truly equal education. As James Nuechterlein recently observed, however, "No one ever satisfactorily explained why racial balance was necessary to achieve decent education for black children, and the apparent assumption that those children could only learn effectively in the presence of some critical mass of white children struck many blacks as condescending at best."[2]

Interestingly, that great, powerful engine of compulsory school integration, the U.S. Supreme Court, never once relied formally on the various rationales used by integration's nonjudicial proponents. Throughout the entire series of busing cases from *Swann* through *Keyes*, the Court disingenuously insisted that it was not integration or racial balance that it sought to achieve, but only the disestablishment of "dual" school systems, and their replacement with school systems that were "unitary." A "dual" system, according to a majority of the justices, was one that was segregated *de jure*—that is, by law. The Court purported to find no equal protection violations with respect to schools that were segregated *de facto*—where racial imbalance arose due to social or demographic factors unrelated to government policy. After having made the crucial distinction between *de jure* and *de facto* segregation in the 1971 case of *Swann v. Charlotte-Mecklenburg*—the first case in which the Supreme Court authorized the use of race-based pupil assignment and compulsory busing as a valid judicial remedy for curing segregation—the Court increasingly enervated that distinction as it issued ruling after ruling upholding the use of busing as a remedy for racial imbalance regardless of whether the complained-of imbalance was actually brought about by segregative governmental policies.

To be sure, the Court, by resorting to the sort of baroque reasoning so characteristic of its decisions upholding the use of affirmative action in employment, declined to admit that its rulings upholding race-conscious pupil assignment constituted anything more than an attempt to bring an end to *de jure* segregation in the nation's schools. Yet the conclusion is unavoidable that the Court had, in effect, amended the Constitution to require racially balanced schools where at all feasible. The "constitutional mandate," as Lino Graglia has observed, "was changed from a prohibition of racial discrimination to separate the races to a requirement of racial discrimination to mix them."[3]

Not all federal judges were as reluctant as the Supreme Court's integrationist majority to acknowledge that this was what had happened. Writing for a panel of the Court of Appeals for the Fifth Circuit in the 1966 case of *United States v. Jefferson County Board of Education*, Judge John Minor Wisdom sententiously declared that "no army is stronger than an idea whose time has come,"[4] and went on to suggest that judges were obliged to incorporate such ideas into the Constitution. Therefore the Constitution should henceforth be interpreted as recognizing that the "racial mixing of students is a high-priority educational goal."[5] There was thus no need for Wisdom and his colleagues to justify his admission that "in this opinion we use the words 'integration' and 'desegregation' interchangeably"; if integration was "an idea whose time had come," then it followed that it must now be required by the Constitution.

The case of one Supreme Court justice in particular, Thurgood Marshall, provides an exceptionally clear illustration of how the legal meaning of "desegregation" was transformed during the twenty-year period following the Court's decision in *Brown*. As a young NAACP attorney representing the black plaintiffs in that historic case, Marshall engaged in the following colloquy with Justice Felix Frankfurter:

> *Frankfurter*: It would be more important information in my mind, to have you spell out in concrete what would happen if this Court reverses and the case goes back to the district court for entry of a decree.

> *Marshall*: I think, sir, that the decree would be entered which would enjoin the school official from, one, enforcing the statute; two, from segregating on the basis of race or color. Then I think whatever district lines they draw, if it can be shown that those lines are drawn on the basis of race or color, then I think they would violate the injunction. If the lines are drawn on a natural basis without regard to race or color, then I think that nobody would have any complaint.[6]

Twenty years later, in his dissenting opinion in *Milliken v. Bradley*,[7] the same Thurgood Marshall delivered himself of a much different understanding of the meaning of "desegregation":

> We held in *Swann* that where *de jure* segregation is shown, school authorities must make "every effort to achieve the greatest possible actual degree of desegregation." . . . If these words have any meaning at all, surely it is that school authorities must, to the extent possible, take all practicable steps to ensure that Negro and white children in fact go to school together. This is, in the final analysis, what desegregation of the public schools is all about.[8]

A majority of Marshall's colleagues on the Court would not go quite this far; in the case at hand they refused to authorize interdistrict busing where a history of *de jure* segregation—even according to the Court's by now quite expansive definition of "*de jure*"—could be found in only one of the districts involved. The *Milliken* decision, however, seemed less rooted in a principled adherence to the *de jure/de facto* distinction than in a pragmatic recognition of the limits of what the traffic would bear. Drawing the predominantly white suburbs of Detroit into a busing plan to correct racial imbalance in the inner-city schools would, aside from the social and economic costs involved, have exposed with absolute clarity the integrationist underpinnings of court-ordered desegregation.

To many observers it was already clear that integration had supplanted desegregation as the principal rationale for court-ordered busing. One telltale indication of this was the Court's reliance on statistical breakdowns of the racial composition of student bodies as evidence of segregation (a pattern repeated, as we have seen, in the Court's Title VII rulings). Is numerical data showing the ratio of black students to white students attending a particular school a valid indicator of segregation? To illustrate the peculiar connotation that the word "segregation" has taken on in the context of education, the economist Walter Williams asks that we consider, as an example, the water fountains at Washington National Airport. Are they segregated or desegregated? "Most people would first establish whether blacks had unimpeded access to any fountain," says Williams. "If so, the fountains would be deemed desegregated."[9] Next he asks us to consider whether the nation's public schools are segregated or desegregated. For many civil rights activists, and for the federal courts, the answer is not nearly as simple and straightforward as in the case of the water fountains. Williams writes:

> The confusion is caused by the shifting definition of desegregation. The test people used to determine whether water fountains were desegregated was whether a black was *able* to use the facility. But the test for desegregated public schools has become whether blacks *are* using the facility in proportion to their numbers in society. No one would employ a numbers-based criterion to determine whether water fountains were segregated. Moreover, having found statistical disparities, such as blacks being 75 percent of the District of Columbia's population but, let us say, 15 percent of the airport's fountain users, no one would propose to remedy the situation by a busing plan.[10]

It is easy to see why civil rights activists would attach greater importance to achieving racial balance in public schools than in the use of public water fountains. Given the state of public opinion, however, proponents of the use of busing to achieve school racial balance could not have hoped to realize their will through the legislative process. They therefore resorted to an increasingly familiar stratagem: They sought to persuade courts to recognize what was essentially a cherished public policy goal as a constitutional right. The transformation of public policy goal into constitutional right was achieved chiefly through a kind of rhetorical legerdemain by which "integration" and "desegregation" became synonymous.

The Position of the Justice Department

The Reagan Justice Department might have been expected to challenge compulsory racial busing and race-conscious pupil assignments in the federal courts, especially in light of statements made by William Bradford Reynolds such as the following:

> In constitutional terms, no child can be denied the opportunity to attend any public school in the system because of his or her race; nor can he or she be deprived on account of race of an educational opportunity equal to that afforded others in the school system. The constitutional command is that, to the extent such school attendance barriers or educational barriers have been erected, they must be removed "root and branch"; that is the "desegregation" imperative. If that is accomplished, the fact that there might remain in the school district a school that continues, by choice, to be predominantly one race, offends no law.[11]

This view, however, had been presented to the federal courts, including the Supreme Court, on numerous occasions during the 1970s, and had for the most part been rejected. With so many busing plans already in place throughout the country by the time the Reagan administration took office, the Justice Department might have developed a strategy of supporting the growing number of school districts around the country that, after experiencing years of court-ordered busing, were now going to court seeking relief from the remedy—that is, permission to end busing on the theory that whether or not racial balance could be permanently maintained in the absence of busing, the school district had at least seen to it that putatively segregative barriers had been removed "root and branch."

Apart from devising its own particular litigation strategy, important decisions had to be made regarding cases that the Justice Department had inherited from the Carter administration. Because the process of litigation in America is notoriously tortuous and protracted, the Justice Department under a new administration will typically find itself burdened with many active cases in which department involvement was initiated at the behest of the previous administration. (As noted in the previous chapter, *Connecticut v. Teal* was such a case.) Department officials under the new administration must decide what role the new administration will play in such actions—whether to continue in the same vein as the previous administration; to modify its position somewhat; to withdraw from the case altogether; or to reverse the position taken under the previous administration and thus, in effect, switch sides.

Racial Busing as Irreversible Public Policy: The Case of Seattle

A "holdover" case in the school desegregation area was *Washington v. Seattle School District No. 1*, the resolution of which would serve to demonstrate a zealous judicial commitment to the integrationist ideal. In November 1978, voters in the state of Washington passed by a 2-to-1 margin a ballot initiative that would have prohibited local school boards from "requiring any student to attend a school other than the school which is geographically nearest or next nearest the student's place of residence—and which offers the course of study pursued by such student."[12] The proposal, known as Initiative 350, did, however, set forth several exceptions to this requirement: a student could be assigned to a school outside his neighborhood if he "requires special education, care, or guidance . . . , if there are health or safety hazards between the student's place of residence and the nearest or next nearest school"; or if "the school nearest or next nearest to his place of residence is unfit or inadequate because of overcrowding, unsafe conditions, or lack of physical facilities."[13] The initiative would have permitted busing for racial purposes only insofar as it did not purport to "prevent any court from adjudicating constitutional issues relating to the public schools." In other words, racial busing would be permitted only as part of a judicial remedy for a constitutional violation.

Initiative 350 had been placed on the statewide ballot by residents of a Seattle school district who were opposed to a plan adopted by the school board calling for mandatory reassignment and extensive busing of elementary school children for the purpose of racial integration. The plan had been prompted, not by any judicial finding of *de jure* segregation in the Seattle public schools, but rather by a school board resolution to eliminate "racial imbalance" from the schools by the beginning of the 1979 academic year.[14] When the initiative passed and became state law, the Seattle School District, together with two other school districts in the Seattle metropolitan area, sued the state of Washington on the grounds that the new law violated the Fourteenth Amendment's equal protection clause. The law was invalidated by a district court, whose decision was subsequently affirmed by the Court of Appeals for the Ninth Circuit.[15]

In view of Assistant Attorney General Reynolds's publicly stated opposition to compulsory busing for racial purposes, it is not surprising that when the case was appealed to the Supreme Court he reversed the position taken before the lower courts by the Carter administration, which had supported the plaintiffs. It is important to note that the case was not about the constitutionality of race-conscious student assignments. Rather, the issue was whether a state could prevent units of local government from making a certain kind of decision with respect to issues having a "racial nature." In terms of equal protection doctrine, the question was whether Initiative 350, in implicitly proscribing busing for racial purposes—while permitting busing for certain specified nonracial purposes—had created a constitutionally invalid racial classification. A majority of five justices (Blackmun, Brennan, Marshall, White, and Stevens) decided that it had, and thus affirmed the judgment of the Court of Appeals.

In his opinion for the majority, Justice Harry Blackmun relied heavily on *Hunter v. Erickson*,[16] a 1969 case concerning use of the referendum procedure by voters in Akron, Ohio to disestablish a fair-housing ordinance enacted by the Akron City Council, and to require furthermore that any future fair-housing ordinances first be approved by an electoral majority before becoming effective. In *Hunter*, the Court found that this initiative, which took the form of an amendment to the city charter, served as an "explicitly racial classification treating racial housing matters differently from other racial and housing matters."[17] It also found that the charter amendment significantly altered the structure of the policy-making process in Akron where racial housing matters were concerned, thus "making it more difficult for certain racial and religious minorities to achieve legislation that is in their interest."[18]

The facts in the *Seattle* case, however, differed from the facts in *Hunter* in at least two important respects. First, while it is reasonably clear that fair-housing legislation benefits minorities, it is not so clear who, if anyone, benefits from compulsory school integration, especially where extensive busing is involved. Recent polling data suggest that slightly more than half of all blacks oppose school busing for racial integration,[19] and unless one is prepared to make the condescending argument that half of all blacks have thereby demonstrated an inability to identify and support policies that are ostensibly in their interest, the question of whether busing benefits blacks (either as individuals or as a group) must remain open to debate. This is especially so given the inconclusive results of social science research on the effects of integrated versus nonintegrated schooling.[20] Even if it were possible to substantiate the claim that blacks benefit from busing, it is something of a historical novelty to base constitutional adjudication on the question, "Who benefits?" Yet this, as we have already seen, is precisely the mode of adjudication now fashionable in the leading law schools.

In addressing the question of who benefits from busing, the Justice Department was undoubtedly correct when it asserted in its brief that the proponents of mandatory integration cannot be classified by race. Blacks and whites could be counted among both the supporters and the opponents of Initiative 350.[21] Indeed, of the two Seattle legislative districts in which the initiative failed to pass, one was predominantly black and the other was predominantly white.[22] This did not, however, deter Justice Blackmun from concluding, apparently on the basis of nothing more than his own preconception, that "for present purposes, it is enough that minorities may consider busing for integration to be legislation that is in their interest. . . . Given the racial focus of Initiative 350, this suffices to trigger application of the *Hunter* doctrine."[23]

As we have noted, the *Hunter* doctrine proclaimed the unconstitutionality of *structural alterations* in the governmental decision-making process solely where racial issues are concerned, and therein lies the other difference between the *Seattle* and *Hunter* cases. Whereas an amendment to a city charter mandating the use of popular referenda with respect to certain discrete policy matters almost certainly amounts to a "restructuring" of an existing political process, it is by no means clear that anything analogous to this had occurred in the *Seattle* case. As Justice Powell repeatedly stressed in his dissenting opinion, the Washington state constitution, like all state constitutions, locates final authority over public education at the state, rather than the local, level.[24] The authority of local school boards thus being derivative, state officials could legally abolish them altogether and not be said to have "restructured" the political process; it would be simply an instance of state authority overriding local authority. This point also failed to impress the Court's majority, prompting a dismayed Justice Powell to describe the effects of the Court's *ad hoc* improvisation on the *Hunter* doctrine:

> Under today's decision this heretofore undoubted supreme authority of a State's electorate is to be curtailed whenever a school board—or indeed any other board or instrumentality—adopts a race-specific program that arguably benefits racial minorities. Once such a program is adopted, *only* the local or subordinate entity that approved it will have authority to change it. . . . It is a strange notion—alien to our system—that local governmental bodies can forever preempt the ability of a State—the sovereign power—to address a matter of compelling concern to the State.[25]

The Court's decision was yet another example of result-oriented jurisprudence, in the sense that it relied upon a manifestly inapplicable precedent to protect a public policy that a majority of the justices favored. Moreover, it established as constitutional principle a kind of "ratchet effect" pertaining *exclusively* to policies having to do with race. Once again, the Justice Department did not seek a repudiation of existing legal precedent; it did not challenge the validity of the *Hunter* doctrine, although it might have in view of the expansive interpretation of the equal protection clause that doctrine represents. Rather, the Justice Department sought merely to distinguish between the *Hunter* and *Seattle* cases, arguing that the rule of decision that governed the former case could not reasonably be applied to the latter. Once again, however, its efforts failed to contain race-conscious civil rights doctrine within existing parameters.

Denial of Tax Exemptions as a Civil Rights Imperative: Bob Jones University and the IRS

On May 24, 1983, the Supreme Court provided yet another example of the extent to which it would distort legal precedent or ignore statutory law in pursuit of racial integration. The case was *Bob Jones University v. United States*, but the issues it raised are best understood in light of the recent history of federal tax policy toward predominantly white private schools.

Given the history of "massive resistance" to school desegregation in the South following the Supreme Court's decision in *Brown v. Board of Education*, it is perhaps understandable that civil rights activists would suspect any Southern private school with an exclusively or even predominantly white enrollment of representing yet another attempt to circumvent desegregation. The fact that by the middle of the 1970s a significant proportion of these private schools—labeled "segregated academies" by the media—were sectarian institutions catering to the burgeoning movement of fundamentalist Christians did nothing to alter the perception that the schools were essentially outgrowths of white racism. It is important to note, however, that by 1976 the Supreme Court had made it unlawful (under the 1866 Civil Rights Act) for private schools to discriminate against blacks in admissions, and had, in the case of *Runyan v. McCrary*, established the right of black students to enforce their right to equal consideration at any private school through litigation in the federal courts. Thus, when the civil rights lobby began in the late 1970s to mount a campaign against the all-white private academies, it was not to gain an already-established right of access to the schools, but rather to undermine the operation of schools that had failed—for whatever reason—to conform to the integrationist ideal. According to one scholar who has studied the genesis of the "tax-exempt schools debate," the challenge to the schools was rooted mainly in the inability of civil rights activists to comprehend why any parent would want to remove his child from a public school, except to avoid exposing the child to an integrated classroom.[26] Only racism, it seemed, could explain such behavior, and racist behavior could not go unchecked.

The solution was to discourage the spread of such schools, and perhaps to bring about the demise of those already in existence, by requiring them to pay federal taxes. Since its inception, the federal tax code has explicitly authorized tax exemptions for non-profit religious, educational, and charitable organizations; this fact, however, would not prevent the bureaucrats who managed the Internal Revenue Service from interpreting the tax code to deny exemptions to schools that they suspected of racial discrimination. Nevertheless, if IRS officials were to infuse the tax code with a mandate for school integration, they first needed to reconcile this action with the plain language of the relevant statute. The principal statutory provision relating to tax-exempt organizations is Section 501(c)(3) of the United States Tax Code, Title 26, which grants exempt status to:

> Corporations and any community chest, fund or foundation, organized and operated exclusively for religious, charitable, scientific, testing for public safety, literary, or educational purposes, or to foster national or international amateur sports competition . . . , or for the prevention of cruelty to children or animals, no part of the net earnings of which inures to the benefit of any private shareholder or individual, no substantial part of the activities of which is carrying on propaganda, or otherwise attempting, to influence legislation . . . , and which does not participate in, or intervene in (including the publishing or distributing of statements), any political campaign on behalf of any candidate for public office.

In attempting to determine whether a specific organization would qualify for a tax exemption under Section 501(c)(3), the first thing that a reasonably alert judge or IRS administrator might have noticed in reading the section is its use of the disjunctive "or" in listing the kinds of organizations to be recognized as tax-exempt. For example, according to this language, exemptions would be available to religious organizations, to educational organizations, or to charitable organizations, among others. Private sectarian schools would thus appear to qualify for tax-exempt status in their capacity as both religious organizations *and* educational institutions. Because for tax purposes the term "charitable" historically has been understood in light of its somewhat vague common-law definition, the schools' inclusion in the category of charitable organizations is problematic. Since they already fall into two of the other specified categories, however, the question of whether they should be regarded as "charitable" institutions for tax purposes would appear to be immaterial.

In any case, a literal reading of the tax code's provisions was first abandoned by the judiciary in the 1970 case of *Green v. Kennedy*,[27] wherein a three-judge panel of the U.S. District Court for the District of Columbia announced that the aforementioned provisions of the Internal Revenue Code "must be construed and applied in consonance with the Federal public policy against support for racial segregation of schools, public or private." It happened that the private schools at issue in the *Green* case actually were authentic "segregated academies," but it is also clear that the Court's "construction" of the Internal Revenue Code was based, not on the language of the code itself, but on a series of Supreme Court precedents that were, as Jeremy Rabkin has suggested, not really apposite to the case at hand. For example, in the leading case, *Tank Truck Rentals v. Commissioner of Internal Revenue*,[28] the Court held that a company could not deduct fines paid for violations of state highway laws on the not unreasonable theory that Congress did not intend "to encourage violations of declared public policy." The decision stressed that "the test of nondeductibility is the severity and immediacy of the frustration ['of sharply defined national or state policies'] resulting from allowance of the deduction." In another decision handed down some eight years later, the Supreme Court reaffirmed that the "public policy" limitation applied only "in extremely limited circumstances" because "the federal income tax is a tax on net income, not a sanction against wrongdoing."[29] Although the judgment in the *Green* case went against the IRS, it was only in a legalistic sense that the IRS had lost, for the agency had announced, even before the final decision had been rendered, its own new policy of denying tax exemptions to any private school in the country that practiced racial discrimination in admissions. It was not surprising, then, that the IRS did not appeal the district court's ruling, which after all had the effect of legitimating its own policy. An attempt to appeal the decision was made by a group of white parents in Mississippi who had not been parties to the original case, but the Supreme Court simply issued a summary affirmance of *Green*, refusing to hear oral arguments and declining to offer any opinion of its own.[30]

Evidently the IRS was emboldened by the outcome of the *Green* case. At least one would think so given the zeal with which it began to devise ambitious new standards for applying the federal tax code as a "sanction against wrongdoing." With the encouragement of the U.S. Commission on Civil Rights, the IRS in August 1978 issued proposed guidelines to determine "whether certain private schools have racially discriminatory policies as to students and therefore are not qualified for tax exemption under the Internal Revenue Code." The guidelines stated:

> A *prima facie* case of racial discrimination by a school arises from evidence that the school (1) was formed or substantially expanded at or about the time of desegregation of the public schools, and (2) has an insignificant number of minority students. In such a case, the school has the burden of clearly and convincingly rebutting this *prima facie* case of racial discrimination by showing that it has undertaken affirmative steps to secure minority students. Mere denial of a discriminatory purpose is insufficient.[31]

Moreover, the IRS specifically refused to exempt church-sponsored schools, in effect challenging the religious sincerity of any such schools that manifested the two incriminating characteristics specified in the guidelines.*

The guidelines defined "an insignificant number of minority students" as "less than twenty percent of the percentage of the minority school age population in the community served by the school." Not only would the so-called "reviewable schools" lose

---

*Later, during congressional hearings, the IRS proposed two exemptions from its guidelines. One applied to any school that was "part of a system of commonly supervised schools"—provided the entire system satisfied the guidelines; the other applied to schools with "special programs or special curricula which by their nature are of interest only to identifiable groups which are not composed of a significant number of minority students." "What became evident during the congressional hearings," observed Peter Skerry, "was that the first exemption was directed primarily at Catholic schools operating as part of a diocesan system and the second at Jewish day schools." See Peter Skerry, "Christian Schools versus the IRS," *The Public Interest* (Fall 1980), p. 36.

their exemption from federal taxes (including social security and unemployment contributions), but the right of individual donors to deduct charitable contributions to the schools from their federal income taxes would also be denied. As Peter Skerry has noted, these sanctions, especially the latter one, would tend to be particularly catastrophic for the countless small, fledgling institutions that constitute the informal network of Christian schools.[32]

After the proposed IRS guidelines came under attack by congressional allies of the Christian fundamentalist community such as Senator Jesse Helms, the IRS in February 1979 issued "revised proposed guidelines." Apparently designed to demonstrate the ease with which a truly nondiscriminatory "reviewable" school could regain its tax-exempt status, the revised guidelines offered six examples of the kind of "affirmative steps" that such a school would need to take:

- active and vigorous minority recruitment programs

- tuition waivers, scholarships, or other financial assistance to minority students

- recruitment and employment of minority teachers and other professional staff

- minority members on the board or other governing body of the school

- special minority-oriented curricula

- participation with integrated schools in sports, music, and other events and activities[33]

Like so many agency regulations and court decisions issued under the rubric of "ending discrimination," the IRS guidelines are symptomatic of the bizarre set of meanings so often imputed to the word "discrimination." No attempt was made to explain, for example, why it would be necessary for the schools to "actively" and "vigorously" recruit minority group members in order to demonstrate an absence of racial bias on their part. What is more, at least one of the suggested "affirmative steps"—offering tuition waivers and scholarships to minority students—would appear, in addition to being manifestly supererogatory (assuming that its purpose is indeed merely to ensure nondiscrimination in admissions), almost calculated to bankrupt the fledgling Christian schools, whose typical profile is that of a small, understaffed, modestly equipped institution operating on a shoestring budget and supported mostly by working-class parents and church members.[34]

Congress finally acted to prohibit the IRS from enforcing the 1978–79 guidelines by adopting a pair of legislative amendments that prohibited the use of appropriated funds for any "procedures, guidelines . . . or measure which would cause the loss of tax-exempt status to private, religious, or church-oriented schools . . . unless in effect prior to August 22, 1978."[35] Because the amendments spoke only to the 1978–79 proposed guidelines, however, they did not affect the ability of the IRS to continue to deny exempt status to private schools it judged to be discriminatory. That is, the IRS would not be allowed to proceed with its proposed criteria for establishing a *prima facie* case of discriminatory conduct that would apply automatically to all private schools, but it could still investigate schools on an individual basis and, where it deemed appropriate, deny exempt status, just as it had been doing before 1979.

It was, in fact, on the basis of the original regime established legally by the *Green* ruling that the IRS in November 1970 began notifying private, sectarian colleges of changes it had made in its policy for granting tax exemptions, and announced its intention to challenge the tax-exempt status of private schools practicing racial discrimination in their admissions policies. One of the colleges so notified was Bob Jones University of Greenville, South Carolina, and when, more than six years later, on January 19, 1976, the IRS officially revoked the university's tax-exempt status retroactive to December 1, 1970, the stage was set for the most volatile and widely publicized civil rights lawsuit of President Reagan's first term.

One of the remarkable things about *Bob Jones University v. United States* is suggested by the identity of the parties named in the case. In the lower courts, Bob Jones University and the United States government were clearly at odds, inasmuch as the Carter administration had vigorously defended the 1970 IRS policy on tax exemptions against the legal attack launched by the university. Even the Reagan administration was prepared to defend the IRS initially, and did so in its 1981 brief urging the Supreme Court to grant certiorari in the case.[36] But on January 8, 1982, after the Court had agreed to hear the case, and after hearing pleas from Republican House Whip Trent Lott and Senators Strom Thurmond and Jesse Helms, administration officials (notably Assistant Attorney General Reynolds) decided that Bob Jones University and the lower court judges who had written opinions in the university's favor had the stronger arguments.

As it had done before and would do again, the administration switched sides in an ongoing civil rights controversy inherited from the previous administration. (Actually, the Justice Department did not totally abandon its previous position; it filed a "split brief," supporting Bob Jones' claim that the IRS had exceeded its authority, but disagreeing with the university's position that even if the IRS had acted legally, Bob Jones was protected from its policy by the First Amendment's free exercise clause.) One might have thought that the essential agreement of the two parties—the university and the government—would cause the case to be dismissed for want of a controversy. Instead, however, the Supreme Court took the highly unusual step of inviting William Coleman, Jr., a private attorney who was secretary of transportation in the Ford administration, to enter the case as *amicus curiae*. Since he was unconnected to either of the parties in the case, Coleman evidently was to represent himself. So why invite Coleman? Probably the justices surmised that Coleman, who is black, could be counted on to argue a view of IRS authority adverse to the view shared by the Justice Department and Bob Jones University. As Rabkin observed, "Coleman's introduction into the case was the Court's way of assuring some opposing argument in the absence of a genuine adversary contest—once universally regarded as the precondition for any judicial decision."[37]

Another striking feature of the case was the decision of the Court to combine it with another case that concerned the withdrawal of tax-exempt status from a private religious school, *Goldsboro Christian Schools v. United States*. The Court explained that the Court of Appeals for the Fourth Circuit, which had heard the two cases on appeal, "found an 'identity for the present purposes' between the Goldsboro case and the Bob Jones University case, which had been decided shortly before by another panel."[38] This was no doubt true as far as the central purpose of the litigation was concerned—to challenge the IRS's purported authority to deny the schools tax-exempt status. There were, however, striking dissimilarities in the respective admissions policies of the two schools that had got them into trouble with the IRS in the first place. Since its inception in 1963, Goldsboro Christian Schools, located in Goldsboro, North Carolina, had maintained an explicit racially discriminatory admissions policy, based on its interpretation of the Bible. Bob Jones University, on the other hand, had, at least since 1971, maintained a racially nondiscriminatory admissions policy (and did in fact admit and enroll black students), but also required students to observe a host of religiously based rules governing personal conduct. One of those groups of rules read as follows:

1. Students who are partners in an interracial marriage will be expelled.

2. Students who are members of or affiliated with any group or organization which holds as one of its goals or advocates interracial marriage will be expelled.

3. Students who date outside their own race will be expelled.

4. Students who espouse, promote, or encourage others to violate the University's dating rules and regulations will be expelled.[39]

By a vote of 8 to 1, the Court approved the IRS policy on tax exemptions for private schools. In his opinion for the majority, Chief Justice Burger repeatedly defended the IRS action on the theory that racial "discrimination" is contrary to "national public policy." Yet only in the final brief paragraph of his nineteen-page opinion did he even so much as allude to the distinction that could arguably be made between the kind of discrimination practiced by Bob Jones and that practiced by Goldsboro. Burger disposed of the distinction this way:

Petitioner Bob Jones University, however, contends that it is not racially discriminatory. It emphasizes that it now allows all races to enroll, subject only to its restrictions on the conduct of all students, including its prohibitions of association between men and women of different races, and of interracial marriage.

> Although a ban on intermarriage or interracial dating applies to
> all races, decisions of this Court firmly establish that discrimi-
> nation on the basis of racial affiliation and association is a form
> of racial discrimination.[40]

Following this passage are citations to three Supreme Court
cases that apparently constitute the basis of the Court's "firm establishment." Two are cases in which the Court invalidated *state
laws* prohibiting interracial marriage, and one of these, the landmark case of *Loving v. Virginia*, was decided as recently as 1967. The
only cited case that involved a policy against interracial marriage
by a private organization was decided in 1973, three years *after* the
date at which Bob Jones University became liable for unpaid back
taxes. Thus, for all the righteous indignation in Burger's opinion
about the evils of "racial discrimination in education" and its con-
trariness to "fundamental public policy,"* the Bob Jones rule against
interracial marriage and dating appeared to violate little more than
the collective wisdom of a majority of the justices of the Supreme
Court—and a collective wisdom of fairly recent vintage at that.

With its gratuitous incantation of familiar shibboleths citing
"the stress and anguish of the history of efforts to escape from the
shackles of the 'separate but equal doctrine' of *Plessy v.
Ferguson*,"[41] the Court completely ignored the reality of Bob Jones
University. It was a private, voluntary association of like-minded
people who shared a discrete set of religious beliefs, one of which
happened to be an interpretation of Biblical scripture to proscribe
marriage and dating between the races. Within the community of
Christian fundamentalists, the university apparently had little difficulty attracting students, both black and white, who subscribed
to its reading of the Bible. It is perhaps worth noting, too, that even
in the modern secular world there is widespread ambivalence

---

*For example, "But there can no longer be any doubt that racial discrimination in
education violates deeply and widely accepted views of elementary justice."—76
L.Ed.2d 157, 174. "Given the stress and anguish of the history of efforts to escape
from the shackles of the 'separate but equal' doctrine of *Plessy v. Ferguson*, . . . it
cannot be said that educational institutions that, for whatever reasons, practice
racial discrimination, are institutions exercising 'beneficial and stabilizing influ-
ences in community life,' . . . "—Ibid., p. 175. "Whatever may be the rationale for
such private schools' policies, and however sincere the rationale may be, racial
discrimination in education is contrary to public policy."—Ibid., p. 176.

about interracial marriage and dating. A 1985 public opinion poll, for example, disclosed that nearly one-fourth of all black Americans disapprove of marriage between blacks and whites.[42] Moreover, one may observe that even in progressive journals and newspapers such as the *Village Voice*, the lovelorn sophisticates whose romantic entreaties fill the "Personals" section of the classified advertisements will typically indicate a preference for a member of their own race. It would thus appear that the most that can be said is that there is a "fundamental public policy" against state laws prohibiting interracial marriage and dating, but even this policy has so far been enunciated only by the Supreme Court itself, and only as recently as 1967.

The Court's eagerness to engage in an ostentatious display of its resolve in the battle against what it took to be the residual manifestation of separate-but-equal doctrine in Bob Jones' ban on interracial marriage is evident in its treatment of the central issue in the case as well. What made the Bob Jones case so important to the success of the Reagan agenda—not just in civil rights policy, but to the entire philosophy of representative self-government implicit in that agenda—was its attempt to curtail public policy making by the least accountable and least representative institutions of government—in this case, an agency of the federal bureaucracy. Section 501(c)(3), the provision of the Internal Revenue Code from which the IRS claimed to derive its authority to deny tax exemptions to private schools, was quoted above. As noted, a careful reading of that provision clearly discloses that "there is nothing in the language of Section 501(c)(3) that supports the result obtained by the Court," to quote from Justice Rehnquist's lone dissent.[43] Indeed, Chief Justice Burger's majority opinion is yet another perfect example of result-oriented jurisprudence, in that it virtually ignores the statute it is supposed to be construing and instead selectively quotes a litany of past Supreme Court opinions, the cumulative effect of which is to show that, notwithstanding its detailed listing of the activities and enterprises that are to receive tax-exempt status, Congress, in drafting the instrument, *really* intended to denote only "charitable" institutions by this language, and furthermore, that "charities were to be given preferential treatment because they provide a benefit to society."[44]

Having thus established the intent of Congress, Burger could proceed to the conclusion that an institution could not be said to provide a benefit to society, and therefore could not, by definition, be considered "charitable," if it did not "demonstrably serve and be in harmony with the public interest," did not comport with "the common community conscience," or was "affirmatively at odds with [the] declared position of the whole government."[45] The Chief Justice could then go on to conclude that Bob Jones University was definitely not such a charitable institution by indulging in the crude tactic of equating the school with the worst of Jim Crow: "stress and anguish . . . escape from the shackles . . . 'separate but equal' . . . *Plessy v. Ferguson*," and so on.

In the latter half of his opinion, Burger painstakingly attempted to document congressional approval of the peculiar reading of Section 501(c)(3) by the IRS and the Court. He notes that "during the last 12 years there have been no fewer than 13 bills introduced to overturn the IRS interpretation of Section 501(c)(3)."[46] Solemnly averring that "ordinarily, and quite properly, courts are slow to attribute significance to the failure of Congress to act on particular legislation,"[47] he nevertheless concludes his analysis with the observation that "in view of its prolonged and acute awareness of so important an issue, Congress's failure to act on the bills proposed on this subject provides added support for concluding that Congress acquiesced in the IRS rulings."[48] In light of this statement, it is interesting to note that on January 18, 1982, President Reagan, as if to demonstrate in no uncertain terms that the administration's main reason for opposing the IRS's position in the case was to restore to Congress the exclusive authority to make fiscal policy, introduced a bill to Congress that would have empowered the IRS to deny exemptions to discriminatory schools. It quickly became apparent that there was little congressional enthusiasm for the measure; House Speaker Thomas O'Neill, for example, called the president's action "outrageous,"[49] and Senate Majority Leader Howard Baker and Finance Committee Chairman Robert Dole both expressed doubt that the legislation would pass.[50] There is thus considerable irony in Burger's remarks equating congressional inaction with congressional acquiescence. The refusal of Congress to pass legislation empowering an administrative agency must be construed as tacit acceptance of the agency's impotence.

The transcendent significance of the Court's decision, as suggested above, lay not in its implications for Bob Jones University or even for similarly situated private schools. Far more important was the Court's grant of vast legislative authority to an unelected and unaccountable administrative agency. It was in this regard that the Court's 8-to-1 ruling struck a major blow against a critical component of the Reagan agenda, the effort to establish limits on bureaucratic governance. The usurpation of legislative authority by the IRS had been a concern of the Reaganites long before the *Bob Jones* case came to public attention. During the 1980 presidential campaign, candidate Reagan expressed his concern about IRS "harassment" of private schools, and soon after taking office, he declared that "the taxing power of the government must not be used to regulate the economy or bring about social change."[51] It is arguable that what the Supreme Court did in the *Bob Jones* case was to expand the scope of IRS authority well beyond the capacity to harass private schools. This point was not lost on Justice Powell, who set forth his reservations about the Court's decision in a concurring opinion:

> Even more troubling to me is the element of conformity that appears to inform the Court's analysis. The Court asserts that an exempt organization must "demonstrably serve and be in harmony with the public interest," must have a purpose that comports with "the common community conscience," and must not act in a manner "affirmatively at odds with [the] declared position of the whole government." Taken together, these passages suggest that the primary function of a tax-exempt organization is to act on behalf of the government in carrying out governmentally approved policies. . . . As Justice Brennan has observed, private, nonprofit groups receive tax exemptions because "each group contributes to the diversity of association, viewpoint, and enterprise essential to a vigorous, pluralistic society." [Citation omitted.] Far from representing an effort to reinforce any perceived "common community conscience," the provision of tax exemptions to nonprofit groups is one indispensable means of limiting the influence of governmental orthodoxy on important areas of community life.[52]

Indeed, it is easy to imagine any number of currently tax-exempt groups whose activities could be considered in violation of a declared government policy. On the basis of the precedent laid down in the *Bob Jones* case, could a church or religious organization that advocates unilateral disarmament or an end to nuclear weapons research be denied tax-exempt status? How about a religious group that sent aid and volunteers to assist the Sandinista government in Nicaragua? Or a private college that employs a professor who teaches the desirability of Marxist revolution? And now that sex discrimination has become as repugnant to "the common community conscience" as race discrimination, how can the IRS justify the continuation of tax-exempt status for private women's colleges such as Smith and Mount Holyoke—institutions that categorically refuse to admit men? The resolution of these and other particular cases would evidently be left to the discretion of the career civil servants who run the IRS. Their decisions would stand as long as Congress "acquiesced"—that is, as long as it failed to pass legislation disestablishing the IRS policy.

Though they address different issues and different circumstances, the *Seattle* and *Bob Jones* cases both illustrate how pronounced is the desire among judges and civil rights activists to eradicate racial imbalance. If integration, conceived as balance or parity, is always "good," then its opposite, racial imbalance, is always "bad," and hence must be remedied through government coercion. In the 1980s this view was so entrenched among the civil rights elite that the slightest challenge to it automatically placed one beyond the bounds of respectable opinion. Thus it was that Lino A. Graglia, who has the distinction of being the only law professor in the country to have written a book criticizing the legal and constitutional basis of court-ordered busing, could for that reason not even be nominated (much less confirmed) to fill a vacancy on a federal court of appeals, so negative was the reaction to reports that the Justice Department was planning to appoint him.[53] A similar fate befell Charles J. Cooper, an aide to Assistant Attorney General Reynolds whose nomination for a promotion within the Justice Department was approved by the Senate in 1985, but not without a fight. When it emerged during confirmation hearings before the Senate Judiciary Committee that he had once written a memorandum offering his opinion that "a principled analysis could be devised in support of the proposition [that] antibusing bills are constitutionally sound," he was upbraided by Senator Joseph Biden (D–Del.) for expressing a legal rationale for circumventing the Constitution.[54] Of course it was not the Constitution per se that Cooper was trying to circumvent, but rather the values and beliefs of those who purport to represent the Constitution on civil rights issues.

With the integrationist ideal elevated to the level of a universal good whose attainment therefore was held to be required by law, Constitution, and common decency, the Reagan administration could still seek to represent the aspirations of a public largely disaffected by compulsory racial busing by trying to curtail that most odious means of pursuing racial balance in the schools, but as its own experience and that of others indicated, it could not dare to challenge the conceptual underpinnings of busing—that racial imbalance equals racial segregation, that achieving racial balance in the schools is a proper end of government, and so on. What it did instead, resulting in its only moderately successful attempts to reformulate civil rights policy in the area of school desegregation, was tacitly to accept (at least in public) the premises upon which compulsory integration was based, but at the same time to advance an alternative, less onerous means of effecting integration—the creation of so-called "magnet schools." Moreover, where busing plans were already in operation, the Justice Department would support local officials who argued, in accordance with Supreme Court precedent,[55] that they were not obliged to maintain busing in perpetuity once busing had achieved its formally prescribed objective of disestablishing a "dual" school system. A gradual return to racially imbalanced schools due to normal demographic shifts unrelated to government action should not be held to require a "remedy" that consisted of further busing. This approach resulted in an end to busing certain categories of students in Norfolk, Virginia, and in Oklahoma City, Oklahoma. In both cases, however, the Justice Department took care to emphasize that the results it had sought were in no way inconsistent with the pursuit of integration. Commenting on the federal appeals court ruling that permitted the disestablishment of busing in Norfolk, Reynolds called it "a much needed breath of fresh air in our continuing efforts to achieve meaningful desegregation that is more fully sensitive to the educational needs of public school students not only in Norfolk but throughout the country."[56] The problem with the cross-town busing of pupils in Norfolk, Reynolds averred, was that it had interfered with "meaningful parental participation in the education of their children."[57] Hence recourse was made to the familiar lawyer's expedient of "balancing" competing "values."

The magnet-school approach to integration was adopted in Bakersfield, California, under a consent decree negotiated between the Justice Department and the Bakersfield City School District, expressly as an alternative to court-ordered busing, which appeared inevitable had the Justice Department suit against the school district gone to trial. The Bakersfield Plan, which was endorsed by local black and Hispanic groups, was typical of the magnet-school approach: Bakersfield would try to attract white students to predominantly black and Hispanic schools by establishing special programs in science, computer-assisted instruction, and the creative and performing arts, as well as special classes for gifted or talented youngsters.[58] This approach thus substitutes a carrot for a stick as the means to school integration.

In trumpeting the Bakersfield Plan, Reynolds again revealed an inclination toward what modern journalists might call a "New Pragmatism" in his handling of the integration issue:

> This is a blueprint for desegregation in the future without relying on mandatory busing, which does not work anywhere in a very meaningful way. We continue to believe that school systems can be desegregated by voluntary means that eliminate racial isolation and improve education programs. Mandatory busing is not acceptable.[59]

Notice how easily Reynolds slips into the linguistic habits of "civil rightsspeak"[60]—a blueprint for integration is held up as a blueprint for "desegregation," and "desegregation" is to be achieved through "means that eliminate racial isolation. . . . " Racial isolation, not government-enforced segregation, is the evil to be combated. Reynolds seemed to change his tack when asked, at a news conference, what would happen if the racial balance in the city's schools did not change significantly after three years of voluntary desegregation efforts.* Reynolds replied:

---

*Magnet schools can sometimes have the perverse effect of attracting *too many* white students, which is good for integration but bad for minority students who would like to take their place. The City of Los Angeles, which introduced magnet schools in the 1970s as a means of voluntarily achieving school racial balance, initially established a numerical ratio of 60 percent minority students to 40 percent white students for each of its 86 magnets. By November of 1987, however,

The Supreme Court has told us, I don't know how many times, that there is nothing wrong with a school that is racially imbalanced. That's not unconstitutional at all. It's only unconstitutional when that's a forced situation because the school board has basically put in place, intentionally, certain practices and procedures that preclude children from going to one school because of their race.[61]

If that is what is meant by "segregation," then why the need for busing schemes or magnet schools? Why not simply get a court injunction against those "practices and procedures that preclude children from going to one school because of their race"? Answer: Because that strategy would not meet the requirement of racial balance, the absence of which is called "segregation."

The point here is not to chide Assistant Attorney General Reynolds for inconsistency or failure to adhere to principle. It is rather to suggest that the prejudices and policy preferences of the civil rights elite had become so predominant that changes in the public policies governing race and the schools could only be achieved in an attenuated and episodic fashion, and only then if the advocates of change succeeded in framing their initiatives in terms that showed fidelity to the prevailing integrationist orthodoxy.

That orthodoxy, as we have seen, includes the proposition that achieving racial balance in the schools is nothing less than a

---

82 percent of the students in the school district were minorities, as were fully two-thirds of those on waiting lists for the magnet program. Minority group representatives and their white allies presently moved to lower the minority-white ratio to 70–30 in order to accommodate more minority students at the obviously more attractive magnet schools. As one white board member explained, "It seems somehow inequitable to me that a district that is 20 percent Anglo should have 40 percent of the magnet school space reserved for us [whites]." This suggestion immediately raised a sobering question: Would reducing white enrollment to 30 percent mean that the magnet schools would now be segregated? The question . . . was deemed to be so critical that, following weeks of heated debate, the board finally voted to allow a survey to be conducted in magnet school communities to determine whether parents and staff would consider a school to be integrated if it were only 30 percent white.

In sum, magnet programs have the virtue of dispensing with busing's coerciveness, but there is always the danger that insofar as they are regarded primarily as mechanisms for promoting integration, they may under some circumstances end up excluding members of the very groups on whose behalf the integrationists make their moral and legal claims.

constitutional, not to mention moral, imperative. In both the *Seattle* case and the *Bob Jones* case, the Justice Department took positions that challenged the prevailing orthodoxy. In *Seattle* the Civil Rights Division supported the right of a state's electorate to ban the busing of students for the purpose of achieving racial balance. In the *Bob Jones* case it argued that a department of the federal bureaucracy did not have the authority unilaterally to use the taxing power to punish deviation from the integrationist orthodoxy. Both initiatives would have subjected that doctrine to some measure of popular scrutiny and control; the processes of representative self-government would have been brought to bear. That is a far more radical departure from present practice than is the substitution of magnet schools for busing as a vehicle for "desegregation," or permitting local school boards finally to bring an end to years of court-ordered busing. Even these developments would prove too much for many within the civil rights establishment; predictably, the disestablishment of busing in both Norfolk and Oklahoma City was opposed by the NAACP in the courts.[62]

We must now assay the reasons behind the continued predominance of the integrationist orthodoxy and, more generally, the race-conscious version of civil rights to which it belongs.

CHAPTER FIVE

The Failure of
Civil Rights Reform

It was a mark of the departure of the civil rights movement from its original meanings that issues like busing and quotas arose. Nonetheless, by the 1980s they had become identified as the very essence of the movement; to oppose them was to be perceived by many as being opposed to civil rights itself.

—James Nuechterlein,
"A Farewell to Civil Rights"

Twenty years ago Americans certified their credentials as enlightened, forward-thinking citizens by proudly and publicly declaring their allegiance to the principle that discrimination on the basis of race, sex, religion, or ethnicity is categorically wrong, and that no one should be either favored or disfavored on the basis of these immutable characteristics, least of all by government or at government's command. Because enlightened opinion regarded this principle not merely as good public policy—as, for example, it might have regarded the progressive income tax or the Clean Air Act—but as a matter of right, most people felt it only proper that the responsibility for upholding and protecting this principle should be vouchsafed to the federal judiciary, which had performed so admirably throughout the 1950s and 1960s in the struggle for racial justice. The preceding chapters have examined a number of cases in which the Justice Department under the Reagan administration attempted, in various ways, to restore the nondiscrimination principle to national civil rights policy following twenty years of steady erosion. The story told has largely been one of frustration and failure at the hands of the federal courts.

Having seen *how* the administration failed to reformulate civil rights policy, we must now try to explain *why* it failed.

Although this work has examined attempts to reformulate civil rights policy through the courts, any attempt to account for the *general* failure of the Reagan civil rights initiatives must also address, at least cursorily, the administration's inability (or, as the case may be, unwillingness) to pursue reform through nonjudicial channels.

The policy-making process as undertaken by Congress and the executive branch has been the subject of intense study by an entire generation of political scientists. One can choose from a variety of compelling models, paradigms, frameworks, and typologies developed and refined over the years to explain how public policy is made and unmade. As good as any, and arguably one of the best, is James Q. Wilson's schema for "clarifying and explaining the politics of different policy issues."[1] Wilson identifies four types of policy issues, each of which is defined by its actual or perceived benefits and costs. If, with respect to a particular policy initiative, both the benefits it confers and the costs it exacts are widely distributed throughout the electorate, the disposition of that initiative will be characterized by "majoritarian politics." When costs are widely distributed, but benefits are narrowly concentrated—that is, when the result of a policy would be to benefit a relatively small, well-defined group—it is the subject of "client politics," so named because policy makers have adopted some discrete group as a "client" deserving special legislative solicitude.

If the cost-benefit equation is reversed, so that costs are narrowly concentrated while benefits are widely distributed, the result is "entrepreneurial politics." Here policy entrepreneurs, often from outside the formal structure of government (Ralph Nader and Howard Jarvis are two prominent examples cited by Wilson), "find ways of pulling together a legislative majority on behalf of interests not well represented in the government" in order to enact a policy that will supposedly benefit the majority while adversely affecting some discrete group, either by reducing benefits presently enjoyed by the group or by imposing new costs on it.[2] Finally there is "interest-group politics," in which well-defined, usually well-organized groups lock horns over a policy issue that entails both concentrated costs and concentrated benefits. The general public is usually indifferent to the vagaries of interest-group politics, because the outcomes of these struggles generally affect only the interest groups involved.[3]

Which of these four types of policy making can be applied to the battle over civil rights policy in the 1980s? It is tempting to say that the movement *toward* affirmative action and busing—what we have called the race-conscious regime of civil rights—is an example of client politics, because benefits are concentrated upon a relatively small and identifiable segment of the population, while costs appear to be distributed among a large mass of people who "may be either unaware of any costs or indifferent to them because, per capita, they are so small."[4] This definition, however, is misleading when applied to affirmative action because affirmative actions' "costs" are *not* distributed evenly among the white majority (or even among the cohort of white males, itself a numerical minority within the total population), in a way that affects each individual but only in slight, nearly imperceptible ways. In fact the costs are borne *entirely* by certain unfortunate individuals whose total number is no greater than the number of those receiving affirmative action benefits. Those costs are hardly inconsequential, either, as the white litigants in any of the cases examined in the preceding chapters would surely attest.

It is true that those who bear the cost of affirmative action do not constitute an identifiable or organized group (thus ruling out interest-group politics as a dominant paradigm), but that is not to deny that they share certain characteristics. Often, as the cases examined here suggest, they are moderate-income public sector employees, such as police officers, firefighters, and schoolteachers. Among those who are employed or are seeking employment in the private sector, they tend to be white males who are disproportionately young, at that stage in life when people try to establish themselves in a vocation or career by earning an apprenticeship in a trade union, for example, or a place in a law, business, medical, or academic graduate school. Those white males least likely to bear the costs of affirmative action are affluent, middle-aged professionals and executives—bank and corporation vice-presidents, partners in law firms and brokerage houses, medical doctors and psychiatrists, senior journalists, and tenured university professors.* In short, a white male who has already "made it"

---

*For an informative discussion of affirmative action employment practices in colleges and universities, see George Roche, *The Balancing Act: Quota Hiring in Higher Education* (La Salle, Ill.: Open Court, 1974).

generally has very little to fear from affirmative action. (It is also quite likely that such a person will be able to insulate his family from the effects of compulsory school integration—that, at least, has been the case historically.) Within the population as a whole, the potential victims of affirmative action are decidedly in the minority.

If the movement to enact racial preferences and quotas does not fit neatly into Wilson's typology, what of the Reagan effort to return to race-neutral principles? Of the four types of policy making Wilson discusses, the one that would seem to apply is entrepreneurial politics, where benefits are distributed and costs are concentrated. However, the objections raised above are equally apposite here; the benefits of dismantling affirmative action would not be distributed evenly among all whites. With that said, there are some problematic features of entrepreneurial politics that may help to explain the triumph of the race-conscious regime of civil rights during the 1980s. For example, Wilson calls it "remarkable that policies of this sort [those that distribute benefits and concentrate costs] are ever adopted, and in fact many are not."[5] He goes on to affirm a point made in Chapter 2 in response to those who argue that the failure of Congress to overturn agency and court rulings establishing race- and gender-preference schemes constitutes tacit support for such policies:

> After all, the American political system creates many opportunities for checking and blocking the actions of others. The Founding Fathers deliberately arranged things so that it would be difficult to pass a new law; a determined minority therefore has an excellent chance of blocking a new policy. And any organized group that fears the loss of some privilege or the imposition of some burden will become a very determined minority indeed.[6]

The ability of the civil rights lobby to work its will in Congress cannot be overestimated. During the Reagan years it was widely credited with playing a major role in defeating the administration's effort to promote William Bradford Reynolds to the position of associate attorney general, and to appoint Judge Robert Bork to the Supreme Court. (Later in this chapter we will examine its role in the passage in 1982 of a race-conscious version of the Voting Rights

Act.) There can scarcely be any doubt that the civil rights lobby would have been especially tenacious (and effective) in blocking legislation designed to reaffirm the nondiscrimination principle that inheres in the 1964 Civil Rights Act by specifically prohibiting all public and private racial preference schemes.

The absence of a genuine policy "entrepreneur"—or for that matter any significant organized movement advocating civil rights reform—is also probably linked to the administration's failure to seek a legislative reformulation of civil rights policy. Although Wilson is careful to point out that "entrepreneurial politics can occur without the leadership of a policy entrepreneur if voters or legislators in large numbers suddenly become disgruntled by the high cost of some benefit a group is receiving . . . ," it is nonetheless likely that the administration's efforts would have been greatly assisted by the moral and strategic leadership that such an activist ideally would have provided. Reagan himself provided leadership of this kind on a variety of national defense and economic issues, but beyond an occasional perfunctory statement in support of nondiscrimination, he was largely silent on the question of civil rights, contributing very little to the national debate. Some in the administration emerged as formidable advocates of policy reform—William Bennett on education and Edwin Meese on criminal justice, for example—with the apparent support of the president and the administration as a whole, but those who championed the cause of nondiscriminatory civil rights policies were countered by others who evidently favored the status quo. The Justice Department effort, spearheaded by Reynolds and Meese, to reestablish the nondiscrimination principle was opposed by another cabinet secretary, William Brock of the Department of Labor.

From mid-1985 until mid-1986, Brock led a faction within the administration that opposed the Reynolds-Meese proposal to eliminate numerical goals and timetables from the OFCCP guidelines implementing Executive Order No. 11246.[7] Although as noted earlier this was one of the few areas of civil rights policy in which the administration could have acted unilaterally, the president could not or would not resolve the dispute within his cabinet. Hence the status quo was maintained through inertia, and the Brock forces, in effect, won. Earlier Brock had made known his opposition to the Justice Department's civil rights initiatives through his conspicuous lack of support for Reynolds during the Senate confirmation hearings on his nomination to be associate attorney general. Brock's behavior in the affair was even criticized by the *Wall Street Journal*, one of the few nationally prominent newspapers to support the Justice Department's civil rights initiatives (at least on its editorial page). "Where," the *Journal* asked in an editorial, "were Mr. Reynolds's supporters [during his confirmation hearings]?" The *Journal* continued:

> As for the White House, President Reagan himself has spoken strongly for Mr. Reynolds. Then Monday, new Secretary of Labor Bill Brock, when asked about Mr. Reynolds, quipped, "Never ask an administration to admit it made a mistake." Such backbiting by a cabinet official is symptomatic of this administration's inability to defend its personnel and ultimately its policies against the tactic of nominee-hunting.[8]

The *New York Times*, for its part, praised Brock for "waging a worthy battle to preserve decency in the Administration's civil rights record."[9] The point here is simply to underscore a point made earlier—that the Reagan administration behaved rather like a loose confederation instead of a united front. It stands to reason that civil rights policy entrepreneurs within the administration would find it very difficult to mobilize active public support for their efforts when they could not even gain the cooperation of their administration colleagues. Moreover, the presence of a dissenting faction within the administration itself provided ammunition for supporters of the status quo, making it easier for them publicly to discredit the civil rights reformers.

Outside the administration, the closest thing to a civil rights policy entrepreneur during the Reagan years was Clarence Pendleton, chairman of the United States Commission on Civil Rights. Indeed, given its unique role in civil rights policy discourse, the commission itself might have emerged as a kind of collective policy entrepreneur, and in fact that may have been what the administration had envisaged. In any event, the story of the commission's tribulations during the Reagan years illustrates well the salience of the "client" and "entrepreneurial" models of policy making, and is therefore an appropriate subject for a digression.

The Struggle over the Civil Rights Commission

The U.S. Commission on Civil Rights (CRC) was created by Congress in 1957 as a bipartisan agency whose mission, in President Eisenhower's words, was to "put the facts on the table."[10] The commission was composed of six members, appointed by the president and approved by the Senate. Commissioners' terms were indeterminate, although they generally have served about seven years, being replaced only after voluntarily resigning. (The lone exception occurred when President Nixon requested—and received—the resignation of Theodore Hesburgh as chairman of the commission because of Hesburgh's support for mandatory busing of school children.[11])

By Washington standards the CRC was always a small agency; as of 1980 its annual budget was slightly more than $12 million and its staff numbered roughly 230 people.[12] At its inception in 1957, Congress instructed the commission to investigate complaints that citizens were being denied the right to vote, to analyze court decisions involving discrimination, to serve as a national clearinghouse for information on civil rights, and to report its findings and recommendations to the president and Congress.[13]

Few questioned the need for such an agency in 1957 and in the decade that followed. The modern civil rights movement was still in its infancy, and the cataclysmic changes that it would eventually bring about in voting, school desegregation, and access to public accommodations were still facing strong resistance, especially in the South. Moreover, Congress itself, and the Senate in particular, were dominated by an entrenched southern-based leadership that typically regarded the fledgling civil rights lobby with suspicion if not outright hostility. By the 1980s, however, when groups such as the NAACP, the National Urban League, the Southern Christian Leadership Conference, the National Organization for Women, and the American Civil Liberties Union could join with powerful allies both inside and outside of government to defeat judicial and cabinet-level executive appointments on the grounds of "civil rights," one might have questioned the need for such an agency within the executive branch of the federal government. The commission not only persisted throughout the 1970s and into the 1980s, but gradually became a forceful exponent of the very same expansive race- and gender-conscious, group-oriented civil rights policies that were being advanced by the increasingly influential civil rights establishment outside of government. It is hardly an exaggeration to say that by 1980 the CRC had become, in effect, a governmental lobbying arm of the consortium of civil rights interest groups. Many of the race- and gender-conscious guidelines and regulations adopted by the EEOC and the OFCCP during the 1970s had been recommended by the commission. Indeed, one searches in vain for a single civil rights policy issue during the entire decade of the 1970s on which the commission's official position differed substantially from that of the NAACP. Like the private civil rights interest groups, the CRC broadened its focus considerably, so that by the early 1980s it was undertaking studies of such things as the extent of income inequality between blacks and whites in Alabama, and the effect of budget cuts in student aid on predominantly black and Hispanic colleges.[14]

With the advent of the Reagan administration and its reformist approach to civil rights policy, the CRC abandoned what little pretense remained that it was a neutral fact-finding body and unabashedly assumed the role of inhouse critic of executive branch policies. The accusatory tone of its official pronouncements rivaled the strident denunciations of the Reagan administration's fiercest critics. The following excerpts from two CRC reports, issued in 1982 and 1983, respectively, are illustrative:

Although this administration expresses support for school desegregation, its statements and actions indicate otherwise. A Department of Justice that opposes the most effective remedy for desegregating the public schools—the mandatory reassignment of students—and the most effective tool for implementing this remedy—student transportation—actually stands in opposition to school desegregation. A Department of Justice that supports voluntary methods of desegregation which over time have proved ineffective would have the Nation return to pre-1954 standards. A Department of Justice that appears to stress "quality segregated education" would have the Nation revert to the "separate and unequal" blot that has stained our Nation's credo of equal justice under law.[15]

There is a widespread perception that the Federal Government is relaxing its enforcement posture in the area of civil rights and cutting back on social programs that have benefited many Americans. These retrenchments are viewed by some as a necessary and temporary expedient to ensure long-term economic recovery. Bigots, however, are quick to interpret these initiatives as a lack of government concern for minorities who are now fair game for attacks that are expected to go unchallenged.[16]

One notices how closely these apocalyptic assertions, with their partisan bias and paranoid tone, resemble the indignant rhetoric that one associates with the press releases of the various civil rights interest groups.

In addition to issuing formal reports excoriating administration policies, the CRC sent letters to administration officials such as Assistant Attorney General Reynolds, Attorney General William French Smith, Secretary of Agriculture John Block, and Secretary of Education Terrel Bell objecting to decisions made by their respective agencies affecting civil rights, which given the commission's expansive definition of that term, included virtually the entire gamut of social welfare policy.[17] In the spring of 1983 the CRC publicly quarreled with the administration over the latter's refusal to submit to CRC demands that it furnish statistical data on the race, ethnicity, and sex of top-level executive branch appointees; eventually the CRC voted to subpoena the information from the Departments of Education and Labor.[18] It was as if the commission saw itself as a kind of shadow cabinet on civil rights and social welfare policy within the executive branch.

In early 1982 President Reagan attempted to alter the character of the commission by firing its chairman, Arthur S. Fleming, and Stephen Horn, both Republicans, and naming Republicans Clarence M. Pendleton, Jr. (who was black) and Mary Louise Smith as chairman and vice-chairman, respectively. The CRC's membership had been so unanimous in its opposition to the administration's policies, however, that replacing just two commissioners had little effect, especially since one of the new appointees, Smith, frequently sided with the holdover commissioners to produce 5-to-1 votes critical of administration policy.[19] Moreover, two of the more extreme devotees of the race-conscious version of civil rights—Mary Frances Berry and Blandina Cardenas Ramirez, who would later issue the joint statement asserting that the nation's civil rights laws do not protect white males from discrimination—were still on the commission. On May 20, 1982, the president sent three additional nominations to the Senate to replace Berry, Cardenas Ramirez, and Murray Saltzman. The nominations were approved by the Judiciary Committee over the objections of five dissenting Senators, who complained about the "wholesale replacement of the commissioners." The Senate leadership never acted on the nominations; at the end of 1982 they remained buried in the Judiciary Committee.[20]

In May of 1983 the administration tried again, this time naming three more nominees. One of them, Robert Destro, was one of the three who had failed to gain Senate confirmation the previous year (having been criticized for his opposition to abortion and for criticizing the work of the CRC), but the other two were new, and both carried seemingly impeccable civil rights credentials. John H. Bunzel was a senior research fellow at the Hoover Institution and a former president of San Jose State University; he was reputed to be a "neoconservative" expert on civil rights law. Morris B. Abram was a former president of Brandeis University with a long record of involvement in the civil rights movement, having served on several occasions as Martin Luther King's lawyer, and as chairman of the United Negro College Fund. All three were registered Democrats.[21] What mattered to the civil rights lobby and its allies in Congress, however, was not credentials or party affiliation but whether the nominees supported race-conscious civil rights doctrine, especially employment quotas and busing. All three were on record as being opposed; therefore the civil rights establishment would oppose their nominations. Its congressional allies, however, needed some more principled basis for opposing the Reagan nominees and Reagan's general effort to reconstitute the CRC. Since commissioners did not serve staggered fixed terms, it was clear even to opponents of the nominations that the president had the legal authority to remove sitting commissioners. Opponents were therefore reduced to arguing that he should not exercise that authority, for to do so, they alleged, would violate the independence of the commission.[22] Thus the Leadership Conference on Civil Rights, an umbrella group of approximately 160 civil rights organizations, called on the Senate to prevent the subversion of the "commission's independence and integrity."[23] Representative Parren J. Mitchell (D–Md.) described the appointments as "the political rape of that commission."[24] Representative Don Edwards (D–Calif.) informed the House of Representatives that "the commission you will get will not be an independent commission; it will be a commission with five of the commissioners newly chosen by the president."[25] The national news media were quick to pick up on the theme: "[Reagan-appointed CRC staff director Linda] Chavez dismissed the idea that she is compromising the commission's independence by promoting the administration's perspective," read a typical interview with a Reagan appointee.[26]

The independence issue was a monumental red herring, unless one defines "independence" as near-unanimous opposition to every policy of a sitting president. Few in Congress or the press thought it important to ask whether the CRC that Reagan sought to reshape had been independent from the civil rights lobby. Had that question been raised, the obvious answer would have been that the commission was a perfect example of a "captured" agency. As far as the commission's independence from the administration was concerned, it should have been noted that Reagan, in attempting to appoint commissioners whose ideas about civil rights tended to coincide with his own, was merely following the example set by his immediate predecessor in the White House. Morris Abram's qualifications for service on the CRC were so impressive that he attracted the notice of President Carter, who subsequently offered Abram a position on the commission. Carter hastily withdrew the offer, however, after Abram advised him that he did not support the use of racial quotas.[27] Had Abram been permitted to serve during the Carter years, his would have been the only voice in opposition to quotas on the entire commission. Carter was apparently unwilling to tolerate even one dissenting opinion with respect to this critical civil rights issue.

With the Senate again threatening to block the Reagan appointments, the administration negotiated a compromise with Senate leaders whereby the number of commissioners would be increased to eight, four of whom would be appointed by the president, the rest by congressional party leaders.[28] The result was that the administration finally got a voting majority; only Berry and Cardenas

Ramirez remained from the pre-Reagan commission.* The continued presence of these two on the commission was hardly enough to mollify the organized civil rights lobby, however.

Having grown accustomed to a CRC that was essentially a governmental appendage of itself, the civil rights lobby could only regard the new commission as illegitimate, dominated by people who were manifestly opposed to civil rights. The NAACP's official response to the advent of the new CRC was to issue a report condemning President Reagan for "turning the Civil Rights Commission into a haven for political and social Neanderthals whose views of the Constitution are clouded by distortions of justice and a social Darwinist theory."[29] Ralph Neas, executive director of the Leadership Conference on Civil Rights, assailed Reagan for having "removed some of the commission's conscience. . . ."[30] The national press rapidly assimilated the notion that the new commissioners were opposed to civil rights. In an ostensibly objective account of the negotiated compromise that permitted the installation of Abram, Bunzel, and Destro on the commission, the *National Journal* reported that, according to an early version of the compromise agreement, two of these three, together with Pendleton, would be joined on the commission by what the *Journal* termed "a moderate Republican with a pro–civil rights record,"[31] presumably to counterbalance the anti–civil rights records of the other Reagan appointees.

With the nature and meaning of "civil rights" so ambiguous in the 1980s, one might have thought it healthy and constructive for the commission to become a forum for open debate on the issues that divided adherents of the two competing versions of civil rights. This, at any rate, was the agenda that the new commission set for itself. A clear illustration was the transformation of *Perspectives*, a quarterly

---

*The correlation between the party affiliation and the race, ethnic, and gender characteristics of the eight members of the "new" commission are perhaps worth noting. Of the three black members, none was a Democrat (Pendleton and Francis F. Guess were Republicans; Berry was registered as an Independent.) On the other hand, all three of the white male members were Democrats. There were now two Hispanic commissioners, both female (Cardenas Ramirez and Esther Gonzales Arroyo Buckley); one was a Democrat, the other a Republican. There were thus three female commissioners, no two of whom had the same party affiliation. The new staff director, also appointed by the president, was a Republican Hispanic female (Linda Chavez).

magazine published under commission auspices, into *New Perspectives*. Whereas in its previous incarnation it had been invariably predictable and dogmatic, *New Perspectives* featured articles representing a variety of viewpoints on salient civil rights controversies. On the issue of "comparable worth"—the doctrine which holds that the government should ensure that men and women are paid the same for different jobs requiring comparable skill and responsibility—the CRC held two days of hearings and commissioned independent reports by sixteen experts, eight of whom supported the concept and eight of whom opposed it. Taken together, the reports were a valuable source of information and opinion about a complicated and much misunderstood policy issue.[32] The lack of agreement over the definition of "civil rights" naturally resulted in fewer reports overall, because commissioners often could not agree about what constituted an appropriate subject for inquiry. Many academics who were familiar with the new commission's work nonetheless claimed that its quality and objectivity represented a noticeable improvement over that of the old CRC.[33]

A Civil Rights Commission that devoted itself to debating the nature and meaning of civil rights—devoted itself, that is, to a reexamination of first principles, so to speak—and that issued carefully researched, even-handed analyses of critical civil rights issues, was exactly what the civil rights establishment did not want and could not tolerate. "A debating society, however elegant the debaters," wrote Representative Don Edwards in a letter to the *New York Times*, "is no substitute for a strong, independent Civil Rights Commission." ("Strong" and "independent" were of course code words to describe a commission that was in step with the organized civil rights lobby.) With the Reagan administration out to destroy civil rights, debate was the last thing that the CRC should have been concerned with; what was needed were more angry polemics aimed at the administration and its policies. Indeed, the very suggestion that there should be a debate about the meaning of civil rights was offensive to most professional civil rights activists. In their minds, the Reagan appointees who wanted to debate the meaning of civil rights in the 1980s were interlopers who had dared to challenge the "real" authorities. Clarence Pendleton was, in the words of Representative Parren Mitchell of the Congressional Black Caucus, a "lackey for those who would crush black aspirations."[34]

The demise of the CRC was probably not inevitable, even in light of the intense hostility that it generated among the civil rights establishment. That hostility, however, combined with some apparent administrative malfeasance and internal bickering among the commission's majority, was enough to bring it down. The bickering centered on the public persona of Chairman Pendleton, who was given to delivering audacious broadsides against the organized civil rights community and its leaders. With a combative flamboyance he traveled the country, making public speeches in which civil rights leaders were described as "charlatans" and accused of promoting a "new racism."[35] He was fond of equating quotas, preferences, and set-asides for blacks with the insidious paternalism of the antebellum southern plantation, and he often compared contemporary civil rights leaders with the erstwhile plantation owners. In a widely quoted remark he called the concept of comparable worth "the looniest idea since Looney Tunes came on the screen."[36]

Pendleton's outspokenness apparently grated on fellow Reagan-appointee John Bunzel, so much so that in April 1986, Bunzel publicly called on Pendleton to resign. In a letter to Pendleton that Bunzel released to the press, he charged that Pendleton's "inflammatory rhetoric" and "fulminations" had diverted attention from the work of the commission and tended to "undermine the credibility" of the group. Referring to Pendleton's repeated attacks on civil rights leaders, Bunzel averred that Pendleton had made a mistake "by charging those who do not share your views with fostering a new racism. By dismissing the leaders of civil rights organizations as charlatans, you have clouded a national debate with an inappropriate bitterness." And there was more. Bunzel went on to all but accuse Pendleton of slandering the leaders of the civil rights establishment:

> These men and women, and the organizations they have led, have played a major role in bringing about the legal and peaceful transformation of American life. They have a record of which they can be proud. While I often disagree with their approaches to affirmative action and other issues, I submit that they are not deserving of your contempt or derision.[37]

This criticism of Pendleton, made by a fellow commissioner who nearly always voted with Pendleton on issues that came before the CRC, further reveals why that agency, despite its Reagan-appointed majority, was ultimately ill-equipped to serve as a forum for challenging the entrenched civil rights orthodoxies of the 1970s and 1980s. For not only was the reconstituted commission hindered by a powerful array of external forces that had a large stake in retaining the CRC as one of its own constituent parts, but there were in addition significant differences among the new commissioners themselves, not on substantive issues but on the public role to be played by individual commissioners. Pendleton, a businessman by vocation, was by nature a brash and acerbic activist who sought to use his position on the commission as a bully pulpit from which to speak to the black masses across America. He was not only black himself, but unlike anyone else connected with the Reagan administration or its civil rights policies, Pendleton was capable of speaking to ordinary blacks *as* an ordinary black, in an idiom that blacks understood and that, moreover, identified him as one of them. Realizing better than most whites that lower class black Americans are, like other disadvantaged groups in the past, still very much in the thrall of their putative leaders, Pendleton deliberately tried to undermine the credibility of the leadership, much as the leadership had tried to undermine his legitimacy as chairman of the CRC. When he attacked the same black leadership that had been so merciless in its denunciations of him, Pendleton was engaging in more than tit-for-tat; he was acting on his belief that as a prerequisite to persuading ordinary blacks to abandon the politics of racial preference, he would first need to discredit the icons in whom that idea was embodied.

To be sure, Pendleton's public pronouncements on civil rights frequently invoked legal precedent and constitutional principle, but his disparagement of the black leadership was intended specifically for the black masses, before whom he hoped to demonstrate the emperor's nakedness. His message to blacks was that their leaders had contrived to foster in them a feeling of helplessness and despair, thereby making them increasingly dependent on the leadership and its demonstrated ability to lobby in their behalf for government-sponsored dispensations. In this way the civil rights organizations remained viable, their leaders prosperous and influential, long after the goal of attaining formal civil rights for blacks had been met. It was a provocative argument (especially coming from the chairman of the Civil Rights Commission), inflammatory, as Bunzel observed, by its very nature. Pendleton made it a persistent theme of his public oratory.

To a careful and judicious scholar like Bunzel, the Pendleton approach was anathema. In so sensitive an area as civil rights policy, the last thing that was needed was for the chairman of the CRC to engage himself in a personal vendetta against the leadership of the civil rights establishment. The commission should strive, according to Bunzel, to ensure that the debate was confined strictly to matters of policy and principle, its tone courteous and dispassionate. These, after all, are the norms that ideally prevail in the academic community where Bunzel had spent most of his adult life.

The disagreement between Bunzel and Pendleton was about more than tactics and style, however; at a more fundamental level their disagreement was over which segment of the American public the CRC ought to address. In seeking to advance a common civil rights agenda, the two men had chosen to speak to widely divergent constituencies, making disagreement over tactics inevitable. The Bunzel–Pendleton rift thus personified a major dilemma of civil rights reform under the Reagan administration: whether to take its case to the constitutional intelligentsia or to the broad masses of the American people. In seeking to effect change entirely through the courts, the administration effectively chose the former strategy, partly, we may surmise, because of the extraordinary salience of ideas and of those who create and promote ideas in matters pertaining to the jurisprudence of rights, and partly because it lacked the will, the ability, or the self-confidence necessary to take its case directly to the people.

In any event, it was indicative of the severe constraints under which the reconstituted CRC had to operate that neither Pendleton's combative populism nor Bunzel's scholarly detachment could work as effective strategies for reformulating civil rights policy within that agency. Bunzel's appeal for moderation and civility would have had merit in most government agencies, but it was self-defeating in an agency that he himself described, in his resignation letter of December 1, 1986, as "a little Beirut on the Potomac."[38] As we have seen, that characterization of the CRC was accurate from the moment the Reagan appointees took their seats on the commission, well before Chairman Pendleton began issuing "fulminations." The initial (and most scurrilous) salvo had been fired by the very civil rights leaders whom Bunzel defended in his letter to Pendleton as "not deserving of your contempt or derision." Bunzel acknowledged that he "often disagree[d] with their approaches to affirmative action and other issues . . . ," but he seemed to forget that it was precisely the same disagreement that prompted the NAACP to impugn his own character, as well as the characters of those of his colleagues with whom the NAACP disagreed. That sort of personal opprobrium, coupled with the bogus "independence" issue, had rendered Bunzel's vision of a fair-minded, methodologically rigorous commission whose ineluctable conclusions would gradually be accepted—albeit perhaps grudgingly—by the civil rights establishment, as quixotic at best. Written off as a lapdog of the Reagan administration and its reactionary civil rights agenda, the reconstituted CRC was marginalized by the civil rights elite, something to be alternately pilloried and ignored.

Under these circumstances it may have made sense for the administration to give control of the commission to the likes of Pendleton, someone who would go over the heads of an intransigent elite and speak to ordinary Americans—particularly ordinary black Americans. This too was an impracticable strategy, however. As a government appointee, Pendleton was subject to the official scrutiny of hostile elements in the federal government, notably the Democrat-controlled Congress. Both his personal finances and his administration of the commission came under investigation in early 1986, by the Small Business Administration and the General Accounting Office, respectively. Particularly damaging was the GAO report, conducted at the behest of Representatives Don Edwards, Augustus Hawkins, and Patricia Schroeder—liberal Democrats who had severely criticized the administration's civil rights initiatives. Issued in March 1986, the report found "irregularities in the personnel practices, travel records and financial management of the commission since October 1982."[39] In a departure from its usual practice, the GAO did not permit the target agency to review and comment on the GAO study; ordinarily such responses are included in the final version of a report.[40] The report nonetheless served as the basis for an amendment, drafted by Representative Julian C. Dixon of California and the Congressional Black Caucus, to eliminate all funding for the commission and to require it to cease operations by

December 31, 1986. Though the amendment was passed by the House Appropriations Committee, the full House ultimately settled for a reduction in the CRC's annual appropriation from $11.8 million to $7.5 million.[41] This had the effect of keeping the commission structurally intact but operationally moribund. Presumably Congress stands ready to resurrect the CRC under a future administration with a "pro–civil rights" agenda.

It is tempting to say that the experience of the Commission on Civil Rights under the Reagan administration is instructive for what it tells us about an administration's prospects for effectively utilizing government agencies as vehicles for the practice of entrepreneurial politics, especially when the agency in question has previously operated according to the norms of client politics (which was certainly the case with the pre-Reagan CRC). We must resist such a facile conclusion, if only because there *are* examples of agency-initiated policy reform in areas other than civil rights. A study by Martha Derthick and Paul Quirk, for example, shows how a convergence of prepossessing factors led to successful regulatory reform in three regulated industries during the late 1970s and early 1980s.[42] In each case administrative agencies transcended client politics to initiate policy reform that was strongly opposed by organized interest groups. Significantly, however, one of the factors cited by Derthick and Quirk as most important to the success of the reform movements was the confluence of "expert" and mass opinion regarding the desirability of reform, the implication being that reform was possible only with the assent of elites. The experts who mattered in each of the cases studied by Derthick and Quirk were economists, a preponderance of whom agreed that regulatory reform was desirable, and who could demonstrate, moreover, through empirical research and statistical analysis, that policy reform would have a salutary economic impact on the nation as a whole. Opponents of reform were helpless in the face of such evidence, and they could not question the competence or moral character of those who called for it.

The situation at the Civil Rights Commission was much different. A long-standing tradition had been established there according to which professional competence and expertise were determined primarily by the substance of one's views, whose merits were judged by a larger community of the civil rights elite. Regardless of his objective credentials, a commissioner lacked authority if his views diverged substantially from the collective wisdom of the civil rights elite. Lacking legitimacy, the reconstituted CRC was destined to fail in its policy-reform efforts where other agencies had succeeded; its failure is attributable less to institutional factors than to the peculiar way in which authority is established in the civil rights policy arena.

Interest-Group Politics: Big Business versus Small Business

Because they appear most apposite, we have focused thus far on the entrepreneurial and client models of politics in our discussion of the failure of civil rights reform. One aspect of that failure, however, can be explained in terms of the interest-group model of politics. On more than one occasion we have noted that the one area in which the Reagan administration could have acted unilaterally to alter existing civil rights policy was the Labor Department's guidelines for implementing Executive Order No. 11246. By no longer requiring firms under contract to the federal government to follow rigid numerical goals and timetables for the hiring and promotion of minorities and women, the administration would not only have advanced the cause of nondiscrimination; it would also have relieved employers of what would appear to be an onerous burden. But the American business community is not a political monolith, and hence when the administration began to hint that it might revise or amend the executive order guidelines, business groups began lobbying both for and against the proposed changes.

In August 1985 the administration let it be known that it had drafted an executive order that, as reported by the *New York Times*, "would prevent the Labor Department from requiring any companies to set numerical goals. It would also forbid the use of statistical evidence to measure compliance with laws against discrimination."[43] The *Times* failed to mention, however, that the draft contained a potentially important addendum:

> Nothing in this executive order shall be interpreted to require or provide a legal basis for a government contractor or subcontractor to utilize any numerical quota, goal, or ratio, or otherwise to discriminate against, or grant any preference to, any individual

or group on the basis of race, color, religion, sex, or national origin with respect to any aspect of employment. . . . [44]

Executive orders are not legislative acts; they are essentially strategies for enforcing federal law, to be followed by the relevant enforcement agencies of the executive branch as mandated by the president. The proposed draft would not have prevented employers from using racial goals, quotas, or other forms of preference on a voluntary basis. Its only effect would have been to prevent the Labor Department from *requiring* their use by federal contractors. Nevertheless, it should not have surprised the administration that Richard T. Seymour of the Lawyers' Committee for Civil Rights would call the draft "an astonishingly extreme document," or that Ralph Neas of the Leadership Conference on Civil Rights would simply label it "unconscionable."[45] But the administration was probably dismayed by the response the draft received from a substantial segment of the business community. In a survey taken among chief executive officers of large corporations (most of them in the "Fortune 500"), more than 90 percent—116 out of 127 respondents—said that the "numerical objectives" in their company's affirmative action program were established partly to satisfy "corporate objectives unrelated to government regulations." In response to a related question— "Do you plan to continue to use numerical objectives to track the progress of women and minorities in your corporation, regardless of government requirements?"—slightly more than 95 percent said yes.[46] Like many survey questions, this one is worded ambiguously enough to warrant caution in interpreting the results; to at least some of the respondents, using statistics to "track the progress" of female and minority employees may not have meant the same thing as hiring and promoting members of these groups according to predetermined numerical quotas and timetables.

Many businesses *did* make clear their intentions in no uncertain terms. John L. Hulck, chairman of Merck, a large pharmaceutical company in Rahway, New Jersey, declared that "we will continue goals and timetables no matter what the government does. They are part of our culture and corporate procedures." John M. Stafford, president and CEO of Pillsbury, voiced a similar sentiment: "It has become clear to us that an aggressive affirmative action program makes a lot of sense. So if the executive order is issued, it wouldn't affect us."[47]

If these and other companies intended to proceed with their affirmative action efforts in any event, one might have expected them to be indifferent to the possible removal of a governmental requirement that they practice affirmative action, much as one would be indifferent to the repeal of a law requiring citizens to breathe. Yet many of the nation's largest companies, led by the National Association of Manufacturers, the traditional lobbying arm of "big business," mounted a major campaign to dissuade the administration from adopting the draft proposal.[48] Why should they have bothered? There appear to be two reasons. The first can be deduced from the section of the draft that disclaims a legal basis *in the executive order* for the use of racial preferences. In an increasingly litigious society, employers have an interest in maintaining legal certainty and predictability, in discrimination law no less than in other areas of business-related law. So long as the Labor Department *requires* federal contractors to use goals and timetables that have the effect of favoring minorities and women in hiring and promotion, the firms using these methods will be virtually invulnerable to reverse discrimination suits brought by white males who believe they have been unfairly denied a job or promotion. Remove the governmental requirement, however, and the climate may change. At the very least, more white males may be encouraged to bring such suits, and defending against them would be more difficult—and expensive.

The simple solution for such firms would be to drop their race- and gender-based employment procedures altogether, as the draft proposal apparently intended for them to do. That, too, would create serious problems, however. As a perceptive article in *Fortune* magazine pointed out, "most large companies have an entrenched affirmative action bureaucracy in the personnel department," and many of the people who staff these bureaucracies are themselves minority group members and feminists with close ties to the organized civil rights community.[49] In addition to overseeing their companies' minority and female recruitment, retention, and promotion efforts, these inhouse affirmative action professionals are often given free reign to organize "workshops" and "seminars" to indoctrinate employees and management in the affirmative action mindset. For example, according to the *New York Times*,

> since 1981 all Merck employees have been required to attend a day-long session to discuss such issues as racial stereotypes,

sexual harassment and problems of the handicapped. The company offers "assertiveness training programs" for women and courses in English as a second language. Merck also recruits extensively at historically black colleges and has a special executive program for women, blacks and Hispanic people.[50]

If an IBM or an AT&T or a Merck were suddenly to announce the cessation of its race- and gender-conscious employment techniques—which would, of course, entail the shutting down of the company's in-house affirmative action bureaucracy—these affirmative action professionals would not be likely to leave quietly. To the contrary, one can imagine the outcry, recriminations, demonstrations, and threats of consumer boycotts.

The outrage of the displaced affirmative action professionals would likely be shared by their clients in the company, the minorities and women encouraged in the belief that their fate and the fate of affirmative action are directly linked. As one corporate affirmative action professional put it, "Now that minorities have come in the door, the job of affirmative action is to oversee the upward mobility of these people. That is the focus in the 1980s."[51] According to *Fortune*, "once a company has an affirmative action program in operation, it cannot stop or even retreat noticeably without stirring grievances and impairing morale among women and minorities on the payroll."[52]

If the executive order draft were enacted, large companies with entrenched affirmative action bureaucracies would be faced with a Hobson's choice: They could either retain their affirmative action programs and risk exposure to lawsuits brought by disgruntled white males, or they could eliminate that risk by dropping their affirmative action programs, thereby incurring the wrath of the displaced affirmative action professionals, their clients within the company, and possibly the organized civil rights community in the form of demonstrations and boycotts. That alone would be enough for many large companies to view the executive order draft with alarm, but there is an additional reason why large businesses of the sort represented by the National Association of Manufacturers would have an incentive to keep the existing Labor Department rules intact. That reason becomes easy to discern when one considers that the businesses that lobbied *in favor* of the administration's draft tended to be small firms with low profit margins and hence a heightened interest in maintaining low overhead costs. These firms, whose lobbying arm in the debate over the draft was the United States Chamber of Commerce,[53] tended not to have entrenched affirmative action bureaucracies in their personnel departments; indeed, they might not even have personnel departments per se. For them, staying abreast of changes in particular goals and timetables prescribed by the OFCCP, conducting extensive minority and female recruitment efforts, and filing the reams of government forms that are part and parcel of the compliance effort, often constituted an intolerable burden. The comparatively adverse impact of these compliance costs could put a small firm at a competitive disadvantage against a larger rival in bidding for government contracts. Hence larger firms had a very sound business reason to lobby against any changes that would have the effect of removing the disadvantage under which their smaller rivals were forced to operate. Political scientists Eugene Bardach and Robert A. Kagan have observed this phenomenon across the spectrum of regulated industries, which sometimes makes for strange political bedfellows. They note that in general,

> [a]ntibusiness social groups are often joined in pushing for more protective regulation by distinctly "probusiness" groups and, in fact, by businesses. Regulation usually affects competitors unevenly, imposing relatively higher costs on some than on others and creating advantages for low-compliance-cost firms. It also creates markets for suppliers of whatever is needed to comply with the regulations.[54]

Moreover,

> [t]he available stock of proregulation political sentiments can also be exploited by business interests seeking competitive advantages. While firms may not always be able to predict how they would fare under the specific terms that might emerge in a new regulatory program, once the regulations are in place the distribution of relative advantages and disadvantages becomes apparent. Proposals to ease regulatory restrictions, at that point, stimulate opposition from the specific interests that foresee losing some advantage. This opposition can conveniently ally itself with more diffusely ideological proprotection interests.[55]

Bardach and Kagan developed these rules of thumb in the course of studying the impact of consumer, environmental, and worker health and safety regulations on businesses, but they apply with equal validity to the present case. Here an alliance of large business groups and the already formidable civil rights lobby—combined with internal division within the White House—were enough to kill the executive order draft. "Client politics" had contributed to the failure of a civil rights reform initiative in an important nonjudicial area of civil rights policy.

Voting Rights in the 1980s: Toward Racial Corporatism

We began this chapter by asking why civil rights reform was not aggressively pursued through nonjudicial means, particularly in the form of a sweeping legislative act reaffirming the sanctity of the nondiscrimination principle. We have noted, first, that there was dissension, or at least confusion, within the administration over precisely what its objectives should be. There were episodes involving the reconstitution of the civil rights commission and the revision of a key executive order that revealed the limits of entrepreneurial politics and, conversely, the potency of client politics and interest-group politics in the civil rights policy debate. To borrow a phrase, the correlation of forces did not appear to favor a major legislative initiative to reformulate civil rights policy, notwithstanding the state of unarticulated mass opinion. To the catalog of episodes that boded ill for legislative civil rights reform we must add one more—the controversy that surrounded the extension of the Voting Rights Act in 1982.

Our treatment of this affair must be brief. In order to treat it adequately one would need to discuss the strange evolution of the Voting Rights Act since its initial passage in 1965. That subject would fill another volume, and so lies beyond the scope of this work. Fortunately, however, such a volume has recently been published: *Whose Votes Count?* by political scientist Abigail M. Thernstrom now stands as the definitive study of the history and consequences of the Voting Rights Act. Accordingly, much of what follows is derived from Thernstrom's work.[56]

The Voting Rights Act as passed in 1965 shared many of the characteristics of the Civil Rights Act passed in the previous year. We noted in Chapter 2, for example, that the Civil Rights Act, although national in its scope, was directed mainly at the southern states, where denial of equal opportunity was most pervasive and most virulent; so, too, the Voting Rights Act. The peculiar set of customs and laws that had deprived blacks of the electoral franchise, despite the passage of the Fifteenth Amendment in the immediate aftermath of the Civil War, were indigenous to the South, having been instituted after the withdrawal of federal troops in 1877. These included literacy and "understanding" tests, poll taxes (used elsewhere as well, but not always for racial purposes), intimidation and violence, and the "white primary," which may well have been the most effective means of disfranchising southern blacks. Like the Civil Rights Act, the Voting Rights Act explicitly conferred a right upon *individuals*, and was couched in the language of equal opportunity. The core of the Act was Title I, section 2:

> No voting qualification or prerequisite to voting, or standard, practice, or procedure shall be imposed or applied by any State or political subdivision to deny or abridge the right of any citizen of the United States to vote on account of race or color.

It is clear that, as Thernstrom puts it, "the aim of the Voting Rights Act—the *single* aim—was black enfranchisement in the South. Obstacles to registration and voting, that is, were the sole concern of those who framed the statute."[57] As the agenda of the organized civil rights movement changed, however, so did the judicial and administrative interpretation of the act. Following a pattern that closely paralleled the transformation of the Civil Rights Act, the emphasis shifted from the guarantee of equal opportunity (to register and to cast ballots) to a guarantee of equal results. In the voting rights context an equal result was not held merely to be a state of affairs in which each person's vote counted exactly as much as every other person's vote, but was held instead to be one in which each racial (or language) *group* succeeded in electing candidates drawn from its ranks, in numbers proportionate to the group's number in the general population.

This scheme meant that a state, county, or municipality could be judged in violation of the Voting Rights Act if it used an electoral system (such as the at-large system) in which black candidates running for office in a particular jurisdiction did not get elected in numbers commensurate with the number of blacks residing in that jurisdiction. The offending governmental units were said to be guilty of "minority-vote dilution." The act thus became a tool to force state and local governments to restructure their electoral systems (for example, to substitute district elections for at-large elections) and to engage in racial gerrymandering—the drawing of electoral districts so as to create as many majority-black districts as possible, which would presumably ensure the election of more black candidates.

The Voting Rights Act was originally drafted so that certain of its provisions—most notably section 5, the so-called "pre-clearance" section that required certain jurisdictions, all of which were in the South, to seek the approval of the Justice Department before instituting any electoral changes—would periodically expire, subject to renewal by Congress. In 1982 these "temporary" provisions (as they were called in 1965), which constituted only a small part of the act, were scheduled to expire; Congress was faced with the task of deciding if and for how long they should be extended. With the virtual elimination of the practices that had once barred the access of southern blacks to the polls, a strong case could have been made against renewing the temporary provisions at all. Yet as soon as the House began holding hearings on the issue, it became clear that any argument against renewal was untenable because the issue had been cast by civil rights activists in terms of whether the act per se was to be extended. An argument against renewal of the special provisions was portrayed as an argument in favor of repealing the act itself.

Moreover, the occasion represented an opportunity for civil rights activists to "strengthen" the act by amending section 2. As noted above, the section as originally written banned qualifications and procedures "imposed or applied . . . to deny or abridge the right . . . to vote on account of race or color." In the 1980 case of *City of Mobile v. Bolden* the Supreme Court, in a reversal of precedent, interpreted that language to refer only to qualifications and procedures that were *intentionally* devised for the purpose of diluting the impact of minority votes. *Mobile*'s substitution of an "intent" standard for the previously announced "effects" test in establishing official discriminatory conduct in minority-vote dilution cases had brought sharp criticism from the civil rights lobby. Expiration of the temporary provisions of the Voting Rights

Act in 1982 offered a splendid opportunity to correct legislatively
this errant Supreme Court interpretation of the act. Thus in April
1981 Representative Peter Rodino (D–N.J.) and Senator Charles
Mathias (R–Md.), among others, introduced bills that would not
only extend the life of the temporary provisions but also alter the
wording of section 2. The revised version of section 2 would
change "to deny or abridge" to "in a manner which *results* in a
denial or abridgement of."[58] The potential effect of the new language would be to ban any and all electoral systems (not just in
the South or other regions with a history of voter discrimination)
that tended to dilute the impact of minority votes, measured as
the ability of black and Hispanic candidates to win election in
proportion to the percentage of voting-age blacks and Hispanics
residing in a given jurisdiction. Depending upon how federal
judges and Justice Department attorneys chose to interpret the
amended version of section 2, proportional representation by race
could well have become, to all intents and purposes, the law of
the land.

"For all its potentially radical implications," writes Thernstrom,
"the proposed amendment drew remarkably little attention either
at the press conferences held on April 7, 1981, following introduction of the bills in the House and Senate, or in the House subcommittee hearings that began a month later. The reason," she says,
"is clear":

> [P]otential opponents were asleep at the switch, and enthusiasts
> had nothing to gain from rousing them. Civil rights supporters,
> in fact, downplayed the magnitude of the suggested amend-
> ment. The altered wording was described as a "clarification";
> they argued that, in viewing section 2 as merely a restatement
> of the Fifteenth Amendment, the Court had misconstrued the
> intentions of the statute's framers. Civil rights spokesmen
> claimed that, since the preclearance provision prohibited elec-
> toral changes that were discriminatory in effect as well as in
> purpose, the failure of section 2 to make a similar reference to
> invidious impact was merely an oversight.[59]

The manufacture and dissemination of this misconception
was accomplished by an extremely potent iron triangle consisting
of the organized civil rights lobby, the chairman (Don Edwards)
and staff of the House Subcommittee on Civil and Constitutional

Rights, and the national media. With respect to the first element in this triumvirate Thernstrom writes that

> the civil rights community was . . . organized to an unprece-
> dented degree. Never before, perhaps, had so sophisticated a
> lobbying effort been set up to peddle a product so consistently
> presented as above politics. A meticulously organized national
> effort had been launched to sell that which allegedly should
> need no selling. It was a powerful political potion, the effects of
> which it was the unenviable task of critics to dispel.[60]

The strategic prominence of the House subcommittee's chairman and staff only magnified the influence of the civil rights lobby,
represented in this instance by the ubiquitous Leadership Conference on Civil Rights. If "the Leadership Conference on Civil Rights,
in effect, functioned as an extension of Edward's staff,"[61] then "the
staff's views . . . were indistinguishable from those of the Leadership
Conference. There was nothing extraordinary in this; Edwards had
total confidence in the civil rights lobby, and his hiring practices
legitimately reflected that faith."[62] Most members of the House Subcommittee on Civil and Constitutional Rights did not need to be
persuaded by staff of the correctness of the civil rights lobby's position. "Many committee members came to the issue predisposed to
see the question in the clear moral terms that virulent southern racism had made appropriate in 1965. In fact, most members had undoubtedly requested assignment to the committee precisely because
of their belief in civil rights as an ongoing moral crusade."[63]

Finally there were the media. Where the powerful axis formed
by the civil rights lobby and the House subcommittee was concerned, there would be no "adversary journalism." The media's
performance was characterized instead by a combination of
partisanship, sycophancy, and incompetence. "There seems,"
lamented Senator Orrin Hatch (R–Utah), one of the few who opposed the bill in the Senate, "to be a preoccupation in parts of the
media to define the debate in terms of whether or not the Voting
Rights Act will be extended this year or permitted to expire. . . .
There is nobody that I know of who will not extend the present
voting rights law, at the very least."[64] That the media's coverage
was generally inaccurate and tendentious is suggested by the following lengthy excerpt from Thernstrom's book:

A *New York Times* editorial described the House bill as "well calculated to secure the hard-won rights of blacks and Hispanics." The description gave no indication that the issue before Congress was an expansion of existing protection, not just its retention. Another *Times* editorial implied that the proposal to extend section 2 without modification was a "weakening amendment." . . . Overall, readers of *Newsweek*, *Time*, the *New York Times*, and the *Washington Post* must have thought that time had stood still in the South. David Broder declared that the gap between black and white registration in the South was just as great in 1981 as it was in 1965—a preposterous assertion. News stories commonly profiled black counties with low levels of black political participation, a phenomenon that was always explained by discrimination and inadequate enforcement of the act. Higher participation rates would depend upon continuing (or greater) federal vigilance, such stories implied. Rarely did reporters discuss the respective responsibilities of the federal government and the local black community—precisely how much the [government] should and could do to get out the vote.

In short, the issues were more complicated than the media let on; further, many assertions by the press were simply false.[65]

In the Senate as well as in the House, there was no organized opposition to the amended version of the Voting Rights Act—no group with even a chance of countering the formidable resources and enormous influence brought to bear by the civil rights lobby. The passage of the amended act was an archetypal example of client politics. Unlike the House hearings, however, the hearings before the Judiciary Committee in the Republican-dominated Senate were marked by the appearance of a handful of distinguished witnesses who testified against the amendment. These witnesses, invited largely at the behest of Hatch, the committee chairman, suggested that in a community of equal citizens individuals, not groups, are the appropriate unit of representation. "This is not India," remarked Henry Abraham, professor of government at the University of Virginia. "There is no right to be represented on the basis of group membership."[66] "The amendment . . . inches us along toward a corporate concept of electoral democracy," Donald Horowitz charged.[67] Walter Berns worried that, under section 2 as amended, legislators would "represent not undifferentiated people, people defined only as individuals living in districts of approximately equal size, but groups of people, defined by their race or language preference, and they can be said to represent them only if they are of that race or if they . . . prefer that language."[68] Barry Gross reminded the senators that "the Constitution speaks only of individuals. . . . Individuals choose by election other individuals to represent them from political subdivisions spread out over regions. There is no provision for group representation no matter how shamefully treated they were, nor how tragic their history."[69] Hatch himself asked, "Are individuals elected to office to represent individual citizens or are they elected to office to represent ethnic and racial blocs of voters?"[70]

The testimony of such witnesses was nothing compared to the juggernaut created by the synergy of the civil rights lobby, the House subcommittee, and the media. By the time the amended version of the Voting Rights Act reached the floors of the House and Senate, proponents had succeeded in portraying the amended version of the act as the original, unadulterated act that was passed in 1965; opponents were accused of trying to weaken the act by deleting the "effects" standard for determining if voter "discrimination" (the code-word for minority vote dilution) had occured, which, it was implied, had been an integral part of the act all along. Thus was reality stood on its head. In July 1986 Professor Herman Schwartz could write in the *New York Times* that "despite a barrage of statements and articles by the Attorney General, William French Smith, Congress voted 389–24 and 85–8 *to keep the effects test.*"[71] To keep the effects test? Either Schwartz, a professor of constitutional law, was ignorant concerning the subject about which he presumed to enlighten the *Times*'s readers, or he was engaged in a willful distortion. His reference to a "barrage of statements and articles by the Attorney General" constitutes a somewhat more subtle distortion, with its implication that Congress decided overwhelmingly to approve the amended version of the act despite a one-sided lobbying campaign waged by opponents within the Reagan administration. In fact, the administration's posture was one of studied indifference during the entire time that the bill was being debated before the House and Senate committees;[72] only belatedly did it become involved, and in the end the administration supported the legislation when it became clear that it would pass.[73] On the other hand, Thernstrom's careful research shows that lobbying over the issue was indeed one-sided and intense—and came entirely from the pro-amendment forces.

It became clear almost immediately that the amended version of section 2 would in fact operate as a ban on any electoral system that failed to produce outcomes consistent with the new norm of proportional representation by race. The *National Journal* reported that between 1982 and 1985 roughly two-thirds of the electoral plans challenged in court under the Voting Rights Act were rejected.[74] On June 30, 1986, the amended act produced a landmark Supreme Court ruling, and predictably it served not only to "correct" the *Mobile* decision, but also to effectively nullify language inserted into the act at the Reagan administration's urging which declared that nothing in the provision established "a right to have members of the protected class elected in numbers equal to their proportion of the population."[75] It was precisely the alleged failure of the state of North Carolina deliberately to create majority black legislative districts when the state legislature reapportioned districts statewide following the 1980 census that was at issue in the case of *Thornburg v. Gingles*.[76]

In oral arguments before the Court, Solicitor General Charles Fried, arguing on behalf of the Reagan administration and in support of North Carolina, could do little more than point out that black candidates had recently won several seats in at least three of the five districts that the plaintiffs had alleged were in violation of the 1982 amendment. This fact did not disconcert Julius LeVonne Chambers, director-counsel of the NAACP Legal Defense and Education Fund and Fried's opposite number in the case. He told the justices that the recent election results in the named districts were deceptive because whites had supported black candidates in hopes of undermining the black voters' lawsuit.[77] Moreover, said Chambers, the legislature's failure to create districts with solid black majorities meant that those blacks who were elected had to appeal to white voters and were therefore not the best representatives of black communities.[78] Voter "discrimination," Chambers was clearly implying, should now be understood as including situations in which black candidates had to appeal to white voters in order to get elected. The same Supreme Court that had exerted itself so strenuously in behalf of school integration now endorsed an incipient racial corporatism—the electoral equivalent of the South African system of tribal "homelands"—by a vote of 9 to 0.

Justice Brennan's opinion for the Court rejected the notion "that if a racial minority gains proportional representation in a single election, that fact alone precludes" finding a violation.[79] Julius LeVonne Chambers disingenuously announced that the decision "gives us a powerful new tool for protecting the equal rights of minorities to register, to vote and to have their votes counted with equal weight."[80] In fact, that tool had been available since 1965 and had been used to great effect. The new tool fashioned by Congress and the Court was of a much different kind, to be used for a much different purpose.

With the Supreme Court weighing in on the side of racial corporatism, the formidable iron triangle that shepherded the amended Voting Rights Act through Congress now became an iron rectangle. The administration's failure to seek a legislative redress of race- and gender-conscious civil rights policies may well be attributable in part to internal confusion, dissension, or irresolution, but the story of the Voting Rights Act and the other civil rights episodes recounted in this chapter make clear that any attempt at legislative redress would have been doomed from the start. With the possible exception of Executive Order No. 11246, the administration had no choice but to work through the courts, where it would also fail.

A more conventional analysis might end at this point, with the proffer of a systemic- or institutionally oriented conclusion about the failure of civil rights reform. Such a conclusion would emphasize the limits of entrepreneurial politics and the concomitant salience of client politics and interest-group politics; or it might refer to the influence of the "New Congress" and the rise of "issue networks," and so forth. But none of these explanations gets to the ultimate "Why" question. That is, they tell us why civil rights reform failed, but they neglect to explain why a race- and gender-neutral, nondiscriminatory civil rights policy was so strongly resisted by those who mattered—the politicians, journalists, interest-group activists, and federal judges who constitute America's civil rights elite. What we need is a theory of the attitudes and beliefs that inform this elite's conception of civil rights. Such a theory will be offered in the next chapter.

CHAPTER SIX

The Civil Rights Ideology in Our Time

Those who accept the ideological revelation make the Mosaic decision to identify themselves with the oppressed as historical agents of social transformation, and although most ideological recruitment . . . concentrates upon a pool of potential supporters who are by nature clearly distinct from the rest of the population, there is in principle no natural limit to such identification, as male feminists or White supporters of Black nationalism may testify.

— Kenneth Minogue,
Alien Powers: The Pure Theory of Ideology

The conventional political science literature is of limited use in developing a theory of elite attitudes and beliefs about civil rights, because of the tendency of most political scientists to focus on institutions and processes—and to all but ignore the role of ideas—in their analyses of political phenomena. A key politician such as Don Edwards was not responding to interest-group pressure when he helped the civil rights lobby push through the amended version of the Voting Rights Act. Federal judges did not refuse to reaffirm the nondiscrimination principle in the Civil Rights Act and the Fourteenth Amendment because of interest group pressure. Nor did the national media stand for the most part in opposition to civil rights reform because of the need to sell newspapers and commercial broadcast time. And those within the professoriate who wrote and spoke in support of race- and gender-conscious civil rights doctrine were not responding to the imperatives of political or commercial expedience. All these people behaved as they did because they earnestly *believed* in the position they had staked out.

What was the nature of this belief, where did it come from, and upon what was it based? These questions border on psychology and cannot be answered definitively. We can offer a theory, however, and happily there is at least one political scientist whose work points the way. In a remarkable book published in 1985, Kenneth Minogue limned the essential attributes of modern political ideologies—the systems of thought that inform and animate so many of the modern world's political movements. It is to Minogue's work that we now turn in our attempt to describe the foremost impediment to civil rights reform in the 1980s—the contemporary civil rights ideology.

At the outset we must acknowledge that to speak of a "civil rights ideology," or of any kind of ideology for that matter, risks alienating some readers. That is because no precise definition of the term is universally agreed upon. Publicists tend to use it as a pejorative word to denote ideas that they happen to dislike ("I have principles; you have an ideology"). Explains Minogue,

> Political scientists use the word to describe any of the more evolved bodies of political doctrine in which theory is combined with a project for political action. It thus refers to isms. I shall use it more narrowly, to denote any doctrine which presents the hidden and saving truth about the world in the form of social analysis.[1]

In this narrow and admittedly idiosyncratic sense of the term, then, ideology is distinguished from more conventional modes of political thought by its reliance on a central idea "so abstract that it is less a doctrine than a machine for generating doctrines, and its simplest formulation is that all evils are caused by an oppressive system."[2] The paradigmatic ideology, thus defined, is of course Marxism. The genius of Minogue's book lies in its demonstration of how the basic analytic categories and discursive tactics that are indigenous to Marxism have been successfully adopted by latter-day political movements, including communism, third world nationalism and, most especially, feminism. Drawing on this insight, we want to suggest that a major reason for the persistence of race- and gender-conscious civil rights policies is that the ideologically derived mode of analysis and discourse has been successfully grafted onto the civil rights movement (which originally bore none of these characteristics). Before developing this idea any further, let us return to Minogue's "pure theory" of ideology. Here are seven fundamental elements of the ideological worldview:

1. Society is seen as divided between oppressor and oppressed, and the continuing ascendance of the oppressor class is facilitated by a hidden structure of domination. The structure of domination is comprehensive and universal—it includes not only law and public policy, but morality, manners, religion, and social custom. Indeed, all social institutions and conventions are the products of either the willful self-interest of the oppressor class or the false consciousness of the oppressed class. Often they are identified with both. Depending upon the particular species of ideology under consideration, the concealed structure of domination may be called by any of several names: for example, capitalism, patriarchy, racism, imperialism, or modernity.

2. All political thought and action is determined by "interests," which by definition strive for self-maximization and self-aggrandizement. There is no such thing as a disinterested party: "Ideology is a form of theoretical conscription: *everyone*, by virtue of class, race or nation, is smartly uniformed and assigned to one side or the other."[3] Hence no government "neutrality" is possible (nor, incidentally, is scholarly neutrality possible), because in choosing an ostensibly neutral policy the state indirectly gives an advantage to the oppressor class, whose interests are in any event protected and advanced by the concealed structure of domination. The government, therefore, necessarily adopts policies that are partial to either the oppressor or the oppressed; any attempt to remain neutral automatically helps the oppressor.

3. It is implicit in the dichotomy of oppressor and oppressed that the interest of the oppressed is associated with justice, and the interest of the oppressor is associated with injustice.

4. The term "minority" is a synonym for "oppressed." It is thus possible for women, who constitute 51 percent of the population of the United States, to be lumped together with "minorities," while Jews (who account for 3 percent) and White Anglo-Saxon Protestants (who account for 15 percent) do not qualify for minority status.

5. The object of politics is to liberate the oppressed, which requires that the structure of domination be altered or destroyed.

6. All species of ideology are necessarily hostile to individualism (and, even more so, to legal and political doctrines that emphasize individual rights) because individuals isolated from the communitarian bonds formed by joint membership in a particular class, sex, or race are incapable of effective citizenship, which is possible only through participation in the collective consciousness appropriate to one's social group.

7. Ideology is unfalsifiable, inasmuch as it considers its opponents to be suffering from a character defect (false consciousness or, alternatively, an interest in preserving one's own privilege). Any empirical evidence that seems to disconfirm the "truth" as represented by ideologists is in the nature of a mystification. Moreover, when considered ideologically such evidence can actually be used to demonstrate the subtle yet immense power of the structure of domination, as, for example, when housewives profess not to regard marriage as a form of slavery; so powerful is the structure of domination that the slave is rendered incapable of understanding her predicament. ("It is interesting," writes the feminist theoretician Kate Millet, "that many women do not recognize themselves as discriminated against; no better proof could be found of the totality of their conditioning."[4] The same might be said of the black majority that has failed to recognize that busing is, to use Justice Blackmun's phrase, "in their interest.")

The Pure Theory of Ideology Applied to Civil Rights

The particular theory to be offered here is derived from the framework delineated above, and can be stated as follows: A very substantial segment of American political and legal elites—that substratum that we have referred to as America's "civil rights elite"—is in thrall to a civil rights ideology that has as its core belief the notion that American society is divided into two distinct classes—an oppressor class and an oppressed class. The oppressor class is predominantly white and male, and maintains a monopoly of wealth, power, and privilege through its manipulation of a concealed structure of domination, which is alternately called "racism" or "sexism" (or "patriarchy" in the parlance of academic feminism). Sometimes, however, the structure of domination is simply referred to as "society." The oppressed class consists of those who systematically are disadvantaged by the concealed structure of domination. In civil rights discourse this class is commonly denominated by the catchall phrase, "minorities and women." The sole object of civil rights policy must therefore be to effect the liberation of the oppressed.

Liberation is equated, not merely with the attainment of formal or procedural rights—"civil rights" as they were commonly understood before 1970—but with the advent of substantive group parity. Put differently, formal rights are a necessary, but not a sufficient, predicate of liberation; genuine liberation consists in the attainment of substantive parity as well. The civil rights elite have discovered that liberation can be realized through the skillful manipulation of the federal civil rights statutes and the equal protection clause of the Fourteenth Amendment. These have effectively been transformed into instruments for confounding the hidden structure of domination, thereby advancing the goal of liberation.

This may strike some as a rather breathtaking thesis, and so a caveat is in order. When we say that a substantial segment of the civil rights elite is "in thrall" to this civil rights ideology, we do not mean to suggest that large numbers of judges, politicians, journalists, and so forth consciously subscribe to each of the ideology's tenets as starkly rendered above. In any given time and place relatively few people will fully embrace the ideological style of analysis and discourse in its purest form. Minogue himself acknowledges that

> the influence of ideology in the West can be easily exaggerated. The political movements it has generated, such as communism and feminism, have had to take on a political form and have necessarily had to become responsive to what actual people want. All such movements are marked by revisionist tendencies. The pure theory of ideology appears only in areas of pure intellectuality, or among small extremist groups. There is no major change over the last two centuries which can be exclusively attributed to it.[5]

Certainly this is true of the civil rights ideology; in its pristine form it is consciously embraced only by those engaged in "pure intellectuality" and by "small extremist groups." Given sufficient incentive, however, people can be induced to internalize the essential precepts of an ideology, even if they have never consciously reflected on those precepts. Accordingly we may distinguish among different types of adherents to the civil rights ideology. Experience suggests that three types may be identified and described as follows:

True believers. This category, as suggested above, consists mainly of intellectuals and members of extremist groups. The civil rights ideology's true believers include academic theoreticians such as those whose work was discussed in Chapters 2 and 3, as well as virtually the entire leadership of the organized civil rights community. The written opinions of certain federal judges, especially Justices Marshall, Brennan, and Blackmun and Judge Wisdom, would also seem to qualify them for membership in this group. Civil rights commissioners Berry and Cardenas Ramirez belong here, too. Their public declaration that the civil rights laws do not protect white males because they are a "favored" group, and that the civil rights laws should be interpreted to protect only members of "disfavored" groups, is a perfect shorthand statement of the central tenets of the civil rights ideology: the division of society into two distinct classes; the belief that somehow one class is "favored," the other "disfavored," evoking the specter of a hidden structure presumably responsible for this state of affairs; and the idea that civil rights laws are properly understood exclusively as instruments for liberating the oppressed, or "disfavored," class.

Guilt managers. In one of his frequent appearances on the television program, "This Week with David Brinkley," the *New York Times* columnist Tom Wicker found himself engaged in an exchange with George Will on the subject of affirmative action as manifested in a recent Supreme Court decision. Will complained about the adverse impact of affirmative action on innocent white males, to which Wicker replied that it was "intellectually indefensible" to maintain that white males as a group have not benefited from discrimination against blacks and women. Then, apparently for emphasis, he quickly added, "I know *I* have."

What is interesting about this form of argumentation is Wicker's reflexive extrapolation from his own experience to that of every other white male. One can readily surmise that Wicker, a son of the South who was sixty years old at the time he made this statement, did indeed benefit, at least indirectly, from discrimination against blacks and women. He entered adulthood as a white Southerner during the heyday of Jim Crow; seemingly a thoughtful and compassionate man, he may be haunted by memories of his coming of age under a social system in which he—especially if his family was at all afflu-ent—belonged to a privileged caste. Perhaps he now suspects that too much of what he has achieved in his life can be traced to the privilege that was his as a young man in the old South.

What Wicker needs is a palliative to soothe his troubled con-science. By citing his own experience as a basis for generalizing about the experience of a vast number of other, disparately situated white males, Wicker is able to diffuse responsibility—and hence guilt—for having participated in a system that conferred unfair advantages upon white males of his generation and regional ori-gin. Moreover, by expanding the pool of alleged beneficiaries of discrimination, he can enjoy the peculiar moral satisfaction that comes with advocacy of compensatory policies for which the ad-vocate personally bears no cost. White males in their twenties and thirties, most of whom will have come of age in the North and the West, and in any case long after the demise of the system of oppres-sion that had benefited Wicker's cohort, may now be pressed into service as surrogates for that cohort, to be sacrificed on the altar of compassion in order to assuage Wicker's sense of guilt. Mean-while, Wicker's personal wealth, position, and influence remain undiminished, and may even be enhanced.

For such people, then, the civil rights ideology conveniently serves as the underlying basis of an elaborate project for cost-free guilt management.

Moral fashionplates. In Tom Wolfe's magnificent novel, *The Bonfire of the Vanities*, there is a character named Lawrence Kramer who, as a thirty-two-year-old assistant district attorney in the Bronx, New York, is consumed by chronic status-anxiety. A grad-uate of the Columbia Law School, he finds that he is increasingly envious of his law school classmates who entered private practice and who now earn more and live better than he does. With the arrival of their first child, Kramer and his working wife hire a British baby nurse, who lives with them in their cramped

Manhattan apartment. Kramer discovers that the presence of this
very proper middle-aged Englishwoman in his modest home only
increases his sense of inadequacy:

> Glenda was the very picture of gentility, having tea, while Mr.
> Kramer, lord of the ant colony, came tramping through to the
> bathroom barefooted, bare-legged, tousle-headed, wearing a
> tattered old plaid bathrobe. . . . What on earth was she really
> thinking, this British arbiter sitting in judgment (on an appalling
> fold-out sofa) upon the squalor of *chez* Kramer?[6]

Then a remarkable thing happens. While watching the *Today* show
one morning, Kramer, his wife, and Glenda are shown a videotape
of a near-riot that occurred in Harlem the night before, in which
militant blacks chased New York's white mayor from a public
meeting hall.

> When it was over, the three of them looked at one another, and
> Glenda, the English baby nurse, spoke up, with considerable
> agitation.
> "Well, I think that's perfectly disgusting. The colored don't
> know how good they've got it in this country, I can tell you that
> much. In Britain there's not so much as a colored in a police
> uniform, much less an important public official, the way they
> have here. Why, there was an article just the other day. There's
> more than two hundred mayors that are coloreds in this country.
> And they want to bash the mayor of New York about. Some
> people don't know how well off they are, if you ask me."
> She shook her head angrily.
> Kramer and his wife looked at each other. He could tell she
> was thinking the same thing he was.
> Thank God in heaven! What a relief! They could let their
> breaths out now. Miss Efficiency was a bigot. These days, the
> thing about bigotry was, it was undignified. It was the sign of
> Low Rent origins, of inferior social status, of poor taste. So they
> were the superiors of their English baby nurse, after all. What a
> . . . relief.[7]

The Kramers' attitude is quite prevalent in America today, particularly among middle-brow, college-educated members of the
"baby-boom" generation. Such people are often not thoughtful
enough to probe the intricacies of the civil rights debate, much less

to assimilate consciously the civil rights ideology. They have learned, however, from school and the media (especially television and its caricature of the quintessential "Low Rent" bigot, Archie Bunker) that to dissent in any way from the orthodox shibboleths on matters of race is *déclassé*, the intellectual equivalent of wearing blue socks with brown shoes. Notice that there is nothing in Glenda's commentary that is truly racist, or that could even be cited plausibly as an example of bigotry, strictly speaking. The ironic message that Wolfe conveys in this ingeniously crafted scene is that the real bigots are in fact the Kramers.

Manifestations of the Civil Rights Ideology

As with most sociological categories, there is with respect to the three types of civil rights elite a good deal of overlap, as individual members of the elite may appear from time to time to manifest characteristics associated with this or that category. It must be emphasized, too, that some will not fit into any of the categories proposed here. The relevance of the categories in assessing particular statements made by individual members of the elite is unmistakable, nonetheless.

When, for example, the columnist Anthony Lewis cites with approval a statement by the Lawyers' Committee for Civil Rights under Law, his conclusion is heavy with the theoretical baggage of the true believer in the civil rights ideology:

> The United States Government has essentially changed sides under Mr. Reynolds: That is what the statement makes so clear. Instead of fighting for the blacks and women who have been the historic victims of discrimination, the Justice Department is now "emphasizing the rights of white males."[8]

American society is conceived as a battleground in which two opposing "sides" are at war. The Justice Department "fights for" one side or the other. Naturally it is supposed to fight for the side of the oppressed, whose members are without exception "the historic victims of discrimination." That the Justice Department might be attempting simply to enforce the letter of the law on behalf of specific individuals, without regard to which "side" it is supposedly helping, is inconceivable to Lewis.

True belief in the civil rights ideology was reflected in a slightly different way in a 1985 decision of the California Supreme Court, unanimously overturning the murder conviction of a black defendant on the grounds that no black women served on his jury. The trial judge had refused to declare a mistrial for that reason, explaining that black women were no more a recognizable group than men who wear toupees. In his opinion for the Supreme Court, Justice Allen Broussard disagreed, declaring that black women "share a common perspective arising from their life experience."[9] Although it may strike some as a particularly crude form of stereotyping, the notion that people share a "common perspective" solely by virtue of their membership in a class defined by race and gender is perfectly consistent with the civil rights ideology. In throwing out the murder conviction, the court implied that the "common perspective" of black women is indeed so unusual that it might have led one of them to reach a verdict that differed from that of all other jurors.

It is the nature of the true believer that he will resolutely continue the struggle against oppression even within the context of the most seemingly benign and open institutions, because of his steadfast belief in the universality of the hidden structure of domination. The modern university has thus become one of the foremost battlegrounds on which the struggle against oppression is waged. This is not because universities are comparatively more racist or sexist than other major institutions; it has rather to do with the proliferation of true-believing civil rights ideologists on university campuses. Shelby Steele, a black professor of English, observed the phenomenon firsthand as a participant at black faculty meetings at San Jose State University:

> Since victimization was not our primary problem—the university had long ago opened its doors to us—we had to continue to make it so. . . .
>
> At our black faculty meetings, the old equation of blackness with victimization was ever present—to be black was to be a victim; therefore, not to be a victim was not to be black. As we contrived to meet the terms of this formula there was an inevitable distortion of both ourselves and the larger university. Through the prism of victimization the university seemed more impenetrable than it actually was, and we more limited in our powers. We fell prey to the victim's myopia, making the univer-

sity an institution from which we could seek redress but which we could never fully join. And this mind-set often led us to look more for compensations for our supposed victimization than for opportunities we could pursue as individuals.[10]

Sometimes evidence of true belief in the civil rights ideology during the 1980s came from unexpected sources. A case in point was William Hudnut, the Republican mayor of Indianapolis, perhaps the most Republican city in America. When the Justice Department asked Indianapolis to eliminate its 25 percent hiring goal for blacks in the city's police department following the Supreme Court's decision in the *Stotts* case, Hudnut refused. When the Justice Department filed suit to force Indianapolis to change its program, Hudnut, backed by the city council, vowed to fight the Reagan administration in court. Appearing on the PBS television program "Frontline," Hudnut addressed the charge that Indianapolis discriminated against white males in the competition for jobs and promotions in the police department:

> People say we're guilty of reverse discrimination. It is conceivable that some people could interpret it that way.
> But you know, I get a little upset when we have a promotion list that's put out, for example. Nine white males are promoted and a black male is promoted, or maybe it's eight white males and a female and a black male.
> You know, and then they tell us we're guilty of reverse discrimination when the whites have gotten 80 percent of the jobs, the white males.[11]

Hudnut acknowledges that some white males are denied promotions because of their race and sex, but that is not unfair because most of the promotions went to other white males. The communitarian bonds of race and gender are so strong and so immutable that the unfortunate victim of discrimination should find solace in the knowledge that his "white brothers" accounted for most of those who were given promotions. This view is so contemptuous of individual autonomy and self-determination, so dangerous in its promotion of a potentially incendiary racial solidarity, that it is simply astonishing.

An example of guilt management, on the other hand, can be seen in a remark addressed to William Bradford Reynolds by

Representative Don Edwards (D–Calif.) during an appearance by Reynolds before the House Judiciary Subcommittee on Civil and Constitutional Rights. Reynolds had told the subcommittee that he saw his job as evenhandedly "challenging those practices that unfairly disadvantage women, Hispanics, and whites," to which Edwards retorted:

> You and I are white male attorneys. We came from families with some money and were educated in the right schools. Unless we behaved very stupidly, the family and institutional support systems guaranteed places for us. We benefited from a racial spoils system.[12]

Edwards's sense of shame at having been the beneficiary of a "racial spoils system," which "guaranteed" his personal success, was great enough for him to betray, through his persistent advocacy of affirmative action, the legitimate aspirations of the vast majority of white males who are totally without the financial and familial resources with which Edwards was blessed.

Senator Howard Metzenbaum (D–Ohio) exemplified the moral fashionplate variety of adherence to the civil rights ideology in an exchange with Reynolds during the latter's confirmation hearings before the Senate Judiciary Committee in June 1985. Following Reynolds's testimony concerning his performance as assistant attorney general for civil rights, Metzenbaum stared at Reynolds and said:

> I do not understand. You are intelligent, you appear to be a decent human being and yet you come down in some of these cases on the side of the bigots.[13]

There is no need for Metzenbaum to reflect on the cases under discussion from the standpoint of principle, or in light of what the relevant statutes and constitutional amendments actually say. The fashionplate knows only that if one is "intelligent" and "decent," one automatically adopts the point of view of the oppressed. If, on the other hand, you "come down on the side of the bigots" (those vulgar, beer-swilling yahoos who are the eternal bogeymen of the civil rights elite), then surely you cannot be intelligent or decent. Affecting the right attitudes, the proper sensibilities, is like dressing in a tastefully coordinated ensemble of designer-label clothes—it sets one apart from the unwashed.

The imperatives of the civil rights ideology were ultimately responsible for the refusal of the ideology's true believers to surrender absolute control of the Civil Rights Commission. Lacking any regulatory or adjudicatory authority, the CRC's main function was tutorial. That function, however, is of particular importance to those in the ideological vanguard, for it is their duty to "teach the masses (and sometimes, indeed, one another) the appropriate consciousness, and until the lesson has been learned, the power must continue in the right hands."[14] The intolerance of dissent from the civil rights ideology that was demonstrated in the struggle over the commission, as well as in virtually every other area of civil rights controversy, was rooted in the ideologist's belief that all political opposition is inherently subversive and illegitimate.

> For the practice of political opposition depends upon a logical presupposition which [the ideologists do] not share: namely, that understanding and responding to problems of public policy is an inherently contestable business, upon which men of good will may quite legitimately disagree, and in which discussion even across party boundaries might be expected to generate decisions of a wiser kind than those likely to be made by a single group of politicians all of one mind. The last thing any of our ideologists could take seriously was this kind of co-operation by debate, because, regarding themselves as philosophers, or as scientists of a sort, they believed that they had arrived at a truth about the conduct of society such as would entirely supersede the blunderings of rhetoric.[15]

This of course explains the tendency of civil rights ideologists to attribute all disagreement to the flawed characters of their opponents. Morris Abram, John Bunzel, and Robert Destro were dismissed as "Neanderthals" by the NAACP,[16] and the NAACP's president, Benjamin Hooks, assailed the sinister machinations of a "right-wing clique" within the administration that was composed of "newly empowered bigots who desire to 'return to the good old days' when society was run totally by and for white males at the expense of everyone else."[17] Because he disagreed with Anthony Lewis, Assistant Attorney General Reynolds was "lawless and heartless."[18] Because he disagreed with Ira Glasser of the American Civil Liberties Union, Reynolds was "the moral equivalent of those southern segregationists of a generation ago standing in the schoolhouse door to defend segregation."[19]

To engage the oppressor in a civilized debate would be to concede the legitimacy of his point of view, which was unthinkable. Hence debate was eschewed in favor of character assassination and apocalyptic rhetoric about spinning clocks and "hostility to civil rights." According to the civil rights ideology, that alleged hostility could have only one explanation; it was neatly summarized by Herbert Hill, professor of industrial relations and Afro-American Studies, in a *New York Times* op-ed piece:

> Affirmative action is opposed because it is the most effective remedy to end the preferential position that whites have traditionally enjoyed at the expense of nonwhite groups.[20]

Affirmative action is opposed because it is harmful to the interest of the oppressor. Opposition is therefore illegitimate.

It was not only the civil rights ideology's intrinsic appeal as a belief system that ensured the triumph of the race- and gender-conscious regime of civil rights during the 1980s; also critical was the capacity of its adherents to stifle the kind of informed debate that is vital to the practice of politics in a liberal democracy. Only if one understands the nature of the civil rights ideology in our time, and appreciates the extent of its influence, can one begin to make sense of the politics of civil rights during the 1980s.

The Civil Rights Ideology and the Supreme Court:
Johnson v. Transportation Agency

Traces of the civil rights ideology can be found in virtually all of the court cases discussed in previous chapters, but one case decided by the Supreme Court during the Reagan years provides an exceptionally clear illustration of the extent to which the civil rights ideology had been embraced by a majority of the justices. On March 25, 1987, the Supreme Court handed down a decision that represented its most forceful repudiation yet of the nondiscrimination principle in civil rights policy.[21] The decision not only repealed Title VII of the Civil Rights Act where white males are concerned— thereby affirming the Berry-Ramirez postulate—but, as Justice Antonin Scalia noted in dissent, actually "inverted" it.

The case, *Johnson v. Transportation Agency*, tested the validity under Title VII of an affirmative action plan that resulted in the promotion of a female over a more qualified white male. Pursuant to a comprehensive affirmative action plan adopted by Santa Clara County, in California, the county's Transportation Agency had implemented, in December 1978, a plan to achieve "a statistically measurable yearly improvement in hiring, training and promotion of minorities and women throughout the Agency in all major job classifications where they are underrepresented."[22] In December 1979 the agency announced a vacancy for the position of road dispatcher, which had recently been reclassified as a "skilled craft" position, and for which the agency's affirmative action plan had set a "long-term goal" of 36 percent female representation. None of the skilled craft positions was then held by a female.[23]

Twelve county employees applied for the promotion, nine of whom were deemed qualified for the job; seven of these received a score of at least 70 in an oral interview, which certified them as eligible for selection by the appointing authority. The interview was conducted jointly by one man and one woman.

Included in the group of seven finalists were a man named Paul E. Johnson and a woman named Diane Joyce. Johnson's score of 75 tied him for second place after the initial interview; Joyce ranked third with a score of 73. According to a rating scale used by the county to interpret numerical interview scores, a score between 70 and 74 meant "would appoint with hesitation"; a score between 75 and 84 meant "would appoint without hesitation." (Interestingly, of the two interviewers it was the woman who had the lower opinion of Joyce. After she checked "yes" to the question, "Would you hire this person as a road dispatcher?" the woman wrote "but marginal," with marginal underlined for emphasis.)[24]

A second oral interview was conducted among the seven applicants who met the minimum score cutoff in the first exam. In this exam, conducted by three supervisors from the road operation division, Johnson ranked first; indeed, he was unanimously recommended by the board as the best qualified. Joyce ranked third, behind Johnson and another white male.[25] As the Road Operation Division director (the usual appointing authority) prepared to announce the promotion of Johnson, the merit selection process was abruptly derailed by the intervention of the county affirmative action coordinator, who appealed to the Transportation Agency director to overrule the division director and appoint Joyce to the position.[26] This he did, causing Johnson to file a lawsuit claiming that he had been a victim of sex discrimination in violation of Title VII of the Civil Rights Act.

In the district court, which ruled in Johnson's favor, two important facts emerged. One was that Santa Clara County's affirmative action plan was not intended to remedy past or present discrimination against women by the County. Indeed, the court could find no evidence that Santa Clara County had ever discriminated against women. Instead the plan was intended to eliminate a "'manifest imbalance' that reflected underrepresentation of women in 'traditionally segregated job categories.'"[27]

The other significant fact concerned the central role of gender in the decision to award the promotion to Joyce. In circumventing the painstaking merit selection procedure that would obviously have concluded with the promotion of Johnson, the agency director who instead selected Joyce for promotion "did not inspect the applications and related examination records of either [Paul Johnson] or Diane Joyce before making his decision" and moreover "did little or nothing to inquire into the results of the interview process and conclusions which [were] described as of critical importance to the selection process."[28] The district court thus concluded that Diane Joyce's gender was *the determining factor* in her selection for the position.[29] Specifically, it found that "[b]ased upon the examination results and the departmental interview, [Johnson] was more qualified for the position of Road Dispatcher than Diane Joyce," that "[b]ut for [Johnson's] sex, male, he would have been promoted to the position of Road Dispatcher," and that "[b]ut for Diane Joyce's sex, female, she would not have been appointed to the position. . . . "[30] The district court's judgment in favor of Johnson was reversed by the Court of Appeals for the Ninth Circuit, but the appellate court did not reject these factual findings.

Justice William Brennan, in a majority opinion joined by Marshall, Blackmun, Powell, and Stevens (O'Connor wrote a separate opinion concurring in the judgment), characterized the agency affirmative action plan as "a moderate, flexible, case-by-case approach to effecting a gradual improvement in the repre-sentation of minorities and women in the agency's workforce."[31] As the facts of the case make clear, however, it was also a machine for generating sex- and race-based discrimination of the most bla-tant kind. There can hardly be any doubt that the agency violated Section 703(a) of Title VII of the Civil Rights Act, whose exact language it is once again useful to quote:

> It shall be an unlawful employment practice for an employer—
>   (1) to fail or refuse to hire or to discharge any individual . . . with respect to his compensation, terms, conditions, or privi-leges of employment, because of such individual's race, color, religion, sex, or national origin; or
>   (2) to limit, segregate, or classify his employees or applicants for employment in any way which would deprive or tend to deprive any individual of employment opportunities or other-wise adversely affect his status as an employee, because of such individual's race, color, religion, sex, or national origin.

Earlier we saw how the Court had justified "voluntary" affir-mative action plans and judicial orders that had the effect of clearly violating Title VII, on the grounds that such measures were temporarily necessary to remedy previous discrimination. In-deed, in the *Sheet Metal Workers* case, the Court emphasized that discrimination against innocent white males could be justified only as a necessary by-product of efforts to remedy "egregious" discrimination against blacks. We also observed that discrimina-tion as understood by the Court—be it "egregious" or otherwise—might involve the use of virtually any standards or criteria that tend to yield a disparate outcome among races or sexes.

Perhaps that is why the *Johnson* decision was not hailed as a landmark case of monumental proportions, for in dispensing al-together with the ostensible requirement that past discrimination alone justifies "remedial" affirmative action, the case was pre-cisely that, at least in terms of the change in formal doctrine that it announced. Now the evil to be combated was "traditionally segregated job categories," defined as all job categories showing a statistical imbalance between the percentage of minorities or women in a given employer's workforce and the percentage of minorities or women in the area labor market or general population.

As a practical matter, however, the decision merely continued the theme of previous Title VII cases. It was novel only because it made explicit what was previously implicit: that a statistical imbalance favoring white males as a group is in itself sufficient to justify employment discrimination against individual members of the group.

This is not to say, however, that the *Johnson* ruling simply continued the status quo, for when considered against the backdrop of "disparate impact" Title VII case law beginning with the 1971 *Griggs v. Duke Power* decision, the *Johnson* ruling carried new and especially ominous implications for white males. The "disparate impact" line of cases, as we have seen, made it increasingly easy for minorities and women to establish *prima facie* discrimination against them by recourse to group statistics. The incentive that employers had thus been given to discriminate against white males in order to prevent or reduce the incidence of statistical disparities among groups—and hence the possibility of costly Title VII litigation—was bolstered by the Court's ruling in *Johnson* that any such discrimination was permissible under Title VII so long as it was carried out pursuant to an affirmative action plan. As Brennan explained:

> Once a plaintiff [such as Johnson] establishes a *prima facie* case that race or sex has been taken into account in an employer's employment decision, the burden shifts to the employer to articulate a nondiscriminatory rationale for its decision. *The existence of an affirmative action plan provides such a rationale.* If such a plan is articulated as the basis for the employer's decision, the burden shifts to the plaintiff to prove that the employer's justification is pretextual and the plan is invalid. As a practical matter, of course, an employer will generally seek to avoid a charge of pretext by presenting evidence in support of its plan. That does not mean, however, as petitioner suggests, that reliance on an affirmative action plan is to be treated as an affirmative defense requiring the employer to carry the burden of proving the validity of the plan. The burden of proving its invalidity remains on the plaintiff.[32]

Obviously none of this is authorized by Title VII. According to the judicial improvisation announced here, a white male who is the victim of race- or sex-based discrimination pursuant to an affirmative action plan can vindicate his Title VII right to non-discriminatory treatment *only* if he can prove that the plan is "pretextual," by which the Court apparently means unnecessary because of the absence of a statistical imbalance among groups. The ease with which minorities and women could bring Title VII suits under the disparate-impact theory of discrimination had now been combined with what was to all intents and purposes a judicial moratorium on reverse discrimination suits by white males. The probable effect of this was forecast by Justice Scalia:

> Thus after today's decision the *failure* to engage in reverse discrimination is economic folly, and arguably a breach of duty to shareholders or taxpayers, wherever the cost of anticipated Title VII litigation exceeds the cost of hiring less capable (though still minimally capable) workers. . . . A statute designed to establish a color-blind and gender-blind workplace has thus been converted into a powerful engine of racism and sexism, not merely *permitting* intentional race- and sex-based discrimination, but often making it, through operation of the legal system, practically compelled.[33]

In a separate opinion concurring in the Court's judgment, Justice John Paul Stevens took note of the inconsistency between the language of Title VII and the Court's purported interpretation of it, explaining the latter as follows:

> Antidiscrimination measures may benefit protected groups in two distinct ways. As a sword, such measures may confer benefits by specifying that a person's membership in a disadvantaged group must be a neutral, irrelevant factor in governmental or private decisionmaking or, alternatively, by compelling decisionmakers to give favorable consideration to disadvantaged group status. As a shield, an antidiscrimination statute can also help a member of a protected class by assuring decisionmakers in some instances that, when they elect for good reasons of their own to grant a preference of some sort to a minority citizen, they will not violate the law. The Court properly holds that the statutory shield allowed respondent to take Diane Joyce's sex into account in promoting her to the road dispatcher position.[34]

This explication of the purpose of "antidiscrimination measures" is clearly a reflection of Stevens's adherence to the civil
rights ideology. Antidiscrimination measures are not conceived as
measures to ensure that no one may legally be discriminated
against, but are understood rather as weapons with which to liberate the oppressed, in whatever way seems efficacious—be it as
sword or as shield. In trying to decide which construction of the
Civil Rights Act to follow—literal or ideological—Stevens writes
that "the only problem for me is whether to adhere to an author-
itative construction of the Act that is at odds with my understanding of the actual intent of the authors of the legislation. I conclude
without hesitation that I must answer that question in the affirmative. . . . "[35] In thus acknowledging the willful substitution of his
(and the majority's) own policy preference for that of the Congress
that passed the legislation he is now supposedly construing,
Stevens's opinion at least has the virtue of candor. He has all but
admitted his deliberate complicity in the repeal of Title VII, and
in the judicial enactment of the civil rights ideology in its stead. It
is possibly the most forthright admission of judicial malfeasance
ever made by a sitting justice.

None of the other pro-affirmative action justices has admitted
violating the intent of Congress; at most they acknowledged adhering to a less than literal construction of Title VII, but have
claimed nevertheless to be following the "spirit" of the statute.[36]
Before *Johnson*, that rationale had been repeated most recently in
the 1986 case of *Firefighters v. Cleveland*:

> It would be ironic indeed if a law triggered by a nation's concern
> over centuries of racial injustice and intended to improve the lot
> of those who had "been excluded from the American dream for
> so long" constituted the first legislative prohibition of all volun-
> tary, private race-conscious efforts to abolish traditional pat-
> terns of racial segregation and hierarchy.[37]

There can be no doubt that the intent of a majority of those in
the 88th Congress who voted for the Civil Rights Act was to enact
legislation that would have the effect of improving the lot of blacks
(and subsequently women), but it is also true that the sole reason
Congress engaged in the protracted exercise of drafting, debating,
and redrafting the Civil Rights Act was to fashion a bill that a

majority could accept. To do that, the bill had to specify in excru-
ciating detail just how its legislative purpose was to be achieved.
By the same token, Congress was abundantly clear in specifying
those measures that were *not* permissible to achieve the bill's purpose—and discrimination against *any individual* on the basis of
race or sex is one of them.

There is nothing ironic or exceptional about this outcome, as
an analogy to the criminal law will illustrate. Over the years, Congress and the state legislatures have enacted a vast body of law
prohibiting various forms of criminal conduct, and providing for
the punishment of those who commit criminal acts. The overall
purpose of these laws is to deter and punish criminal behavior. At
the same time, however, we have chosen not to authorize every
exercise of police power to achieve that purpose. Some uses of the
police power have been specifically proscribed; that is what the
federal rules of criminal procedure, not to mention the Fourth,
Fifth, and Sixth Amendments to the Constitution, are all about. It
is important to keep in mind that certain uses of police power are
proscribed *even though* their use would definitely serve the end of
deterring and punishing criminal behavior. In the same way, the
Civil Rights Act's exclusive focus on the individual, its failure
even to mention any specific groups, and its unqualified prohibition of race- and sex-based discrimination per se, constitute a set
of "procedural safeguards" designed to protect individual rights
against the egalitarian designs of public and private decision makers, even though such designs may arguably comport with the
overall purpose of the act. The justices' refusal to accept their responsibility to vindicate explicitly codified individual rights is, of
course, consistent with the civil rights ideology's stricture that the
only legitimate function of antidiscrimination law is to liberate the
oppressed class.

The Court's majority demonstrated its belief in the hidden
structure of domination as well, as its casual substitution of "traditional segregation" for "egregious discrimination" makes clear.
In *Weber*, the term "traditionally segregated job category" was
used to refer to the construction trades, from which blacks had
undeniably been excluded for generations. In *Johnson*, as Justice
Scalia observed, the position of road dispatcher in Santa Clara
County was "a 'traditionally segregated job category' *not* in the
Weber sense, but in the sense that, because of longstanding social

attitudes, it has not been regarded *by women themselves* as desirable work."[38] Scalia then proceeds to the heart of the matter—the hidden structure of domination that keeps women from participating in certain areas of life, and the liberation movement in which his colleagues have enlisted to dismantle the oppressive structure:

> There are, of course, those who believe that social attitudes which cause women themselves to avoid certain jobs and to favor others are as nefarious as conscious, exclusionary discrimination. Whether or not that is so (and there is assuredly no consensus on the point equivalent to our national consensus against intentional discrimination), the two phenomena are certainly distinct. And it is the alteration of social attitudes, rather than the elimination of discrimination, which today's decision approves as justification for state-enforced discrimination. This is an enormous expansion, undertaken without the slightest justification or analysis.[39]

Scalia is surely correct when he notes that "it is absurd to think that the nationwide failure of road maintenance crews, for example, to achieve the agency's ambition of 36.4 percent female representation is attributable primarily, if even substantially, to systematic exclusion of women eager to shoulder pick and shovel."[40] Whether individual women are themselves eager to shoulder pick and shovel is, however, merely a reflection of their subjective consciousness; it is the ideologist, rather than the actual oppressed, who is solely capable of grasping the objective conditions of oppression, and of identifying the structural impediments to liberation. If most women do not currently desire to work on road maintenance crews, then the hidden structure that nourishes such retrograde attitudes must be altered or destroyed. The *Johnson* decision is part of that historic campaign.

What of the eggs that must be broken in quest of the ideological omelette? Justice Scalia has proven himself so adept as a judge and as a political scientist that we can do no better than to let him have the last word on the meaning of the *Johnson* decision:

> It is unlikely that today's result will be displeasing to politically elected officials, to whom it provides the means of quickly accommodating the demands of organized groups to achieve concrete, numerical improvement in the economic status of

particular constituencies. Nor will it displease the world of corporate and governmental employers (many of whom have filed briefs *amici* in the present case, all on the side of Santa Clara) for whom the cost of hiring less qualified workers is often substantially less—and infinitely more predictable—than the cost of litigating Title VII cases and of seeking to convince federal agencies by nonnumerical means that no discrimination exists. In fact, the only losers in the process are the Johnsons of the country, for whom Title VII has been not merely repealed but actually inverted. The irony is that these individuals—predominantly unknown, unaffluent, unorganized—suffer this injustice at the hands of a Court fond of thinking itself the champion of the politically impotent. I dissent.[41]

CHAPTER SEVEN

Epilogue: The Supreme Court and Civil Rights in the Post-Reagan Era

During the last eight years, the Supreme Court has repeatedly joined Congress in rejecting attempts to turn back the clock on civil rights enforcement. Regrettably, over the past few months, some elements of the Reagan Administration Justice Department's views have found favor in the Supreme court.

—Ralph G. Neas, quoted by Charles Mohr

This book has examined the development of civil rights policy during the Reagan administration. Our treatment of this subject would not be complete, however, if we failed to attend to three cases decided by the Supreme Court in the spring of 1989, several months after the Reagan administration had left office. In one case, *Richmond v. J. A. Croson Co.*,[1] the Court considered whether legislatively mandated set-asides for minority-owned businesses in the letting of government contracts violated the equal protection clause of the Fourteenth Amendment. In *Wards Cove Packing Co. v. Atonio*[2] the Court revisited the nettlesome question concerning the proper scope and distribution of the evidentiary burden in "disparate impact" cases. In the third case, *Martin v. Wilks*,[3] the Court attempted to specify the circumstances under which adversely affected third parties would have legal standing to challenge an affirmative action consent decree under Title VII of the Civil Rights Act. Even though the administration had left office well before these cases were decided, it is arguable that each of the decisions was in some sense a product of the Reagan years. We shall elaborate this argument shortly—but first, the cases.

Richmond v. Croson: Curtailing the Use of "Set-Asides"

Undeterred by the Reagan administration's assault on race-conscious civil rights policies during the decade of the 1980s, many local governments around the country adopted so-called set-asides for minority- and female-owned businesses in the letting of public works contracts. One such local government was the Richmond, Virginia, city council, which in 1983 enacted something called the "Minority Business Utilization Plan." The plan altered the traditional practice of awarding construction contracts to the firm submitting the lowest bid by adding the stipulation that, as a further condition of doing business with the city, prime contractors must subcontract at least 30 percent of the dollar amount of the contract to one or more Minority Business Enterprises. An "MBE" was defined as "a business at least fifty-one percent of which is owned and controlled by minority group members." Minority group members were defined as "citizens of the United States who are Blacks, Spanish-speaking, Orientals, Indians, Eskimos, or Aleuts." It was not necessary for an MBE to be based in the Richmond area to qualify for the 30 percent set-aside, since there was no geographic limit to the plan. The avowed purpose of the plan was "remedial," in that it sought to promote "wider participation by minority business enterprises in the construction of public projects."[4]

The case of *Richmond v. J. A. Croson Co.* was brought by a contractor whose low bid on a city project was rejected because of his failure to comply with the plan's 30 percent minority set-aside requirement. The suit challenged the set-aside on equal protection grounds, and a panel of the Fourth Circuit Court of Appeals ruled that the plan did indeed violate both prongs of "strict scrutiny," the standard of review used by the Supreme Court in judging equal protection claims made against laws that contain "suspect classifications"—classifications based on race or ethnicity. There was no doubt that the Richmond set-aside program made use of a suspect classification. Writing for the Court, Justice Sandra O'Connor observed that the plan

> denies certain citizens the opportunity to compete for a fixed percentage of public contracts based solely upon their race. To whatever racial group these citizens belong, their "personal

rights" to be treated with equal dignity and respect are implicated by a rigid rule erecting race as the sole criterion in an aspect of public decisionmaking.[5]

The question before the Court was whether such a criterion was justified under the circumstances that prevailed in Richmond[*]—a city whose general population was 50 percent black, but where only 0.67 percent of municipal prime construction contracts were awarded to minority-owned firms between 1978 and 1983.[6]

To review, the Court had thus far employed a rule whereby the presence of a race-based classification in a law or government policy automatically triggers the application of an especially demanding standard of review, which the justices have termed "strict scrutiny." According to this doctrine, the law or policy in question can only survive the Court's strict scrutiny if each of the following questions can be answered in the affirmative: Does the law in question serve a "compelling" governmental objective? If it does serve a compelling governmental objective, are the means chosen by government to achieve said objective "narrowly tailored"? These two questions constitute the two prongs of strict scrutiny.

By a vote of 6 to 3, the Court affirmed the Court of Appeals judgment that the Richmond set-aside plan violated both prongs of strict scrutiny. The city argued that insofar as its plan was remedial, it unquestionably served a compelling public purpose. Further, the city interpreted the Court's decision in *Fullilove v. Klutznick* as conferring broad powers upon legislative bodies to remedy the effects of prior discrimination within a local industry.

---

[*]As an aside, it is interesting to note the prevailing circumstances of the construction industry both in Richmond and throughout the nation. The 30 percent set-aside for MBE's was adopted at a time when only 4.7 percent of all construction firms in the United States were minority-owned, and of these, 41 percent were located in California, New York, Illinois, Florida, and Hawaii. One would therefore expect that the ordinance would result in a higher percentage of city contracts being awarded to out-of-state firms, to the detriment of local contractors. Presumably many of the non-MBE firms in Richmond who would be losing business to out-of-state MBE's employ minorities, and hence these minority employees would also be hurt by the loss of business to out-of-state firms. The potentially perverse effects of the Richmond set-aside, while casting doubt on the wisdom of the legislation, do not properly affect the question concerning its constitutionality, however.

The J. A. Croson Company argued that while remedying the effects of past discrimination may indeed be a "compelling" governmental objective, the city was barred by the Supreme Court's decision in the *Wygant* case from attempting to remedy the effects of general societal discrimination. The *Wygant* decision made it clear, said Croson, that such remedies can be valid only if they were put in place for the express purpose of remedying the *city's own* discrimination.[7]

Justice O'Connor's plurality opinion attempted to steer a middle course. She noted that in the *Fullilove* case, where the Court upheld a set-aside plan adopted by Congress, the Court's decision was based heavily on the language of the Fourteenth Amendment, which assigns to Congress the exclusive authority to enforce legislatively the amendment's various provisions.* When the Court upheld the set-aside scheme in *Fullilove*, O'Connor implied, it did so largely out of deference to this constitutionally mandated congressional power. She then arrived at the obvious conclusion that the Court's reasoning in *Fullilove* could not be applied to the present case, which concerned the validity of legislation enacted by a city council.

Justice O'Connor also refused to embrace the position taken by the Croson Company (and by the Court of Appeals). It is true that the *Wygant* Court demanded "some showing of prior discrimination by the governmental unit involved" in order to justify a race-based layoff plan for its own employees, she wrote. The situation in *Richmond* was different, however, because Virginia state law gives the city of Richmond "legislative authority over its procurement policies, and [thus it] can use its spending powers to remedy private discrimination, if it identifies that discrimination with the particularity required by the Fourteenth Amendment."[8] The city could thus use its power to regulate local commerce to remedy past discrimination. But what degree of "particularity" did O'Connor believe was required by the Fourteenth Amendment in identifying such discrimination?

> If the city could show that it had essentially become a "passive participant" in a system of racial exclusion practiced by ele-

---

*Section 5 of the Fourteenth Amendment reads as follows: "The Congress shall have power to enforce, by appropriate legislation, the provisions of this article."

ments of the local construction industry, we think it clear that the city could take affirmative steps to dismantle such a system.[9]

It is important to point out that when Justice O'Connor used the pronoun "we" in the passage above, she was referring only to herself and Justices Rehnquist and White; her opinion was divided into several enumerated sections, and the section wherein this language appears (as well as the rest of her attempt to chart a middle course between *Wygant* and *Fullilove* on the "compelling objective" prong of strict scrutiny) was not part of the opinion of the Court.

Five of the other justices did, however, agree with Justice O'Connor's opinion that whatever the requisite degree of particularity in identifying prior discrimination for the purpose of defending a "remedial" set-aside quota, the city of Richmond had not even come close to meeting that burden. One might have thought that the adoption of a 30 percent quota—as opposed to, say, a 60 percent quota or 5 percent quota—reflected some empirically verifiable projection of the percentage of subcontracts that would have gone to minority construction firms in the absence of any previous discrimination. The Court, however, said

> it is sheer speculation how many minority firms there would be in Richmond absent past societal discrimination, just as it was sheer speculation how many minority medical students would have been admitted to the medical school at Davis absent past discrimination in educational opportunities. Defining these sorts of injuries as "identified discrimination" would give local governments license to create a patchwork of racial preferences based on statistical generalizations about any particular field of endeavor.[10]

We might pause here to consider a potentially significant question raised by this analysis. Suppose the city had given "bonus points"* to minority contractors in the competitive bidding process, rather than adopting a rigid numerical set-aside for them.

---

*Bonus points could take the form of a percentage reduction (say 10 percent) in the dollar amount of the bids submitted by minority-owned firms. Thus, an MBE's bid of $100,000 on a construction project would be treated as a $90,000 bid for competitive bidding purposes, even though all parties concerned would understand that the "real" bid was $100,000.

That scheme would constitute a "racial preference based on statistical generalizations," but it is not clear that the Court would
view such a preference as harshly as it viewed the 30 percent set-
aside. It is perhaps telling that the passage quoted above refers to
the numerical quota that was struck down in the *Bakke* case—a
case in which the Court nevertheless endorsed the use of race as
one "factor" in public decision making. Justice O'Connor's opinion leaves much room for doubt as to whether the Court's aversion
to numerical quotas and set-asides applies to racial preference
schemes in general.

That is perhaps one reason why Justice Antonin Scalia thought
it necessary to contribute a separate concurring opinion in the
case. "In my view," wrote Scalia, "there is only one circumstance
in which the States may act *by race* to 'undo the effects of past
discrimination': where that is necessary to eliminate their own
maintenance of a system of unlawful racial classification."[11] He
approved of O'Connor's distinction between "societal" discrimination and "identified" discrimination, and of her suggestion that
only the latter could be remedied in a manner consistent with the
demands of strict scrutiny. But Scalia took issue with the notion
that such a remedy could take the form of a general racial preference. Referring to the distinction between societal and identified
discrimination, he argued that

> the reason that would make a difference is not, as the Court
> states, that it would justify race-conscious action but rather that
> it would enable race-neutral remediation. Nothing prevents
> Richmond from according a contracting preference to identified
> victims of discrimination. While most of the beneficiaries might
> be black, neither the beneficiaries nor those disadvantaged by
> the preference would be identified *on the basis of their race*. In
> other words, far from justifying racial classification, identifica-
> tion of actual victims of discrimination makes it less supportable
> than ever, because more obviously unneeded.[12]

In other words, Scalia would adopt as an absolute rule the victim-
specific approach to remedying equal protection violations that
was urged on various occasions by the Reagan administration.
Such a remedy would not even be subjected to strict scrutiny because, by definition, it would not involve the use of a racial

classification or preference. However, in evaluating the scope of the Court's decision in the *Richmond* case, it is important to bear in mind that Scalia wrote only for himself; his views do not reflect those of a majority on the Court.

If the first prong of strict scrutiny was violated by Richmond's inability to demonstrate that its racial set-aside served a compelling governmental objective, it hardly mattered whether the second prong—inquiring into the propriety of the means used to achieve the city's objective—could be satisfied by the city. It stands to reason, after all, that once the end of a policy is declared illegitimate, the policy cannot be redeemed simply by showing that the means used to accomplish the end were benign. Nevertheless, the Court extended its inquiry to include a brief examination of the city's means of remedying discrimination—the 30 percent set-aside quota. Justice O'Connor observed that all the city's arguments concerning the need to remedy past discrimination in the construction industry were cast in reference to the experience of blacks. She pointed out, however, that "there is *absolutely no evidence* of past discrimination against Spanish-speaking, Oriental, Indian, Eskimo, or Aleut persons in any aspect of the Richmond construction industry."[13] A program that offered a "remedial" benefit to groups that had not experienced discrimination of any kind could hardly be characterized as a "narrowly tailored" remedy. What is more, said O'Connor, is that there was no evidence that the city had considered the adoption of some race-neutral means—such as offering a partial subsidy to small construction firms—as a way of increasing minority business participation in city contracting. Finally, the adoption of rigid 30 percent quota reflected either a commitment to "outright racial balancing"[14] or a desire for administrative convenience, since the alternative to a quota would likely have been a case-by-case review of each request for relief. Either motive, said the Court, was incompatible with the requirement that the means used to remedy past discrimination must be narrowly tailored.

The three dissenting justices consisted of the reliable triumvirate of Thurgood Marshall, William Brennan, and Harry Blackmun. Writing for all three, Justice Marshall took aim at certain inconsistencies he found between the Court's decision in *Fullilove* and its decision in the present case. Beyond that, he chastised the majority for its lack of deference to the legislative wisdom of local public officials, thus making a curious "states' rights" argument—curious, that is, considering the reputation of its author:

> [By] disregarding the testimony of local leaders and the judgment of local government, the majority does violence to the very principles of comity within our federal system which this Court has long championed. Local officials, by virtue of their proximity to, and their expertise with, local affairs, are exceptionally well-qualified to make determinations of public good "within their respective spheres of authority."[15]

If Marshall found it useful suddenly to transform himself into an advocate of "states' rights," he apparently found it just as expedient to dissociate himself from a one of the more well-worn arguments in support of judicial deference to legislatively enacted affirmative action plans. The argument holds that when non-minority-dominated legislative bodies enact racial preference schemes that favor minorities, the Court should adopt a more relaxed standard of review on the theory that the majority group's decision to, in effect, disadvantage itself constitutes a relatively benign form of discrimination. A generally unarticulated corollary of this argument, however, is that if a legislative body dominated by members of one group enacts a racial preference scheme that favors *that* group and disadvantages *other* groups, a more rigorous standard of review is called for, since such discrimination has the appearance of being anything but benign. In her opinion for the Court, Justice O'Connor called attention to this when she noted that blacks had a voting majority on the nine-member Richmond city council that voted to adopt the 30 percent quota. Not surprisingly, Justice Marshall and his co-dissenters took umbrage at the suggestion that the city council was practicing "simple racial politics":

> The majority's view that remedial measures undertaken by municipalities with black leadership must face a stiffer test of Equal Protection Clause scrutiny than remedial measures undertaken by municipalities with white leadership implies a lack of political maturity on the part of this Nation's elected minority officials that is totally unwarranted. Such insulting judgments have no place in constitutional jurisprudence.[16]

It would appear that for Marshall, however, all racial preference schemes are "remedial" *if* they benefit minorities. Hence, a majority-black city council that adopts a quota for blacks will never be regarded by Marshall in the way that he would regard a white-majority city council that adopted a quota for whites. Surely he would not label as "insulting" the suspicion that the white-majority city council was practicing simple racial politics. Marshall wants to accuse the majority of using a racial double standard, whereby "black leadership" and "white leadership" are subjected to different levels of judicial scrutiny when each leadership adopts policies that favor blacks. But since the central premise in the original argument is that a decision by a group to disadvantage its *own members* is, by definition, never invidious, it would appear that the dissenters, rather than the Court's majority, are the ones who want it both ways. That is, they want the central premise of the original argument to be honored whenever white political leadership enacts policies that favor blacks, and they want the presumption of invidious discrimination to be applied when white political leadership enacts measures aimed at favoring whites. But they do not want the presumption of invidious discrimination to apply to black political leadership that enacts measures aimed at favoring blacks.

From the perspective of Marshall, Brennan, and Blackmun, it is inconceivable that discriminatory policies that favor blacks and disfavor whites could ever be invidious or malevolent; whether the levers of political power are controlled by white politicians or by black politicians makes not a bit of difference. Equal protection jurisprudence, like civil rights jurisprudence generally, is all about liberating the oppressed. Policies such as Richmond's 30 percent set-aside for minority-owned construction firms could hardly be regarded by the dissenters as *violations* of equal protection.

Wards Cove: Narrowing the Meaning of Discrimination

In *Wards Cove Packing Co. v. Atonio*, the Supreme Court was once again called upon to clarify a lingering ambiguity in the disparate-impact theory of illegal discrimination, as it had done on numerous occasions since it first invented the doctrine in the course of deciding *Griggs v. Duke Power* in 1971. In Chapter 3 we saw the

Court's most recent improvisation on the disparate-impact theory: In *Connecticut v. Teal* (1982) the Court ruled that the disparate racial impact of any particular stage of an employer's hiring or promotion process would suffice to establish a *prima facie* case of illegal discrimination—notwithstanding "bottom-line" results that show statistical parity among racial groups.

In our general discussion of disparate-impact analysis we noted that one recurrent problem (not addressed by the Court in *Connecticut v. Teal*) concerned the selection of an appropriate cohort for purposes of statistical comparison when courts and administrative agencies attempt to determine the extent of disparate impact resulting from a particular employment practice. Generally courts have favored an approach that compares the percentage of successful minority job candidates to the percentage of minorities in the local labor market, although they have failed to agree on a common definition of the "local" labor market. For jobs that require specialized skills or training, some courts—but not all—have insisted that the appropriate comparison for establishing disparate impact is between the percentage of successful minority candidates and percentage of minorities in the general labor market who possess the requisite training or skills.*

In the *Wards Cove* case, however, the Supreme Court was asked to endorse a novel method of establishing disparate impact. According to this method, adopted by the Ninth Circuit Court of Appeals, disparate impact—and thus a *prima facie* case of discrimination in violation of Title VII—could be established simply by showing that the percentage of minority-group members holding low-paying, unskilled jobs in a particular firm was substantially greater than the percentage of minority-group members employed in higher-paying, skilled or semi-skilled jobs in the same firm. To be sure, the teleological view of equal opportunity that is captured in the Ninth Circuit's formulation of disparate impact has been a driving conceptual force behind the affirmative action movement for years, as we noted in Chapter 2.

The general idea that a group's statistical representation within the upper echelon of an organization should be roughly equal to its statistical representation within the organization's

---

*See the discussion of *Wygant v. Jackson Bd. of Education* in Chapter 3.

lower echelon is obviously the basis for much of the widespread criticism of professional major league football and baseball over the relative paucity of blacks in coaching and "front office" positions. It is one thing, however, for the National Football League's critics to use the argument from the teleological view of equal opportunity to urge the NFL to adopt preferential hiring criteria to increase rapidly the percentage of blacks in these positions, but quite another for the statistical disparity between black players and black coaches to be the sole basis for establishing a *prima facie* case of illegal discrimination in the hiring of coaches. If the Court had affirmed the Ninth Circuit's ruling in *Wards Cove*, it would have paved the way for hundreds of such cases.

The Wards Cove Packing Company was a salmon cannery operating in remote, sparsely populated areas of Alaska. Because of the seasonal nature of the salmon industry, the cannery operated only during the period of the salmon run; during the rest of the year it lay idle. These two factors—the cannery's remote location and its sporadic operation—caused the cannery's management to hire most of its workers from outside of Alaska, primarily from Washington and Oregon. Jobs at the Wards Cove Packing Company fell into two general categories: cannery line jobs, which were generally unskilled positions, and noncannery jobs, which for the most part were skilled positions. The noncannery jobs generally paid more than the cannery jobs. Noncannery workers were predominantly white and were hired through the company's offices in Washington and Oregon. The cannery workers, on the other hand, consisted mostly of Filipinos and Alaska Natives, the former having been hired through a hiring hall agreement with a predominantly Filipino union local in Seattle, and the latter having been hired from local villages.

In 1974 a group of current and former nonwhite cannery workers brought a suit against their employer, charging that the racial stratification of the Wards Cove workforce was directly attributable to the company's hiring and promotion practices. According to the plaintiffs, the challenged practices—which included nepotism, a "rehire preference," a lack of objective hiring criteria, separate hiring channels for cannery and noncannery jobs, a practice of not promoting from within—were in violation of Title VII on the basis of both the disparate-treatment and the disparate-impact theories discrimination. The "disparate-treatment" theory of discrimination—where an individual is treated differently from other individuals *because of* his race, ethnicity, or sex—is, as we have seen, the only form of discrimination addressed by the actual language of Title VII. Neither the district court nor the Court of Appeals found any merit in the plaintiffs' disparate-treatment claim. After all, none of the challenged practices involved the use of race or ethnicity as a determining factor in hiring and promotion decisions; indeed, the challenged practices were undoubtedly responsible for the inability of many whites to obtain cannery jobs. The district court also found the plaintiffs' disparate-*impact* argument unpersuasive, but on this point the Court of Appeals reversed the district court's judgment. Wards Cove appealed, and the Supreme Court agreed to hear the case.

On June 5, 1989, the Court handed down a 5-to-4 decision that overturned the judgment of the Court of Appeals. Writing for the majority,* Justice Byron White repeatedly attacked the Ninth Circuit's unorthodox use of statistical evidence in the case. Quoting from an earlier decision[17] in which the Court had discerned a "comparison [that] fundamentally misconceived the role of statistics in employment discrimination cases," Justice White reiterated that the "proper comparison is between the racial composition of the at-issue jobs and the racial composition of the qualified population in the relevant labor market."[18] As for the statistical comparison that had informed the Ninth Circuit's decision in the case, White at times seemed astonished at the enormity of the lower court's error:

> Most obviously, with respect to the skilled noncannery jobs at issue here, the cannery work force in no way reflected the "pool of *qualified* job applicants" or the "*qualified* population in the labor force." Measuring alleged discrimination in the selection of accountants, managers, boat captains, electricians, doctors, and engineers—and the long list of other "skilled" noncannery positions [. . .]—by comparing the number of nonwhites filling cannery worker positions is nonsensical.[19]

White offered an example to illustrate the absurdity of the Court of Appeals' theory. He pointed to the plaintiff's own

---

*The justices in the majority were White, Rehnquist, Scalia, O'Connor, and Kennedy.

statistics, which showed that 17 percent of the most recent hires for medical jobs and 15 percent of the new hires for office jobs were nonwhite. Suppose, White suggested, that fewer than 15–17 percent of the applicants for these jobs were nonwhite.[*] The Court of Appeals' theory would nevertheless have permitted the establishment of a *prima facie* case of racial discrimination under Title VII, for the simple reason that nonwhites comprised 52 percent of the workers employed in "cannery jobs." To avoid this result, said White, an employer might be led to "adopt racial quotas, insuring that no portion of his workforce deviates from the other portions thereof. . . . "[20] Paradoxically—and perversely from the standpoint of unskilled minority workers—the recourse to quotas in this scenario could take the form of covert *limiting* quotas for nonwhites in cannery jobs just as readily as it could take the form of preferential quotas for nonwhites in noncannery jobs. Remember that Wards Cove used a predominantly Filipino union local as its main hiring channel for noncannery jobs. If it were to switch to a predominantly white union local, the statistical disparities between whites and nonwhites in the two job categories might vanish altogether. This possibility was not lost on the Court's majority. "Under the Court of Appeals approach," wrote Justice White, "it is possible that *with no change whatsoever* in their hiring practices for noncannery workers—the jobs at issue in this lawsuit—petitioners could make respondents' prima facie case of disparate impact 'disappear.'"[21]

To this point the Court had done nothing that would have constituted a "rollback" of previous disparate-impact cases. It had simply declined an invitation to take disparate-impact theory further down a road leading ultimately to *de facto* mandatory quotas in the American workplace. However, when the Court reversed the decision of the Ninth Circuit Court of Appeals after rejecting its unorthodox approach to disparate-impact claims, it remanded the case so that a determination could be made as to whether the district court record would support a disparate-impact claim made on more conventional grounds. The Court then set out to clarify the means by which a valid disparate-impact claim might

---

[*]We may go White one better and imagine that only 5 or 6 percent of the applicants were nonwhite, but that Wards Cove had a preferential hiring policy for nonwhites who applied for these positions.

be made. The result of this exercise was the assignment to plaintiffs of a somewhat more demanding burden of proof than they were heretofore accustomed to. Ironically—and, it must be said, ingeniously—the rationale behind the Court's partial rollback of disparate-impact doctrine was rooted in the logic of *Connecticut v. Teal*—the very case that the Court had used to accomplish its most recent *expansion* of the doctrine.

In the *Teal* case, the Court had ruled that an employer could not point to racial parity at the "bottom line" of its hiring or promotion process as a way of avoiding liability under Title VII if there were a disparate impact in any particular component of the employment practice used by the employer. Now, in *Wards Cove*, the Court declared that even if on remand the plaintiffs were able to establish that nonwhites are statistically underrepresented in the jobs in question, "this alone will *not* suffice to make out a *prima facie* case of disparate impact."[22] The plaintiffs, the Court explained,

> will also have to demonstrate that the disparity they complain of is the result of one or more of the employment practices that they are attacking here, specifically showing that each challenged practice has a significantly disparate impact on employment opportunities for whites and nonwhites.[23]

One could appreciate the fairness of such a rule, the Court implied, by placing it in the context of the *Teal* case:

> Just as an employer cannot escape liablity under Title VII by demonstrating that, "at the bottom line," his workforce is racially balanced (where particular hiring practices may operate to deprive minorities of employment opportunities) [. . .], a Title VII plaintiff does not make out a case of disparate impact simply by showing that, "at the bottom line," there is racial *imbalance* in the workforce.[24]

Anticipating criticism that this new "specific causation requirement" (as the Court called it) would be unduly burdensome on Title VII plaintiffs, the Court cited "liberal discovery rules," which, in combination with federal regulations requiring most employers to maintain records showing the impact that their tests and other selection procedures have had on various groups, would make it possible for plaintiffs to avail themselves of the data and information they would need to meet the new standard. True, Title VII plaintiffs might have to spend more, and their lawyers work harder, than before, but no more so than plaintiffs in non-Title VII lawsuits.

Finally, the Court added one more revision to the disparate-impact doctrine, this one having to do with the "business necessity" requirement. Previously, employers with respect to whom a *prima facie* case of disparate impact had been established would, as a consequence, be required to prove to a court's satisfaction that the challenged procedure was "substantially job-related." Now, said the Court, although such employers would still carry "the burden of producing evidence of a business *justification* for his employment practice," the plaintiff would henceforth be assigned the "burden of *persuasion*"[25]—that is, the burden of persuading a trial court that the employer's "justification" for utilizing the challenged practice is untenable. This was certainly a departure from the Supreme Court's own precedents, although the Court pretended as though it was merely correcting lower court error. "There is no requirement," wrote Justice White, "that the challenged practice be 'essential' or 'indispensable' to the employer's business for it to pass constitutional muster: this degree of scrutiny would be almost impossible for most employers to meet, and would result in a host of evils [such as recourse to quota hiring]."[26] White phrased this part of his opinion as if he were speculating about what would happen prospectively, but there can be little doubt that he was actually describing a phenomenon that had already occurred.

The dissenters in the case were Brennan, Marshall, Blackmun, and Stevens; the latter two justices wrote opinions. Justice Stevens, whose opinion in *Johnson v. Transportation Agency* enthusiastically endorsed what Stevens acknowledged as the Court's departure from the original meaning and purpose of Title VII, now chided the *Wards Cove* majority for "turning a blind eye to the meaning and purpose of Title VII. . . . "[27] The apparent inconsistency between Stevens' two opinions disappears, however, as Stevens' *Wards Cove* dissent goes on to equate the "meaning and purpose of Title VII" with "a longstanding rule of law."[28] Judicial decisions that substantially revise legislative enactments undertaken by Congress are one thing, but decisions that, in turn, revise *those* decisions cannot be countenanced: "I cannot join this latest sojourn into judicial activism," Stevens solemnly announced.[29]

Whereas Stevens complained about the majority's revision of the Court's disparate-impact analysis, Justice Harry Blackmun's brief dissent was concerned mostly with setting forth his own revisionist account of the facts surrounding the case, based on his impressionistic reading of the lower court record. "The salmon industry as described by this record takes us back to a kind of overt and institutionalized discrimination we have not dealt with in years . . . ," he declared. "This industry long has been characterized by a taste for discrimination of the old-fashioned sort: a preference for hiring nonwhites to fill its lowest-level positions, on the condition that they stay there."[30] In effect, Blackmun had accused both the district court and the Court of Appeals of erring in their dismissal of the plaintiff's disparate-treatment claims, although he offered no legal analysis of his own to counter theirs.

The case before the Supreme Court, however, came on appeal from a Court of Appeals ruling that was adverse to the *employer* with respect to the disparate-*impact* claim, so the plaintiff's unsuccessful disparate-*treatment* claim is not even an issue in the case. No matter. Making it appear as if the case was really about "discrimination of the old-fashioned sort" afforded Blackmun an opportunity gratuitously to question the majority's faithfulness to the civil rights ideology, and hence its competence to adjudicate civil rights cases: "One wonders whether the majority still believes that race discrimination—or, more accurately, race discrimination against nonwhites—is a problem in our society, or even remembers that it ever was."[31*]

Martin v. Wilks: Affirming the Right to One's Day in Court

A week later, on June 12, 1989, the Court announced its decision in the case of *Martin v. Wilks*. The circumstances that led to this case were all too familiar: A group of white firefighters in Birmingham,

---

*Writing for the majority, Justice White responded to Blackmun's "hyperbolic allegation" as follows: "Of course, it is unfortunately true that race discrimination exists in our country. That does not mean, however, that it exists at the canneries —or more precisely, that it has been proven to exist at the canneries." See 104, L.Ed. 2d at 746, n.4.

Alabama had challenged a Title VII consent decree that gave preference to blacks in the competition for promotions in the Birmingham Fire Department, with the result that black firefighters were being promoted over more qualified whites. The specific issue presented by *Martin v. Wilks* did not, however, concern the validity of the consent decree per se. Rather, the question before the Court was whether the adversely affected white firefighters had legal standing to sue the city for allegedly practicing reverse discrimination pursuant to the terms of the decree. Despite a virtually uninterrupted, twenty-year trend toward a general liberalization of the rules of standing, the right of the *Wilks* plaintiffs to bring *their* lawsuit was upheld by a bare majority of five Supreme Court justices. Not surprisingly, the Court divided along exactly the same lines as it had in *Wards Cove.*

The consent decree had been entered in 1981, following years of litigation between the City of Birmingham and black plaintiffs who claimed that the city's fire department had discriminated against them with respect to both hiring and promotion. Two trials were held. In one, judgment was entered in favor of the plaintiffs —to screen job applicants the city had used a test that was biased, said the district court. The second trial examined the allegation of discrimination with respect to promotions, and it was this trial that culminated in the 1981 consent decree. The decree, which established a 50 percent promotion quota for blacks, was approved by the court over objections filed by a group of white firefighters, as well as by a group of black firefighters who charged that the decree was an inadequate remedy. City authorities thus began to implement the terms of the decree.

Several months after implementation was begun, the city announced the promotion of several black firefighters who, according to at least some of the whites in the department, were less qualified than certain white candidates for promotion. The whites who had been passed over for promotion—a different group of whites from the ones who had filed objections to the decree before it was entered—now sought to bring a Title VII suit against the city, alleging reverse discrimination. A district court judge ruled that if the promotion of blacks was required by the terms of the decree, the city would in effect be immunized from a "collateral attack" launched by third parties such as the white firefighters in *Wilks.* The trial then focused exclusively on the question of whether the disputed promotions were required by the terms of the decree. Finding the answer to be yes, the district court granted a motion to dismiss the plaintiffs' suit on the grounds that it constituted an impermissible collateral attack on a valid consent decree.

The Court of Appeals for the Eleventh Circuit reversed the district court's judgment, specifically rejecting the doctrine of "impermissible collateral attack." Such a doctrine, the court observed, would contravene "the policy against requiring third parties to submit to bargains in which their interests were either sacrificed or ignored."[32] The court thus remanded the case for trial of the discrimination claims, with the suggestion that methods of evaluating race-conscious measures in employment ought not to vary—consent decrees should be judged in the same way that voluntary affirmative action plans are judged.[33] It was this ruling that the Supreme Court was asked to review on appeal.

The Supreme Court's inquiry focused on two questions: First, did the white firefighters forgo their day in court when they failed to intervene voluntarily at the "fairness hearing" that preceded the entering of the consent decree, or should they have been formally "joined" in the proceedings, on the premise that their interest in the case was equivalent to that of a formal party? This premise, in turn, necessarily led to the second question: Were the white firefighters legally "bound" by the terms of the consent decree, or were they merely affected by the decisions of those (such as the city's personnel board) who were truly bound by the decree?

In answer to the first question, Justice Rehnquist, writing for the majority, quoted from an opinion written by the venerable Louis Brandeis:

> The law does not impose upon any person absolutely entitled to a hearing the burden of voluntary intervention in a suit to which he is a stranger. . . . Unless duly summoned to appear in a legal proceeding, a person not a privy may rest assured that a judgment recovered therein will not affect his legal rights.[34]

But were the *Wilks* plaintiffs "absolutely entitled" to a hearing? That, according to Brandeis, would seem to depend on whether their "legal rights" were "affected." In other words, it would depend on whether the *Wilks* plaintiffs were "bound" by the consent decree.

In the view of the four dissenters, the quotation from Justice Brandeis was inapt because the white firefighters were not bound by the decree. They were not "actual parties to litigation," wrote Justice Stevens in an opinion joined by Justices Brennan, Marshall, and Blackmun. Rather, the *Wilks* plaintiffs were "persons who merely have the kind of interest that may as a practical matter be impaired by the outcome of a case."[35] As such, they had a right to intervene in the action "in a timely manner." "But," Stevens continued,

> if they remain on the sidelines, they may be harmed as a practical matter *even though their legal rights are unaffected*. One of the disadvantages of sideline-sitting is that the bystander has no right to appeal from a judgment no matter how harmful it may be.[36]

But wait. Didn't the plaintiffs allege that the City of Birmingham violated their legal right to be free from racial discrimination in the workplace, which right is guaranteed under Title VII of the Civil Rights Act? By confidently asserting that the decree did not affect the plaintiffs' legal rights, the dissenting justices would appear to have prejudged the central issue that the district court was supposed to examine on remand. In fact, these justices were simply arguing from a central tenet of the civil rights ideology—white firefighters are by definition not among the oppressed, and therefore they have no legal rights under Title VII. Listen further to Justice Stevens:

> In this case there is no dispute about the fact that the respondents are not parties to the consent decrees. It follows as a matter of course that they are not bound by those decrees. Those judgments could not, and did not, deprive them of any legal rights. *The judgments did, however, have a practical impact on respondents' opportunities for advancement in their profession.*[37]

If this "practical impact" meant that equal opportunity for advancement was denied to certain individuals because of a racial quota that disfavored members of their group, could it be seriously maintained that such individuals suffered no loss of their legal rights under Title VII? Putting the question in a race-neutral way such as this, the obvious answer is no. Adherents of the civil rights ideology, however, refuse to apply race-neutral principles to such questions, so for them the answer is always contingent on the race of the parties.

Recall that the *Wilks* dissenters were the same four justices who, together with Justice White, formed the majority in *Connecticut v. Teal*. In that case, which also involved allegations of racial discrimination in the awarding of promotions, the plaintiffs were black. According to these justices, the alleged denial of equal opportunity in *Teal* had everything to do with the plaintiffs' legal rights under Title VII. There they joined in an opinion which emphasized that "Title VII guarantees these individual respondents the *opportunity* to compete equally with white workers," and that it "speaks . . . in terms of *limitations* and *classifications* that would tend to deprive any individual of employment *opportunities*."[38] Where white firefighters' "opportunities for advancement" are concerned, however, Title VII is utterly unavailing. Such people can have no legal right to nondiscriminatory treatment; they only have "interests." To all intents and purposes, then, the question of whether the *Wilks* plaintiffs were, in fact, victims of reverse discrimination was not even justiciable in the view of Justices Stevens, Brennan, Blackmun, and Marshall.

Reaction to the Decisions

In each of the the three decisions discussed here the Supreme Court stopped well short of repealing any substantial element of existing civil rights doctrine. In *Richmond v. Croson*, the majority refused to heed Justice Scalia's call for the abolition of discriminatory policies in the guise of race-conscious group "remedies," in favor of a race-neutral, victim-specific approach to remedying discrimination. In *Wards Cove v. Atonio*, the Court was presented with an opportunity to fashion a wholesale repudiation of the disparate-impact theory of discrimination, but declined to do so. To the contrary, its revision of disparate-impact doctrine was so minor that it left substantially intact the expansive approach to disparate-impact theory taken by the Court in *Connecticut v. Teal*. In *Martin v. Wilks* the Court cast no aspersions on the propriety of race-conscious affirmative action consent decrees; it simply said that those whose legal rights are impaired by these devices should be permitted to use the civil rights laws to attack them in court.

The civil rights elite responded to the decisions as if the Thirteenth Amendment had suddenly been repealed. The response of the Rev. Joseph E. Lowery, president of the Southern Christian Leadership Conference, was typical: In affirming the right of the *Wilks* plaintiffs to have their day in court, the Court was attempting "to hide racism under a cloak of legalism. . . . This assault on affirmative action reflects the insidiously insensitive nature of the Reagan administration,"[39] Lowery averred. "Night has fallen on the Court as far as civil rights are concerned. We are seeing the unraveling of gains we thought were secure," was the plaintive response of Benjamin Hooks, executive director of the NAACP.[40] At a news conference several days later, Hooks escalated the level of his bombast: The current Supreme Court, he declared, is "more dangerous to this nation than any Bull Connor with a fire hose; than any Jim Clark with a billy club; more dangerous than any Ross Barnett standing, saying, 'they shall not pass;' more dangerous than George Wallace proclaiming, 'Segregation today, segregation tomorrow, segregation forever.'" If Congress did not act to correct legislatively the Supreme Court's execrable behavior, Hooks threatened, "then we think the only recourse left to us is civil disobedience, on a scale which has never been seen in this country before."[41] "Chipping Away at Civil Rights" was the tendentious title that the editors of *Time* magazine chose for their story about the rulings.[42] On and on went the familiar refrain.

The Court's critics were almost certainly right about one thing. Although the Court had not gone so far as to implement the comprehensive reformulation of civil rights policy that had been urged by the Reagan administration Justice Department, the three decisions discussed in this chapter really did reflect to some extent the influence of the administration. What is not so clear is the nature of that influence. Did the Reaganite arguments in support of a race- and gender-neutral regime of civil rights belatedly persuade certain justices on the Supreme Court to change their views? Or was the Reagan administration's influence limited solely to the personnel changes that were effected on the Court during the Reagan years? The media were quick to apprehend that the three newest justices, Sandra O'Connor, Antonin Scalia, and William Kennedy—all of whom were Reagan appointees—had joined with veteran William Rehnquist, who had been elevated to the position of Chief Justice by Reagan, to form part of the majority in *Croson*, *Wards Cove*, and *Wilks*. In particular, William Kennedy, the final Reagan appointee and hence the newest member of the Court at the time these decisions were handed down, distinguished himself as being every bit as much of a reform-minded civil rights jurist as Scalia. In the *Croson* case, he filed a separate concurring opinion that not only praised Scalia's concurring opinion, but also implied that the equal protection clause prevents not just states and municipalities, but Congress as well, from adopting racial set-asides and quotas.[43]*

If civil rights reform was achieved through judicial appointments alone, the efforts of the Reagan Justice Department would appear to have been in vain. One could say in retrospect that the administration might as well have accepted the race-conscious regime of civil rights that it inherited insofar as the behavior of the Justice Department was concerned, while biding its time until presented with the inevitable opportunity to fill Supreme Court vacancies. But this will not do. For one thing, the administration that assumed office in 1981 could not count on having a longevity that would span two terms, which meant that even in light of the advanced age of a majority of incumbent justices, the administration could not realistically expect to be able substantially to remake the Court by replacing retired or deceased justices. If the administration was to use the courts to reformulate civil rights policy, it would have to take its case directly to the Court as it found it, as opposed to sitting on its hands and waiting for the chance to appoint its own reform-minded justices. Besides, as the failure of the Robert Bork nomination would eventually demonstrate, it was by no means certain that the administration would be able to win Senate confirmation for its Supreme Court nominees. Nor could the administration assume that each of its nominees, once confirmed, would consistently support the administration's positions, as the case of Sandra O'Connor demonstrates.

The fact is that even with the three Supreme Court appointments that the administration was able to make, those three, in

---

*Consider the following passage from Kennedy's opinion: "[The] process by which a law that is an equal protection violation when enacted by a State becomes transformed to an equal protection guarantee when enacted by Congress poses a difficult proposition for me; but as it is not before us, any reconsideration of that issue must await some further case."

combination with Rehnquist, amounted to only four votes. To carry the day the administration would need one more vote—one of the other justices would have to be converted. As it happened, one apparently did convert—Byron White. The same Byron White who had voted with the Brennan-Marshall-Blackmun triad to uphold the validity of racial quotas in the *Bakke* case, the same Byron White who had voted with the *Weber* majority to shield race-conscious job apprenticeship programs from Title VII's mandate of equal opportunity, could by the end of the Reagan era be found voting regularly against racial preference schemes. He not only voted with the Reagan appointees in the three cases discussed in this chapter (having written the opinion for the Court in *Wards Cove*), but joined Rehnquist and Scalia in dissent in *Johnson v. Transportation Agency*, the most recent landmark civil rights case prior to the Spring 1989 decisions.

Who is to say that the shift in White's thinking was not spurred, at least in part, by the controversy over civil rights policy that was generated by the Reagan initiatives? One need not go so far as to say that White was finally persuaded by the force of the arguments set forth in the Justice Department's legal briefs. One need only observe that the Reagan initiatives forced the defenders of the status quo to reveal their own peculiar biases and assumptions about the nexus between civil rights and social justice in late twentieth century America. To the extent that people were willing to pay attention to what was revealed, the administration's labors may well have been worth the effort.

Notes

1 INTRODUCTION

Epigraph: John C. Livingston, *Fair Game? Inequality and Affirmative Action* (San Francisco: W. H. Freeman and Co., 1979), p. 7

1. Victoria Sackett, "Ignoring the People," *Policy Review* (Spring 1980), p. 17.
2. Ibid.
3. See, e.g., Tom W. Smith and Paul B. Sheatsley, "American Attitudes toward Race Relations," *Public Opinion* (October/November 1984), p. 14.
4. Linda S. Lichter, "Who Speaks for Black America?" *Public Opinion* (August/September 1985), p. 41.
5. *Facts on File*, Sept. 23, 1973, 808E2, cited in Lino A. Graglia, *Disaster by Decree: The Supreme Court Decisions on Race and the Schools* (Ithaca: Cornell Univ. Press, 1976), p. 339, n. 48.
6. Linda Chavez and Max Green, "A Defense of the Reagan Administration's Civil Rights Policies," *New Perspectives* (Summer 1984), p. 34.
7. 163 U.S. 537 (1896).
8. Washington Council of Lawyers, "Reagan Civil Rights: The First Twenty Months" (unpublished report, 1983), preface.
9. John H. Bunzel, "Principle Isn't Likely to Determine Hiring Rules," *Wall Street Journal*, September 9, 1985.
10. Ibid.
11. Donna St. George, "Administration May Have to Shelve Its Relaxed Minority Hiring Rules," *National Journal* (October 22, 1983), p. 2172.
12. Ibid.
13. Ibid., p. 2173.
14. Ibid.
15. Robert Pear, "Rules to Enforce Voting Rights Due," *New York Times*, September 2, 1985.
16. Philip Shenon, "Meese Sees Racism in Goals on Hiring," *New York Times*, September 18, 1985.
17. Bunzel, op. cit.
18. Ibid.
19. Jeremy Rabkin, "Office for Civil Rights," in James Q. Wilson, ed., *The Politics of Regulation* (New York: Basic Books, 1980), p. 304.

20. Wallace Turner, "'Sexist' Language Tied to Berkeley," *New York Times*, May 10, 1985.

21. Ibid.

22. Robert Bork, "The Struggle Over the Role of the Court," *National Review* (September 17, 1982), p. 1137.

23. Richard E. Morgan, *Disabling America: The 'Rights Industry' in Our Time* (New York: Basic Books, 1984), p. 4.

24. On this point, see, e.g., Herbert McCloskey and Alida Brill, *Dimensions of Tolerance: What Americans Believe about Civil Liberties* (New York: Russell Sage, 1983), passim.

25. Richard Neely, *How Courts Govern America* (New Haven: Yale Univ. Press, 1981), p. 76 (emphasis added).

26. Ira Glasser, letter to the editor, *New York Times*, June 19, 1985.

27. Anthony Lewis, "White Man's Lawyer," *New York Times*, June 6, 1985.

28. *San Francisco Chronicle*, January 25, 1984.

29. *San Francisco Chronicle and Examiner*, February 17, 1985.

30. Lichter, op. cit., p. 41.

31. Rochelle L. Stanfield, "Reagan Courting Women, Minorities, But It May Be Too Late to Win Them," *National Journal* (May 28, 1983), p. 1120.

32. "Statements of Commissioners Blandina Cardinas Ramirez and Mary Frances Berry," *Toward an Understanding of Stotts* (United States Commission on Civil Rights: Clearinghouse Publications 85, January 1985), p. 63 (emphasis in original).

33. Malcolm M. Feeley and Samuel Krislov, *Constitutional Law* (Boston: Little, Brown and Co., 1985), p. 655.

2   CIVIL RIGHTS DOCTRINE FROM 1965 TO 1980: A CRITICAL HISTORY

Epigraph: Norman Podhoretz, quoted in George Roche, *The Balancing Act: Quota Hiring in Higher Education* (La Salle, Ill.: Open Court, 1974), p. 17.

1. Jeremy Rabkin, "A 'Civil Rights' Snare," *New Perspectives*, Vol. 17, No. 1 (Winter 1985), p. 4.

2. Ibid.

3. 347 U.S. 483 (1954).

4. 163 U.S. 537 (1896).

5. Willmoore Kendall, "What Killed the Civil Rights Movement?" in Willmoore Kendall (Nellie D. Kendall, ed.), *Contra Mundum* (New Rochelle, N.Y.: Arlington House, 1971).

6. Ibid., p. 461.

7. Ibid., pp. 461–462.

8. Ibid., p. 463.

9. Ibid., pp. 463–464.

10. Ibid., p. 465.

11. Barry L. Goldstein, "The Historical Case for Goals and Timetables," *New Perspectives*, Vol. 16, No. 1 (Summer 1984), p. 20.

12. U.S. Senate, Labor and Human Resources Committee, "Committee Analysis of Executive Order 11246" (1982), p. 12 (emphasis added).

13. Robert Pear, "Dispute on Policy on Jobs Continues," *New York Times*, January 30, 1986.

14. Title 41, C.F.R., 60–1.40, cited in Nathan Glazer, *Affirmative Discrimination: Ethnic Inequality and Public Policy* (New York: Basic Books, 1975), pp. 46–47 (emphasis added).

15. Title 41, C.F.R., 60–2.11, cited in Glazer, op. cit., p. 49.

16. Kenneth B. Noble, "Hiring Goals: A Big-vs.-Small Business Split," *New York Times*, March 3, 1986.

17. Goldstein, op. cit., p. 22.

18. *Congress and the Nation*, Vol. III (Washington, D.C.: Congressional Quarterly, 1973), p. 498.

19. *Regents of the University of California v. Bakke*, 438 U.S. 265, 407.

20. Goldstein, op. cit., p. 23.

21. Goldstein, op. cit., p. 23.

22. Richard E. Morgan, *Disabling America: The "Rights Industry" in Our Time* (New York: Basic Books, 1984), p. 188.

23. Alan H. Goldman, "Affirmative Action," *Philosophy and Public Affairs*, Vol. 5, No. 2 (Winter 1976), p. 186.

24. Thomas Sowell, *Civil Rights: Rhetoric or Reality?* (New York: William Morrow and Co., 1984), p. 54.

25. Ibid.

26. Ibid., pp. 54–55.

27. Phil Lyons, "An Agency with a Mind of Its Own: The EEOC's Guidelines on Employment Testing," *New Perspectives*, Vol. 17, No. 4 (Fall 1985), p. 20.

28. Ibid.

29. Ibid.

30. Ibid., p. 21.

31. Ibid.

32. Ibid., p. 22.

33. Ibid.

34. Ibid., p. 23.

35. Ibid., p. 24.

36. Ibid.

37. Ibid. (emphasis in original).

38. Ibid.

39. Ibid., p. 25.

40. Ralph P. Davison, "Keep Federal Affirmative Action Strong," *New York Times*, November 25, 1985.

41. Don Edwards, "Keep Affirmative Action," *New York Times*, February 13, 1986, p. 27.

42. *United Steel Workers v. Weber*, 443 U.S. 193 (1979).

43. Ronald Dworkin, "How to Read the Civil Rights Act," in Dworkin, *A Matter of Principle* (Cambridge: Harvard Univ. Press, 1985), p. 325.

44. Ibid., p. 330.

45. 401 U.S. 424 (1971).

46. Ibid.

47. Ibid. (emphasis in original).

48. Sowell, op. cit., pp. 115–116 (emphasis in original).

49. Kenneth T. Lopatka, "Developing Concepts in Title VII Law," in Hausman, et al. (eds.), *Equal Rights in Industrial Relations* (Madison, Wis.: Industrial Relations Research Assoc., 1977), p. 42.

50. *Robinson v. Lorillard Corp.*, 444 F.2d 791, 798 (4th Cir. 1971).

51. *Diaz v. Pan American World Airways*, 442 F.2d 385, 388 (5th Cir.), *cert. denied*, 404 U.S. 950 (1971).

52. *Gregory v. Litton Systems, Inc.*, 316 F.Supp. 401, 403 (C.D. Cal. 1970), *aff'd*, 472 F.2d 613 (9th Cir. 1972).

53. Lopatka, op. cit., p. 40.

54. Ibid.

55. Gary L. McDowell, *Equity and the Constitution* (Chicago: Univ. of Chicago Press, 1982), p. 9.

56. Ibid.

57. Harvey C. Mansfield, Jr., "The Underhandedness of Affirmative Action," *National Review* (May 4, 1984), p. 30,

58. *Bolling v. Sharpe*, 347 U.S. 497 (1954).

59. Owen M. Fiss, "Groups and the Equal Protection Clause," *Philosophy and Public Affairs*, Vol. 5, No. 2 (Winter 1976), p. 108.

60. Ibid.

61. Ibid.

62. Ibid.

63. Ibid., p. 120.

64. Ibid., p. 148.

65. Ibid.

66. Ibid.

67. Ibid.

68. Ibid.

69. Ibid.

70. Ibid., p. 153.

71. 438 U.S. 265, 361.

72. Fiss, op. cit., p. 153.

73. See, e.g., Michael Pertschuk, *Giant Killers* (New York: Norton and Co.: 1986), Chapter 6; James T. Bennett and Thomas J. DiLorenzo, *Destroying Democracy: How Government Funds Partisan Politics* (Washington, D.C.: Cato Institute, 1985), Chapter 10; and Clement E. Vose, *Caucasians Only: The Supreme Court, the NAACP, and the Restrictive Covenant Cases* (Berkeley: Univ. of Calif. Press, 1959).

74. Mary Douglas and Aaron Wildavsky, *Risk and Culture* (Berkeley: Univ. of Calif. Press, 1982), p. 173.

75. Fiss, op. cit., p. 154.

76. Ibid.

77. Ibid., p. 157.

78. Ibid.

79. Ibid., p. 158.

80. Ibid., pp. 159–160.

81. Hardy Jones, "Fairness, Meritocracy, and Reverse Discrimination," in Ellen Frankel Paul and Philip A. Russo, Jr. (eds.), *Public Policy: Issues, Analysis, and Ideology* (Chatham, N.J.: Chatham House Publishers, Inc., 1982), p. 276.

82. Reginald Smith, "San Francisco Debate—Are Spaniards Hispanics?" *San Francisco Chronicle*, August 10, 1985.

83. Elizabeth Kolbert, "Six Officers Claim Minority Status," *New York Times*, December 6, 1985.

84. Aaron Wildavsky, "The 'Reverse Sequence' in Civil Liberties," *The Public Interest*, No. 78 (Winter 1985).

85. Ibid., p. 37.

86. Ibid., p. 41.

3   EMPLOYMENT DISCRIMINATION, THE COURTS, AND THE REAGAN JUSTICE DEPARTMENT

Epigraph: Peter Sherwood, a lawyer for the NAACP Legal Defense Fund, quoted in Fred Barbash, "The Administration Is Batting Zero On Civil Rights in the Supreme Court," the *Washington Post National Weekly Edition*, January 23, 1984, p. 30.

1. Washington Council of Lawyers, "Reagan Civil Rights: The First Twenty Months" (unpublished report), preface.

2. Charles L. Heatherly, ed., *Mandate for Leadership: Policy Management in a Conservative Administration* (Washington, D.C.: Heritage Foundation, 1981), p. 447.

3. Michael Wines, "Administration Says It Merely Seeks a Better Way to Enforce Civil Rights," *National Journal* (March 27, 1982), p. 536.

4. Ibid., p. 538.

5. Rochelle L. Stanfield, "Reagan Courting Women, Minorities, but It May Be Too Late to Win Them," *National Journal* (May 28, 1983), p. 1119.

6. Ibid.

7. Ibid.

8. Ibid.

9. 457 U.S. 440 (1982).

10. Ibid., at 443.

11. Ibid., at 444.

12. 645 F.2d 133, 138 (1981).

13. 401 U.S. 424, 433–436.

14. 457 U.S. 440, 452.

15. Ibid., at 448 (emphasis in original).

16. 457 U.S. 440, 460.

17. Ibid.

18. Washington Council of Lawyers, op. cit., p. 114.

19. 729 F.2d 1554 (1984).

20. 543 F.Supp 662, 668 (E.D. La. 1982).

21. 729 F.2d 1554, 1556.

22. Ibid.

23. Ibid.

24. Ibid., at 1557.

25. Ibid.

26. Ibid., at 1558.

27. Ibid., at 1565.

28. *Congressional Record*, Vol. 110, p. 6549 (1964), cited in ibid., at 1556.

29. 729 F.2d 1554, 1566.

30. Ibid., at 1566–1567.

31. Ibid., at 1569.

32. Ibid., at 1573 (emphasis added).

33. Ibid., at 1572.

34. 109 U.S. 3 (1883). The Justice Harlan whom Judge Wisdom cites in support of a constitutional rationale for race-conscious affirmative action is, of course, the same Justice Harlan who is famous for having declared in his dissent in *Plessy v. Ferguson* that "our Constitution is color-blind. . . . "

35. 729 F.2d 1554, 1580.

36. See *Morgan v. O'Bryant*, 671 F.2d 23 (1st Cir. 1982). Also see Richard H. Fallon, Jr., and Paul C. Weiler, "Firefighters v. Stotts: Conflicting Models of Racial Justice" in Kurland, Casper, and Hutchinson (eds.), *The Supreme Court Review, 1984* (Chicago: Univ. of Chicago Press, 1985), p. 5, n. 18.

37. Ibid.

38. 467 U.S. 561 (1984).

39. Fallon and Weiler, op. cit., p. 5.

40. Ibid., p. 3, n. 11.

41. Ibid., p. 4.

42. Ibid., p. 4, n. 15.

43. Ibid., p. 4.

44. 679 F.2d 541, 561.

45. Fallon and Weiler, op. cit., p. 5, n. 17.

46. Ibid., p. 5.

47. Ibid., p. 6.

48. Ibid.

49. 81 L.Ed. 2d 483, 494.

50. Ibid., at 495.

51. Ibid., at 497.

52. Ibid.

53. Ibid., at 499.

54. Ibid.

55. Ibid., at 500.

56. Ibid. (quoting Senator Humphrey).

57. Ibid., at 501 (emphasis added).

58. Martin Shapiro, *Courts* (Chicago: Univ. of Chicago Press, 1981), p. 121.

59. Fred Barbash and Kathy Sawyer, "A New Era of 'Race Neutrality' in Hiring?" *Washington Post National Weekly Edition*, June 25, 1984, p. 32.

60. Ibid.

61. See Joe Davidson and Linda M. Watkins, "Jobs Debate: Quotas in Hiring Are Anathema to President Despite Minority Gains," *Wall Street Journal*, October 24, 1985.

62. Robert Pear, "Judges Continuing to Uphold Quotas," *New York Times*, February 10, 1985.

63. Ibid.

64. Ibid.

65. Ibid.

66. Ibid.

67. Ibid.

68. Carl Cohen, "Naked Racial Preference," *Commentary* (March 1986), p. 25.

69. Ibid.

70. Quoted in the opinion of Justice Powell, *Wygant v. Jackson Bd. of Education*, 54 LW 4479, 4480 (May 20, 1986).

71. Cohen, op. cit., p. 25.

72. Quoted in Ibid., p. 27.

73. 323 U.S. 214 (1944).

74. 54 LW 4479, 4484.

75. Ibid., at 4481.

76. Ibid., at 4482 (emphasis added).

77. Ibid., at 4486.

78. Ibid., at 4490.

79. 54 LW 4479, 4486.

80. Ibid., at 4485.

81. Ibid., at 4483.

82. Ibid., at 4488.

83. Ibid.

84. Ibid., at 4491.

85. Ibid. (emphasis added).

86. 54 LW 4984.

87. Ibid., at 5000.

88. Ibid., at 4990.

89. Ibid., at 4988.

90. Ibid.

91. Ibid., at 4990.

92. Ibid., at 4988.

93. See Thomas Sowell, *Ethnic America* (New York: Basic Books, 1981), p. 17.

94. 54 LW 4984, 4986.

95. 54 LW 5006.

96. Ibid.

97. Ibid.

98. Ibid., at 5006–5007.

99. Ibid., at 5007.

100. Ibid., at 5007, n. 2.

101. Ibid., at 5007.

102. Ibid., at 5009.

103. 364 U.S. 642, 651 (1961).

104. 54 LW 5005, 5015.

105. Ibid., at 5013.

106. Ibid., at 5015.

107. Linda Greenhouse, "Justice Official Terms Court's Ruling a 'Disappointment' and 'Unfortunate,'" *New York Times*, July 3, 1986.

108. Kelly Conlin, "Minority Hiring Ruling Puts Concerns on Notice," *New York Times*, July 4, 1986.

109. "The Right to Remedy, Affirmed," *New York Times*, July 3, 1986.

110. Ibid.

4 RACE AND THE SCHOOLS

Epigraphs: Harry V. Jaffa, *The Conditions of Freedom* (Baltimore: The Johns Hopkins Univ. Press, 1975), p. 150; Jennifer L. Hochschild, *The New American Dilemma: Liberal Democracy and School Desegregation* (New Haven: Yale Univ. Press, 1984), p. 203.

1. 347 U.S. 483 (1954).

2. James Nuechterlein, "A Farewell to Civil Rights," *Commentary*, August 1987, p. 32.

3. See Graglia, op. cit., p. 59.

4. 372 F.2d 815, 849.

5. 372 F.2d 815, 846–847, n. 5.

6. Quoted in Graglia, op. cit.

7. 418 U.S. 792 (1974).

8. 418 U.S. 792, 802.

9. Walter E. Williams, "Civil Rightsspeak," *New Perspectives* (Winter/Spring 1986), p. 15.

10. Ibid.

11. Interview in *New Perspectives* (Summer 1984), p. 38.

12. Cited at 458 U.S. 457, 462 (1982).

13. Ibid.

14. Ibid., at 460.

15. 633 F.2d 1338 (1980).

16. 393 U.S. 385 (1969).

17. Ibid., at 389.

18. Ibid., at 395.

19. See Linda S. Lichter, "Who Speaks for Black America?" *Public Opinion* (August/September 1985), pp. 41, 43.

20. Norman Miller, "Changing Views about the Effects of School Desegregation: *Brown* Then and Now," in Marilynn B. Brewere and Barry E. Collins, eds., *Scientific Inquiry and the Social Sciences* (San Francisco: Jossey-Bass, 1981), pp. 413–452. See also Thomas Sowell, "Assumptions vs. History in Ethnic Education," *Teachers College Record* (Fall 1981), pp. 48–51.

21. 458 U.S. 457, 472 (1982).

22. Ibid., at 489, n. 2.

23. Ibid., at 474.

24. Ibid., at 494.

25. Ibid., at 494–495.

26. Peter Skerry, "Christian Schools versus the IRS" *The Public Interest* (Fall 1980), pp. 31–33.

27. 309 F.Supp. 1127 (D.D.C., 1970).

28. 356 U.S. 30 (1958).

29. *Commissioner v. Tellier*, 383 U.S. 687 (1966). See also Jeremy Rabkin, "Behind the Tax-Exempt Schools Debate," *The Public Interest* (Summer 1982), pp. 27–28, n. 3.

30. Rabkin, op. cit., p. 28.

31. Quoted in Skerry, op. cit., p. 31.

32. Ibid., p. 31.

33. Quoted in ibid., p. 32.

34. Ibid., passim.

35. Tinsley E. Yarbrough, "Tax Exemptions and Discriminatory Private Schools," in Yarbrough, ed., *The Reagan Administration and Human Rights* (New York: Praeger, 1985), p. 112.

36. Ibid., p. 115.

37. Rabkin, op. cit., p. 35.

38. 76 L.Ed 2d 157, 169.

39. Ibid., p. 166.

40. Ibid., p. 182.

41. Ibid. p. 175.

42. Lichter, op. cit., p. 42.

43. 76 L.Ed 2d 157, 187.

44. Ibid., p. 172.

45. Quoted from opinion of Justice Powell, ibid., p. 184.

46. 76 L.Ed. 2d 157, 179.

47. Ibid., p. 178.

48. Ibid., p. 179. Cf. Justice Rehnquist's dissent, p. 192: "But we have said before, and it is equally applicable here, that this type of congressional inaction is of virtually no weight in determining legislative intent. [Citations omitted.] These bills and related hearings indicate little more than that a vigorous debate has existed in Congress concerning the new IRS position."

49. *Washington Post*, January 15, 1982.

50. *Washington Post*, February 4, 1982.

51. *New York Times*, January 9, 1982, quoted in Yarbrough, op. cit., p. 114.

52. 76 L.Ed. 2d 157, 185–186.

53. Philip Shenon, "Opposed by Bar, Professor Fades as Judge Choice," *New York Times*, August 8.

54. Robert Pear, "Alabama Mayor Assails Nominee on Civil Rights," *New York Times*, October 24, 1985.

55. See *Pasadena City Board of Education v. Spangler*, 427 U.S. 424 (1976).

56. Lena Williams, "Appeals Court Ruling Would Allow End to Norfolk Busing," *New York Times*, February 8, 1986.

57. Ibid.

58. Robert Pear, "U.S. Shifts Tactics on Desegregation of Lower Schools," *New York Times*, January 26, 1984.

59. Ibid.

60. The term belongs to Walter E. Williams (op. cit., p. 15).

61. Patricia Ward Biederman, "School Board Debate Heats Up on Ratio of Minorities," *Los Angeles Times*, November 3, 1987; and Elaine Woo, "Board Permits Study That Could Lead to Increase in Minorities at Magnet Schools," *Los Angeles Times*, November 17, 1987.

62. Lena Williams, "Controversy Is Revived as Districts End Busing," *New York Times*, March 25, 1986.

5   THE FAILURE OF CIVIL RIGHTS REFORM

Epigraph: James Nuechterlein, "A Farewell to Civil Rights," *Commentary*, August 1987, p. 32.

1. James Q. Wilson, *American Government: Institutions and Policies*, 3rd ed. (Lexington, Mass.: D.C. Heath and Co., 1986), p. 430.

2. Ibid., p. 433.

3. Ibid., pp. 431–432.

4. Ibid., p. 432.

5. Wilson, op. cit., p. 433.

6. Ibid.

7. Robert Pear, "Justice Department Says Court Undermines Job Equality Rule," *New York Times*, May 23, 1986.

8. "The Senate's Character," *Wall Street Journal*, June 26, 1985.

9. "This Hiring Tiger Needs Its Teeth," *New York Times*, January 18, 1986.

10. Dan Fagin, "In Winning His Battle for Rights Commission, Did Reagan Lose the War?" *National Journal* (December 17, 1983), p. 2622.

11. Robert J. Thompson, "The Commission on Civil Rights," in Tinsley E. Yarbrough, ed., *The Reagan Administration and Human Rights* (New York: Praeger Publishers, 1985), pp. 181–182.

12. Ibid.

13. Fagin, op. cit., p. 2622.

14. Juan Williams, "Changing Course at the Civil Rights Commission," *Washington Post National Weekly Edition*, January 23, 1984, p. 29.

15. U.S. Commission on Civil Rights, *Statement of the United States Commission on Civil Rights on School Desegregation*, Pub. 76 (December 1982), p. 54.

16. U.S. Commission on Civil Rights, *Intimidation and Violence: Racial and Religious Bigotry in America*, Pub. 77 (January 1983), p. 13.

17. Thompson, op. cit., p. 184.

18. Ibid., p. 192.

19. Fagin, op. cit., p. 2623.

20. Ibid.

21. Thompson, op. cit., p. 193.

22. Ibid., p. 196.

23. Ibid., p. 194.

24. *New York Times*, May 27, 1983.

25. Fagin, op. cit., p. 2625.

26. Williams, op. cit.

27. Fagin, op. cit., p. 2623.

28. Thompson, op. cit., p. 199.

29. "NAACP Slams Reagan, Asks for Meeting," *San Francisco Chronicle*, February 17, 1985.

30. Fagin, op. cit., p. 2626.

31. Ibid., p. 2625.

32. See *Comparable Worth: Issue for the '80s*, A Consultation of the U.S. Commission on Civil Rights, June 6–7, 1984, Vols. 1–2.

33. "Civil Rights Commission: Unwept to the Grave," *The Economist*, August 2, 1986, p. 23.

34. "Rights Hearing Blowup—Critic Stalks Out," *San Francisco Chronicle*, March 7, 1985.

35. "Civil Rights Commission: Unwept to the Grave," op. cit.

36. Robert Pear, "Civil Rights Agency Splits in Debate on Narrowing Definition of Equality," *New York Times*, October 14, 1985.

37. Robert Pear, "Member of Civil Rights Panel Bids Chief Resign as 'Inflammatory,'" *New York Times*, April 7, 1986.

38. *Oakland Tribune*, December 2, 1986.

39. Lena Williams, "House Group Votes to Cut Off Money for Panel on Rights," *New York Times*, June 27, 1986.

40. "Civil Rights Report Is Faulted," *New York Times*, March 25, 1986.

41. *Oakland Tribune*, op. cit.

42. Martha Derthick and Paul J. Quirk, *The Politics of Deregulation* (Washington, D.C.: Brookings Institution, 1985).

43. Robert Pear, "Rewriting Nation's Civil Rights Policy," *New York Times*, October 7, 1985.

44. Quoted in Anne B. Fisher, "Businessmen Like to Hire by the Numbers," *Fortune* (September 16, 1985), p. 27.

45. "Plan to End Minority Hiring Goals Called 'Unconscionable,'" *San Francisco Chronicle*, August 16, 1985.

46. Fisher, op. cit., p. 28.

47. Ibid.

48. Kenneth Noble, "Employers Are Split on Affirmative Action Goals," *New York Times*, March 3, 1986.

49. Fisher, op. cit., p. 28.

50. Noble, op. cit., p. 13.

51. Fisher, op. cit., p. 30.

52. Ibid., p. 28.

53. Noble, op. cit., p. 13.

54. Eugene Bardach and Robert A. Kagan, *Going by the Book: The Problem of Regulatory Unreasonableness* (Philadelphia: Temple Univ. Press, 1982), p. 18.

55. Ibid., p. 200.

56. Abigail M. Thernstrom, *Whose Votes Count? Affirmative Action and Minority Voting Rights* (Cambridge, Mass.: Harvard Univ. Press, 1987).

57. Ibid., pp. 3–4.

58. Ibid., pp. 80–81.

59. Ibid., pp. 82–83.

60. Ibid., p. 113.
61. Ibid., p. 88.
62. Ibid., p. 101.
63. Ibid.
64. Quoted in ibid., p. 118.
65. Ibid., pp. 118–119.
66. Ibid., p. 132.
67. Ibid.
68. Ibid.
69. Ibid.
70. Ibid.
71. Herman Schwartz, "What About Mr. Reagan's Own Judicial Activism?" *New York Times*, July 28, 1986 (emphasis added). As the title of the essay suggests, Schwartz is concerned with demonstrating that the Reagan administration practiced judicial activism by attempting to alter existing statutory and constitutional law. The quoted statement is offered in support of that allegation.
72. Thernstrom, op. cit., p. 107.
73. Stuart Taylor, "Voter Rights Case Heard by Justices," *New York Times*, December 5, 1986.
74. Ronald Brownstein, "Winning the Vote," *National Journal* (August 17, 1985), p. 1918.
75. Thernstrom, op. cit., p. 136.
76. Taylor, op. cit.
77. Ibid. Political scientists who have lamented the ignorance and apathy of the average voter would no doubt marvel at the level of awareness, sophistication, and strategic acumen allegedly demonstrated by white voters in North Carolina.
78. Ibid.
79. "Court Rejects Voting Plan as Biased," *New York Times*, July 1, 1986.
80. Ibid.

6   THE CIVIL RIGHTS IDEOLOGY IN OUR TIME

Epigraph: Kenneth Minogue, *Alien Powers: The Pure Theory of Ideology* (New York: St. Martin's Press, 1985), p. 2.

1. Minogue, *Alien Powers*, p. 2.
2. Ibid., p. 1.
3. Ibid., p. 5 (emphasis in original).
4. Kate Millet, *Sexual Politics* (New York: Doubleday, 1970), p. 55, n. 71. Millet would no doubt find further "proof" of the "conditioning" of the oppressed in opinion polls which show that at least three quarters of American working women, and a majority of American blacks, do not believe they have ever been victims of discrimination. See William R. Beer, "The Wages of Discrimination," *Public Opinion* (July/August 1987), pp. 19, 58.
5. Minogue, op. cit., pp. 222–223.

6. Tom Wolfe, *The Bonfire of the Vanities* (New York: Farrar Straus Giroux, 1987), p. 31.

7. Ibid., pp. 33–34.

8. Anthony Lewis, "White Man's Lawyer," *New York Times*, June 6, 1985.

9. Susan Milstein, "A Ruling on Black Women as Jurors," *San Francisco Chronicle*, August 20, 1985.

10. Shelby Steele, "On Being Black and Middle Class," *Commentary* (January 1988), p. 46.

11. Quoted in transcript of "Assault on Affirmative Action," *Frontline* #418 (Boston: WGBH Educational Foundation, 1986), p. 22. Originally broadcast on June 17, 1986.

12. Rochelle Stanfield, "Reagan Courting Women, Minorities, But It May Be Too Late to Win Them," *National Journal* (May 28, 1983), p. 1120.

13. Neil A. Lewis, "Hostile Questions Greet Nominee for Justice Post," *New York Times*, June 5, 1985.

14. Minogue, op. cit., p. 200.

15. Ibid., p. 36.

16. "NAACP Slams Reagan, Asks for Meeting," *San Francisco Examiner*, February 17, 1985.

17. Letter to *New York Times*, November 27, 1985.

18. Lewis, op. cit.

19. Letter to *New York Times*, June 19, 1985.

20. Herbert Hill, "A Key Affirmative Action Case," *New York Times*, February 18, 1986.

21. *Johnson v. Transportation Agency*, 107 S.Ct. 1442 (1987). The vote was 6 to 3. Those voting in the majority were Justices Brennan, Marshall, Blackmun, Powell, Stevens, and O'Connor. The dissenters were Justices Scalia, Rehnquist, and Powell.

22. Quoted in ibid., at 1447.

23. Ibid.

24. Cited in "Statement of Vice Chairman Murray Friedman," U.S. Commission on Civil Rights, *Toward an Understanding of Johnson* (Clearinghouse Publication 94, October 1987), p. 14.

25. Ibid.

26. Ibid.

27. Ibid., at 1452.

28. Quoted from district court opinion, cited in ibid., at 1468.

29. Quoted from district court opinion, cited in ibid., at 1469 (emphasis in original).

30. Ibid.

31. Ibid., at 1457.

32. Ibid., at 1449 (emphasis added).

33. Ibid., at 1475 (emphasis in original).

34. Ibid., at 1457–1458.

35. Ibid., at 1459.

36. See *Steelworkers v. Weber*, 443 U.S. 193, 201 (1979).

37. 106 S.Ct. 3063, 3072 (citing *Weber*, 443 U.S., at 204).

38. *Johnson*, op. cit., at 1471.
39. Ibid.
40. Ibid.
41. Ibid., at 1475–1476.

7   EPILOGUE: THE SUPREME COURT AND CIVIL RIGHTS IN THE POST–REAGAN ERA

Epigraph: Ralph G. Neas, executive director of the Leadership Conference on Civil Rights, quoted in Charles Mohr, "Minority Advocates Fear Gains Will Be Lost," *New York Times*, June 13, 1989.

1. 102 L.Ed.2d 854 (1989).
2. 104 L.Ed.2d 733 (1989).
3. 104 L.Ed.2d 835 (1989).
4. 102 L.Ed.2d 854, 871–872.
5. Ibid., at 881.
6. Ibid., at 873.
7. Ibid., at 881.
8. 102 L.Ed.2d 854, 881.
9. Ibid.
10. Ibid., at 885.
11. 102 L.Ed.2d 854, 901 (emphasis in original).
12. Ibid., at 903 (emphasis in original).
13. Ibid., at 890 (emphasis in original).
14. Ibid., at 891.
15. Ibid., at 914.
16. Ibid., at 922.
17. *Hazelwood School Dist. v. United States*, 433 U.S. 299 (1977).
18. *Wards Cove*, 104 L.Ed. 2d 733, 747.
19. Ibid., at 748 (emphasis in original).
20. 104 L.Ed. 2d 733, 748.
21. Ibid., at 750 (emphasis in original).
22. Ibid., at 751 (emphasis in original).
23. Ibid.
24. Ibid. (emphasis in original).
25. Ibid., at 753 (emphasis added).
26. Ibid.
27. Ibid., at 755.
28. Ibid.
29. Ibid., at 756.
30. Ibid., at 754–755.
31. Ibid., at 755. See 104 L.Ed.2d at 746, n. 4.
32. *In re Birmingham Reverse Discrimination Litigation*, 833 F2d 1492, 1498 (1987).
33. Ibid., at 1497.

34. *Chase National Bank v. Norwalk,* 291 US 431 (1934), quoted in *Martin v. Wilks,* 104 L.Ed. 2d 835, 845.

35. 104 L.Ed.2d 835, 849.

36. Ibid. (emphasis added).

37. Ibid., at 851 (emphasis added).

38. 457 U.S. 440, 448 (emphasis in original).

39. Quoted in Charles Mohr, "Minority Advocates Fear Gains Will Be Lost," *New York Times,* June 13, 1989.

40. Quoted in ibid.

41. Quoted in Julie Johnson, "High Court Called Threat to Blacks," *New York Times,* July 10, 1989.

42. "Chipping Away at Civil Rights," *Time,* June 26, 1989, p. 63.

43. 102 L.Ed.2d 854, 898.

Index